CHINA OFF
THE BEATEN TRACK

BRIAN SCHWARTZ

edited by
Bill Newlin

St. Martin's Press
New York

Library of Congress number
82-61428
CIP DATA TK

First Edition January 1983
Second Impression October 1983
Reprinted with Supplement July 1985

Preface

This book grew out of the fulfilment of a lifelong dream — a six-month journey through China. Virtually all travel information was obtained on the spot by either me or my editor, Bill Newlin, and the sections on those few cities neither of us was able to visit (in Inner Mongolia, Shandong and Tibet) are based on interviews with other travellers. We have confirmed hotel prices wherever possible, but there are still many towns in China little visited by "foreign friends," and the room rates we list for those places are the result of a single bargaining session. It goes without saying that any information contained in this book is liable to change, particularly the visa and travel regulations. Try the embassy in your home country first, although chances are they will still claim not to know what's happening in Hong Kong!

Several people provided help and encouragement during the conception and gestation of this book, including Dao Badao, David and Judy Bonavia, George Chen, Eugene Gregor, Karen Korow, Chris Iverson, Joan Law, Herman Yiu, our publisher Magnus Bartlett, the entire staff of China Guides, and my parents Professor Bernard Schwartz and Judge Aileen H. Schwartz. Special thanks are due to Larry Spitz. I would be grateful for any additions, corrections and criticism (nor would I turn a deaf ear to praise). Send all letters to China Guides, PO 31395, Causeway Bay, Hong Kong.

Brian Schwartz

Open cities

Anhui Category A: Bengbu, Hefei, Huangshan Tourist Resort, Jiuhuashan Tourist Resort, Maashan, Tunxi, Wuhu. Category B: Chaohu, Chuzhou, Fengyang County, Huaibei, Huaian, Jingxian County, Qingyang County (Jiuhuashan), Shexian County, Tongling, Xiuning County

Beijing Category A

Fujian Category A: Fuzhou, Quanzhou, Xiamen, Zhangzhou

Gansu Category A: Lanzhou. Category B: Dunhuang County, Jiayuguan, Jiuquan County, Yongjing

Guangdong Category A: Foshan, Guangzhou (Canton), Haikou, Huizhou, Shantou, Shaoguan, Shenzhen, Zhanjiang, Zhaoqing, Zhongshan, Zhuhai. Category B: Baisha County, Boating County, Boluo County, Changjiang County, Chaozhou, Chengmai County, Danxian County, Dapu County, Deqing County, Dingan County, Dongfang County, Dongwan County, Fengshun County, Gaoyao County, Haifeng County, Heyuan County, Huaiji County, Huidong County, Huiyang County, Jiangmen Ledong County, Linggao County, Lingshui County, Lufeng County, Luoding County, Maoming, Meixian, Nanhai County, Qionghai County, Qiongshan County, Qiongzhong County, Sanya, Sihui County, Shunde County, Tunchang County, Wanning County, Wenchang County, Xingning County, Xinxing County, Yunfu County

Guangxi Category A: Beihai, Guilin, Liuzhou, Nanning, Wuzhou. Category B: Beilu County, Binyang County, Guiping County, Guixian County, Luchan County, Rongxian County, Wuming County, Wuxu County, Xingan County

Guizhou Category A: Anshun, Guiyang. Category B: Beiliu County, Guixian County, Luchuan County, Rongxian County, Zhenningbu Yi and Miao Autonomous County, Zhuang Autonomous County

Hebei Category A: Chengde, Qinhuangdao, Shijianzhuang, Zhouxian County. Category B: Baoding, Handan, Tangshan, Zunhua County (Dongling)

Heilongjiang Category A: Daqing, Harbin, Qiqihar. Category B: Hegang, Heihe, Jiamusi, Jixi, Mudanjiang, Wudalianchi, Suifenhe, Tongjiang, Wudalianchi, Yichun

Henan Category A: Anyang, Kaifeng, Luoyang, Zhenzhou. Category B: Linxian County, Gongxian County, Nanyang, Xinxiang, Xinyang (Jigongshan)

Hubei Category A: Jiangling County, Shashi, Wuhan, Xiangfan, Yichang. Category B: Danjiangkou, Ezhou, Huangshi, Jingmen, Shiyan, Suizhou, Xianning

Hunan Category A: Changsha, Hengyang, Xiangtan, Yueyang. Category B: Xiangtan County (Shaoshan), Hengshan Tourist Resort

Inner Mongolia Category A: Baotou, Huhhot. Category B: Dalateqi (Xiangshawan), Dongsheng, Tongliao, Xilinhot, Zalantun

Jiangsu Category A: Changzhou, Liangyungang, Nanjing, Nantong, Suzhou, Wuxi, Yangzhou. Category B: Changshu, Huaian County, Xuzhou, Yixing County, Zhenjiang

Jiangxi Category A: Jigdezhen, Jiujiang (including Lushan), Nachang. Category B: Ganzhou, Jinggangshan County, Pengze County (Longgongdong)

Jilin Category A: Changchun, Jilin, Yanji. Category B: Antu County (Changbaishan Nature Reserve), Baicheng, Liaoyuan, Siping, Tonghua

Liaoning Category A: Anshan, Dalian, Dandong, Fushun, Jinzhou. Category B: Benxi, Liaoyang, Yingkou

Ningxia Category B: Yinchuan, Zhongwei County

Qinghai Category A: Xining. Category B: Huangzhong County (Taer Temple)

Shaanxi Category A: Xian, Yanan. Category B: Baoji, Hangcheng

Shandong Category A: Jinan, Jining, Qingdao, Taian, Weifang, Yantai, Zibo. Category B: Kenli County (Shengli Oil Field), Qufu County

Shanghai Category A

Shanxi Category A: Datong, Taiyuan. Category B: Linfen, Yuncheng

Sichuan Category A: Emei County (Emeishan), Chengdu, Chongqing, Leshan. Category B: Dazu County, Fengjie County, Guanxian County, Meishan County, Wanxian, Wushan County, Xindu County, Yunyan County, Zhongxian County

Tianjin Category A

Tibet Category B: Lhasa

Xinjiang Category A: Urumchi. Category B: Kashi (Kashgar), Shihezi, Turfan (Turpan)

Yunnan Category A: Kunming. Category B: Dali, Stone Forest

Zhejiang Category A: Hangzhou, Ningbo, Shaoxing, Wenzhou. Category B: Deqing County (Moganshan), Huzhou, Jiaxing

New open cities will gradually be added to this list.

Contents

v

Transportation

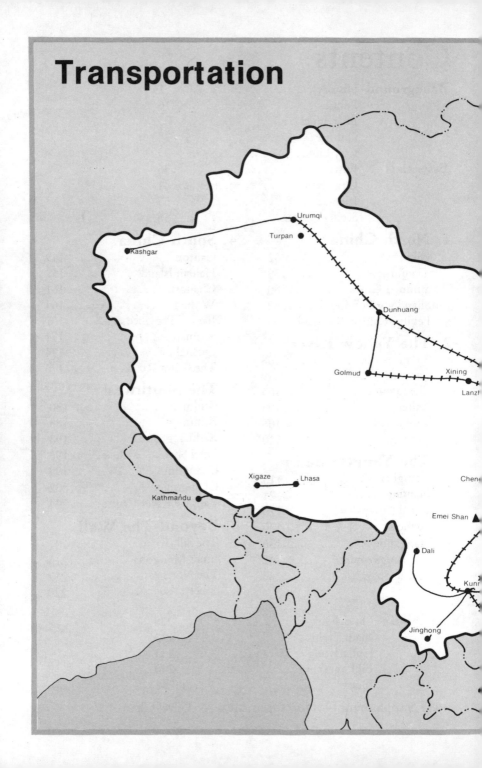

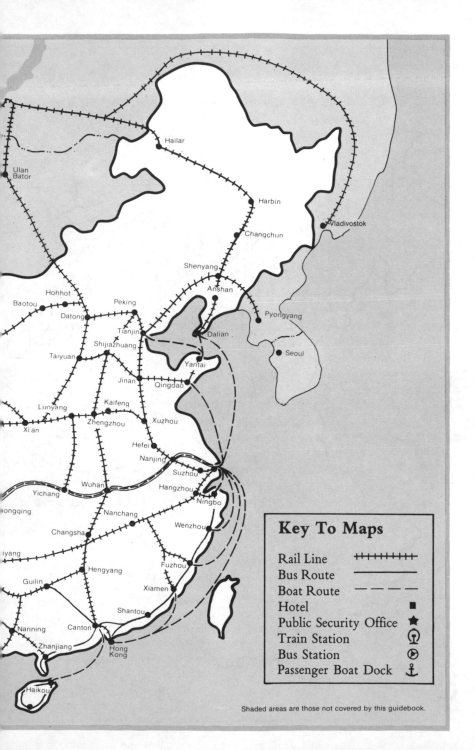

Key To Maps

Rail Line	+++++++++
Bus Route	————
Boat Route	– – – –
Hotel	■
Public Security Office	★
Train Station	⊕
Bus Station	⊗
Passenger Boat Dock	⚓

Shaded areas are those not covered by this guidebook.

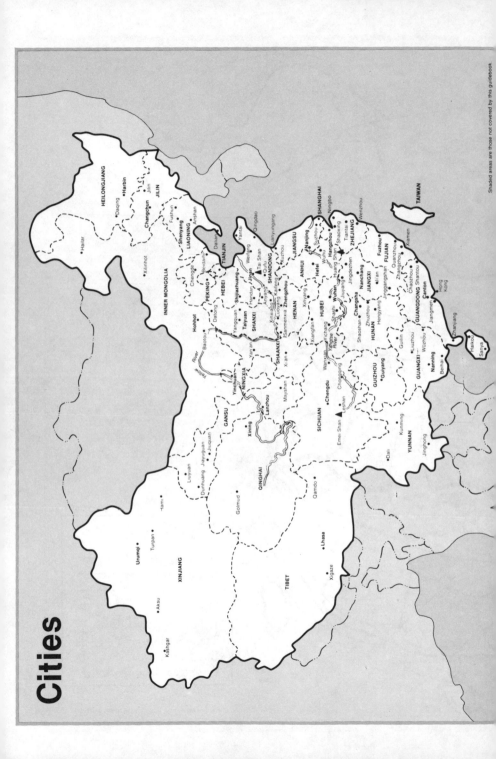

Cities

Shaded areas are those not covered by this guidebook.

History

The Chinese may with justice claim to be the oldest nation on earth. The first Chinese dynasty whose existence is confirmed by archaeological evidence, the Shang, was established no later than the 16th century B.C. When the Shang founded their kingdom, the Jews were a tribe of pastoral nomads led by Abraham and Isaac, the Aryans were herding cows in Persia, Agamemnon and Achilles were generations unborn, and it was well over a millenium before Caesar's legions would first encounter the uncivilized barbarians who inhabited Northern Europe and the British Isles. The contemporaries of the first Chinese rulers, the great agrarian empires of Egypt and Mesopotamia, had by and large decayed by the beginning of the Christian era. Yet China has survived up to the present day.

The Shang kingdom covered only a small fraction of present-day China. It was centered around the Yellow River valley in Henan and included parts of Shandong as well. The society was predominantly agricultural, but there were rudimentary cities. Nobles and other wealthy families lived in colonnaded stone houses, rode in carriages, wore silk clothes and ate from beautifully designed bronze plates and vessels. They employed a system of ideographic writing not unlike that in use today.

In the 12th century B.C. the Shang rulers were overthrown by the Zhou, a people who lived to the west of their kingdom. From then until 771 B.C. the Zhou governed northern China from their capital Hao, located near modern Xi'an. In that year Hao was threatened by barbarian invaders and the rulers moved to Luoyang. Although Luoyang grew to be a huge commercial center of 500,000 people, the Emperor's authority declined almost to nothing, and power was increasingly wielded by local feudal chieftains. Feudalism had been characteristic of Zhou government from the beginning, the king having granted huge fiefs to his generals on condition that they become his vassals and paid tribute to him. By the end of the 8th century many vassal states were strong enough to assert their independence, and the ensuing centuries were a period of war between these new nations. The larger ones annexed the smaller through war and guileful diplomacy, and of the 200 states existing in 700 B.C. only seven remained 300 years later. One of these, Qin, finally emerged supreme, conquering the other six states in a series of wars between 230 and 221 B.C.

The king of Qin became the first Emperor of a united China, Qin Shi Huangdi, who instituted a transformation of Chinese society more profound than any until the present day. He discarded the feudal system in favor of a centralized government under direct imperial control. China was divided into 36 provinces whose governors were appointed by the Emperor and served at his pleasure. A "cultural revolution" was launched to make dissent impossible, and all books, except those dealing with medicine and divination, were ordered burnt. This book-burning was thoroughly carried out, and many of the works of Confucius and his contemporaries are known to us only because they were rewritten from memory after the dynasty fell. At the same time, hundreds of scholars convicted of dissent were executed, and more were exiled. A new nation-wide legal code imposed harsh penalties for a wide range of offenses. Hundreds of thousands of peasants were pressed into work gangs to build such huge construction projects as the Great Wall.

Parallels between the Qin policies and those of the present-day regime are easy to draw, but it must be remembered that the Qin emperor, unlike the Communists, cared nothing for the welfare of the peasants. Indeed, one policy which he instituted was to lead in time to the success of Communism, causing much misery in the intervening two thousand years. This was the introduction of freehold land tenure. Under the Zhou, land could not be bought or sold; farmers were vassals who were, in hard times, supported by their feudal lord. But the beginning of private ownership led to land concentration. Even in good years, farmers grew barely enough to feed their families and pay their debts. In a year of drought or flood, the peasant would be forced to sell his land and, having done so, he could rarely earn enough money to buy it back. Much of the land thus sold would be bought by large landlords. The peasant would become a tenant, forced to give up half or more of his crop as rent. He was at the mercy of landlords, moneylenders and tax collectors. Throughout the centuries, the vast majority of China's population lived on the brink of disaster.

The First Qin Emperor died in 210 B.C. Many of the peasants rebelled against the corvee and heavy taxation. The inexperienced Second Emperor could not contain the revolt, and in 207 B.C. rebels stormed the Imperial Palace. The empty throne was eventually occupied by Liu Pang, who founded the Han Dynasty.

Although repudiating many Qin policies, including the ban on books, the Han rulers continued the centralized form of government. Directly under the emperor were the Three Chancellors, who included a Prime Minister, a Grand Chancellor responsible for military affairs, and a Grand Censor, or government investigator. These three men controlled an elaborate central bureacracy that administered the empire. China was divided into 100 provinces, each of which was governed by an administrator selected by the central government. To train men to fill these posts, a Central University was established at the capital city of Chang'an (Xi'an); bureaucrats were recruited upon recommendation by their province. Thus began a bureaucracy that was to govern China until the modern era.

Like their contemporaries in Rome, the Han emperors, most notably Wu-di, who ruled from 140 to 87 B.C., strived to extend Chinese dominion to the limits of the known world. Their armies engaged in a series of campaigns in which Xinjiang, Guangxi, Guizhou and Yunnan were conquered, and the route to Central Asia and Europe that became known as the Silk Road opened up. Despite this impetus to trade, there were economic recessions caused by heavy taxation. In the countryside, the effects of land concentration were being felt, with many peasants being forced to choose between banditry or starvation. In 9 A.D. the regent, Wang Mang, usurped power and ordered a program of land redistribution. This proved a failure, and a collateral branch of the imperial family recovered the throne in 25 A.D. and moved the capital city to Luoyang. This dynasty, called the Eastern Han, lasted until 220 A.D. In its later years, however, many of the emperors ascended the throne as children, and the central government was greatly weakened by court intrigues and palace conflicts. By the 3rd century the emperors had become puppets of their ministers, and many imperial governors became independent warlords.

In 221 the Han Dynasty officially ended and China split into three kingdoms, Wei, Shu and Wu. The decades of war and intrigue that followed have been immortalized in the classic Ming Dynasty novel *Romance of the Three Kingdoms,* which is still widely read. They ended in 280, when Wei conquered its rivals. Only 26 years later nomadic warriors invaded the newly reunited empire, killed the emperor, and seized the northern half of the country.

The ensuing period was a time of chaos. Hordes of marauders swept through North China, laying waste the great cities of Luoyang and Chang'an and massacring the populace. Millions of Chinese fled southwards to the Yangtse River, where Wei's successors had established a new kingdom. By 439 another Mongolian tribe, the Toba, succeeded in bringing the entire north under its control.

The Toba rulers proved competent and enlightened. Learning and art flourished, as well as an effective program of land redistribution. The Toba, who encouraged interracial marriages, rapidly became sinicized, but still remained open to cultural influences from abroad. This period was the apex of Buddhism's popularity in China, with three million monks living in North China alone.

Both northern and southern regions were, however, politically weak. The central government was rivalled by local strongmen and powerful aristocratic families. In 581 the head of one of these families usurped the Northern throne from its child occupant. The new Emperor conquered the south eight years later and founded the Sui Dynasty, ushering in a 300-year period of relative peace and unity.

The Sui Dynasty itself was short-lived but achieved much. One of its major projects was the "ever-normal granary" scheme, designed to alleviate the recurrent famines which plagued peasants. Farmers were required to contribute a portion of their crops in good years. The grain would be stored in huge depots, one of which, in Hunan, held 1.5 million tons. In years of drought or flood, the stored grain would be sold at low prices or distributed free.

An equally impressive accomplishment, the Grand Canal, was also undertaken in response to the problems of food supply. The soil of North China, once fertile, had by the 6th century become depleted and barren, and food had to be imported from the rich farmlands of the south. To facilitate its shipment, the Grand Canal, the world's largest man-made waterway, was built. Linking Hangzhou with Chang'an and Peking, it served as an important artery of north-south trade until the advent of the railroad.

The Sui ruler's less praiseworthy policies — heavy taxation and a protracted war against Korea — triggered a revolt that overthrew the emperor. In 618 the rebel leader proclaimed a new dynasty, the Tang. Between 627 and 705 the Tang provided China with two unusually able monarchs: Tang Taizong and the Empress Wu. They continued the Han policy of expansion into Central Asia, interrupted during centuries of disunity. Closer to home, they succeeded in breaking the grip of the military strongmen and great families on the reins of power, substituting an effective civil service. A legislative council under a prime minister helped the emperor draft laws, and six ministries, including departments of finance, justice and public works, governed the country. To facilitate local administration, the country was divided into 350 provinces and 1,500 districts. Bureaucrats to staff these organizations were mostly selected by public examination, which meant that candidates were recruited from a far broader stratum of society than before.

The Tang rulers addressed the perennial problem of land concentration with a program of continuous land redistribution. Every man was to receive 15 acres, which was to revert to the state upon his death. Within a few decades, however, the system broke down and the inevitable process of concentration began once more.

Arts and letters, culture and civilization flourished under the Tang, especially during the 40-year reign of Xuan Zong (or Ming Huang), the "Brilliant Emperor," in the 8th century. Chang'an, the capital, sprawled over 30 square miles and had two million inhabitants. The huge markets selling goods from Byzantium and Arabia, the capital's 2,000 companies engaged in foreign trade, and its numerous temples, churches and mosques, all bore witness to the high degree of contact China maintained with the outside world.

Behind the backdrop of cultural splendor, however, the government's power was deteriorating. The emperor created military vice-royalties in the provinces as a defensive measure; in 755 one of these generals revolted and captured the capital. After a short civil war, Chang'an was recovered, but to suppress the rebellion the emperor was forced to cede more power to the provincial governors, who remained independent warlords thereafter. Young, incompetent emperors fell under the influence of their servants, the palace eunuchs. Frequent revolts further weakened the government. Finally, in 907, an especially powerful general forced the emperor to abdicate.

Fifty years of disunity followed. The south seceded, and several short-lived dynasties ruled in the north. In 960 a spontaneous uprising by soldiers disgusted by governmental instability put the army's commander, Chao Kuangyin, on the throne. As much by persuasion as by force of arms, he succeeded in winning the south to his side, eliminating the warlord influence and uniting China under a new dynasty, the Song.

With the power of regional strongmen curbed, that of the bureaucracy grew. All candidates for the civil service had to pass the difficult government examination. Education thus became prized as the key to power and prestige, and it is perhaps for this reason that the Song period is noted both for its unusually efficient bureaucrats and for the flowering of philosophy, painting and science.

During the period of instability the Mongol peoples living in Manchuria had invaded northeast China and made it part of their kingdom, named Liao. Despite a standing army of a million men, Song was no match for its powerful neighbour, and was forced to pay a huge yearly tribute. The massive expenses entailed by this annual payment, the large army, and the salaries of the civil service required taxes to be set at twenty times what they were during the Tang, and the poor peasants bore the brunt of the burden. Wang Anshi, who became Prime Minister in 1070, responded to these pressures by instituting a broad program of economic reform. He founded marketing bureaux in large cities to stabilize prices, and credit agencies to make low-interest loans to carry poor farmers through the lean months before harvest. At the same time the government embarked on extensive projects of irrigation and land reclamation.

These remarkable policies were hundreds of years ahead of their time. Wang Anshi, however, was not a socialist reformer; his economic objectives were primarily to forestall revolt and strengthen the state against the Liao menace. In any event, his influence was short-lived; the emperor died in 1085 and the new ruler, influenced by Wang's powerful opponents, repudiated his program.

Meanwhile Manchuria grew stronger. The Liao rulers were overthrown by the more warlike Nuchen people, whose ruler founded the Jin Dynasty and proceeded to attack China. Kaifeng, the capital, fell to the invader in 1127, and the Song government retreated to Hangzhou. From then until its final fall over a century later, the Song controlled only the southern half of China, while the Jin occupied the north. For this reason, the period after 1127 is known as the Southern Song, while that before the Jin invasion is called Northern Song.

The Southern Song emperors were officially vassals of the much stronger Jin rulers, whom they were forced to address as "lord" and "elder uncle." Despite this humiliation the Song state thrived both culturally and economically. Industries, notably silk and porcelain, grew, and trade in these products with other regions of Asia became so important that excise revenue exceeded that obtained from the tax on land. With a population of one million in 1270, Hangzhou was the richest and most cosmopolitan city in the world. It was also one of the most hedonistic, with entire districts devoted to such entertainments as taverns, restaurants, theaters, storytellers, acrobats and jugglers.

The 13th-century world, however, did not offer a hospitable environment for pleasure-seeking; the Mongol cavalry swept across

Asia under the command of the brutal Genghis Khan. Persia and Russia were occupied and the hordes advanced as far as Venice before falling back. China was not spared. Jin fell in 1234 and Song in 1279 after a surprisingly long and heroic defense. By this time Genghis had been succeeded by his grandson, Kublai Khan, who became first emperor of the Yuan Dynasty.

The Yuan ruled as alien occupiers and were hated by the Chinese. They instituted a caste system with the Chinese assigned the lowest rank and restricted by harsh laws aimed especially at them. The bureaucracy was manned by Mongols, Muslims and other foreigners (including the Italian Marco Polo); its main concern was squeezing as much revenue as possible from the people for the benefit of their overlords.

Mongol rule did have some praiseworthy features. Roads were built from Peking, the capital, throughout the empire. The Mongols practised religious toleration. Easily the most enlightened Mongol policy was the commune system instituted in 1286. Every 100 farm households formed a commune to increase farm production through mutual aid. The system was supplemented by a famine relief scheme.

This progressive agricultural policy did not succeed in overcoming Chinese resentment against Mongol discrimination, however, and when Kublai's death was followed by a string of incompetent successors, revolts spread throughout the country. In 1368 a force of 250,000 rebels converged on Peking, and the weak and frightened emperor fled to the steppes of his native Mongolia.

The leader of the rebellion, Zhu Yuanzhang, came from a peasant family so poor that his parents and brothers died of malnutrition. He was a brilliant military commander, and his followers placed him on the throne. Taking the name of Hong-wu, the first emperor of the Ming Dynasty, he was personally very capable. Nevertheless, his reign is remembered for engendering two ominous developments that ultimately weakened China.

The first of these was a dramatic increase in the power of the Emperor vis-à-vis the bureaucracy. Hong-wu, by inclination a despot, abolished the position of Prime Minister and did not hesitate to have malfeasant bureaucrats flogged or even executed. This precedent did not immediately undermine the integrity of the civil service, due to Hong-wu's tendency to reward the ablest of his subordinates while reserving draconian penalties for those who were demonstrably corrupt or dishonest. His successors, however, were less scrupulous, and were quick to execute any official who offended them: bureaucrats soon learned to tell them only what they wished to hear.

The other, even more dangerous trend was the development of an isolationist attitude towards the world at large. During the Wei, Tang and Song periods, Chang'an, Luoyang, Canton and Hangzhou had sizeable communities of foreign traders. Under the Ming, however, foreign trade was permitted only if disguised as a form of fealty. This epitomized the Ming attitude towards other nations: it saw itself as culturally superior and economically self-sufficient. The new perspective took it for granted that China had nothing to gain from intercourse with the rest of the world.

At the beginning of the 15th century there was a brilliant exception to the isolationist rule. Under Hong-wu's successor, Yong-le, seven naval expeditions were despatched to India, the Middle East, and East Africa. These huge armadas, composed of sixty ships each of which carried a thousand men, brought gifts to and took tribute from the rulers of the nations they visited. Historians still do not agree why the expeditions were undertaken. Some say they were motivated by Yong-le's desire for prestige, to increase the number of his tributaries, while others hold that Yong-le wished to found a commercial empire. In any event, the expeditions did not found colonies or even establish bases and were halted after Yong-le's death. Had Yong-le's successors wished, the fleet, arguably the most powerful in the world, could have founded a colonial empire centuries before Britain and France set up theirs. At the very least, contact with Europe could have been established. But the ships were left to rot in port and China remained closed to outsiders, unaware of the scientific revolution already fermenting in the West.

With the end of Yong-le's reign in 1424, the Ming entered a period of decline. Most of the rulers were youthful and incompetent, and preferred to let their eunuch servants manage affairs of state. These eunuchs were often selfish and corrupt, but because of the emperor's now-absolute powers the bureaucrats did not dare challenge their ascendancy. Instead, many local officials joined the system and vied with the eunuchs in devising new forms of embezzlement. Meanwhile the peasants, already burdened with the increased taxation made necessary by this waste and corruption, suffered further hardships as the usual process of land concentration was given new impetus by the creation of royal plantations. These huge estates were set up by imperial decree as gifts to the ruler's favourites. Their managers often expanded their already-large holdings by hiring thugs to evict peasants from neighboring tracts of land.

A severe famine in Shaanxi in 1628 precipitated the inevitable uprising. The opposition forces slowly moved east, capturing city after city, until in 1644 Peking fell and the dynasty ended. Meanwhile, the Manchus took the opportunity provided by Ming decline to secede. They, too, had a powerful army, but it did not succeed in breaching the Great Wall. Shortly after the rebel occupation of Peking the commander of a loyalist army opened the gates to the northern invaders, hoping that they would crush the usurpers and restore the Ming before returning to Manchuria. The Manchu armies did indeed chase the rebels from the capital, but they stayed and established their own dynasty, the Qing.

The North capitulated to the new rulers without struggle, but the South took 20 years to subdue. Three decades of fighting left a legacy of bitterness that was to persist until modern times. Powerful secret societies, the ancestors of the modern Triads, were formed in the South to resist the outsiders. The Manchus, in turn, viewed the southerners as untrustworthy, and reserved three-quarters of the civil service posts for themselves.

Notwithstanding these conflicts, there followed a period of immense prosperity. From 1662 until 1795 the Imperial Palace was occupied by three of the most able monarchs in Chinese history: Kang-xi, Yong-cheng and Qianlong. Successful military compaigns expanded the empire to its greatest extent ever, and Mongolia and Tibet were included in its suzerainty. The peasants benefited from reduced taxation combined with massive projects aimed at irrigation and flood control. Yet it was during this golden age that the seeds of China's decline were sown.

Because the emperors were so capable, imperial power continued to grow. Yong-cheng created a Privy Council to bypass the six ministries, and made all provincial governors responsible directly to him. The emperor's responsibilities were by now so extensive that they required a man of superhuman ability to discharge them. Qianlong successors were not up to the task.

There were other ominous developments. The navy was totally neglected because it was run by southerners whose loyalties were in doubt. After Kang-xi's time the army, too, was allowed to decline. Moreover the Manchus, in order to bolster their claim to rule China even though they were "barbarians," were forced to adopt a conservative Confucian outlook. Foreign trade, which Confucian scholars looked down on, was restricted to Canton; there was no large-scale attempt to develop industry; and scholarly inquiry leant heavily towards Confucian classics, calligraphy, and the composition of essays. Chinese society became static at a time when Europe was at its most dynamic. China, the most advanced nation in the world at the beginning of the Ming Dynasty, was to become one of the most backward by the time of the eclipse of the Qing.

An even more serious problem facing China was demographic. By 1840 the population had grown to 400 million, almost seven times the Ming high. Since almost all arable land was already in use, and since the farming techniques in Ming times were remarkably efficient, crop yield remained relatively static as population soared. The inevitable result was a rapidly decreasing standard of living. Many farmers were forced to sell their land to buy food, and by the 19th century there was a large army of poor and landless peasants ready to swell the ranks of any rebel force.

The Qing emperors were forced to confront these internal problems against a background of European expansionism. By the end of the 18th century, the British had established a virtual monopoly of trade at Canton. But the conservative Chinese government had little interest in commerce and viewed Britain as a remote, insignificant nation inhabited by uncouth barbarians. Accordingly, the emperor restricted exports, required high duties to be paid on imports, and declared that commerce had to be channelled through one of 12 official trade associations. Most of the British profits came from the sale of opium, the use of which became widespread in China. By 1839 the British were shipping in 2,000 tons of opium annually, and the resulting outflow of silver further weakened China's precarious economy. The emperor accordingly ordered the traffic to cease, and all stocks of opium to be confiscated. In London, the government, pressured by merchants who wanted to force the Chinese to remove trade limitations, sent a fleet to China. The ships bombarded several cities along the coast, seized Shanghai, and threatened to attack Nanjing. China sued for peace and, in the Treaty of Nanjing, agreed to open five ports to British merchants, to slash tariffs on imports and not raise them above 5% without British consent, to end the trade associations' monopoly on commerce, and to cede the barren island of Hong Kong. Later treaties with France and the United States gave those nations similar trading privileges. Twelve years later the British sought negotiations to revise the original agreement. Their demands were refused, and in 1858 Britain and France sent a combined force to attack Tianjin. By the Treaty of Tianjin, China agreed to open ten new ports and to allow British and French ambassadors to reside at Peking. The Chinese concept of diplomacy as a simple matter of receiving tribute was thus definitively repudiated.

The imperial government, meanwhile, had other problems to occupy it. The appalling economic situation engendered the most extensive uprising since Ming times, the Taiping rebellion. Organized by a Chinese Christian mystic during a famine in 1850, the Taipings won widespread support through their program of land redistribution, equality of women, and primitive communism. At their height, the Taiping forces controlled half of China. But the revolt was weakened by rivalry among its generals, and was opposed by the landed gentry and foreign interests, who fielded an army led by European mercenaries. In 1864 the Taiping capital of Nanjing fell to the imperial army and the revolt was over. In the process much of South China had been laid waste, and 20 million people had perished.

With the Taipings defeated, the government devoted its efforts to dealing with the potential threat posed by the seemingly-invincible French and British forces. It was decided that the best way to resist the Europeans was to learn from them. Scientific colleges were set up, munitions factories and naval shipyards created, and a start was made towards industrialization by establishing iron works, coal mines and textile mills. The imperial government did not, however, wish to remould China in Western form, seeking instead to encourage a limited use of Western technology (especially its military aspects) while retaining the basic Confucian social, moral and political framework. The bankruptcy of this program became evident in 1894, when China and Japan went to war over the latter's attempt to make Korea a dependent state. The supposedly modern Chinese army was roundly defeated by the Japanese forces. Many observers took this as a sign that the Confucian system had to be radically altered if China were to survive.

China's humiliation encouraged the Western powers successfully to demand further territorial concessions, and much of the country was carved up into spheres of influence by Britain, France, Germany, Russia and Japan. These mounting foreign demands persuaded the young emperor to heed the advice of scholar-reformer Kang Youwei and embark on a program of liberalization. Kang advocated a constitutional monarchy, and while the initial decrees he drafted were minor, the conservative establishment feared that more drastic enactments were in store. With their support, the reactionary Empress Dowager had the emperor imprisoned, declared herself regent, repudiated the reforms and executed the reformers (except for Kang, who escaped to Japan).

Meanwhile the ever-grim conditions in the countryside sparked yet another peasant uprising in Shandong. However the revolt, led by the Society of the Righteous and Harmonious Fists (Boxers), soon took on an anti-foreign complexion — very likely at the instigation of local government officials, who would otherwise have been the logical targets of the rebellion. In 1899 the Boxers, supported by the xenophobic Empress Dowager, entered Peking, where they laid siege to the foreign diplomatic quarter. The Empress saw this as a chance to rid China of foreign influence, and the government accordingly declared war on eight European powers at once. An allied force marched to Peking, massacred the rebels and sacked the city. China was in grave danger of being partitioned into colonies, but the powers could not agree on a division, and the United States policy, advocating an independent China open to all for commerce, was generally accepted.

Even the Empress was now convinced that China was too weak to survive without reform. The civil service examination, whose 1,000-year-old Confucian curriculum had become increasingly irrelevant, was abolished. At the same time, the court promulgated a draft constitution whose primary feature was that it allowed the emperor to retain absolute legislative and executive powers. In effect an attempt to legitimize rather than curb the emperor's dominion, this constitution convinced many intellectuals that all court-sponsored reform was a sham and that China could not become a modern nation until the Manchus were overthrown. Many revolutionary societies were set up throughout the country. In 1905 several of these merged to form the Alliance for Chinese Revolution, headed by the Cantonese Dr. Sun Yat-sen.

In the following years the imperial government was weakened by the death of the Empress Dowager and the dismissal of Yuan Shikai, the most influential official in the bureaucracy, who had won the loyalty of a large section of the army. In 1911 the court announced that it would nationalize the railroads. Provincial governors as well as wealthy merchants viewed this as an attempt to restrict their autonomy, and many gave their support to the Alliance. Thus, when a hurriedly-organized coup in Wuhan seized control of the local government, the heads of many other provinces declared their loyalty to the revolutionaries. By the year's end, most of southern China had repudiated imperial authority, and on January 1, 1912, Sun Yat-sen was inaugurated as first president of the Chinese Republic.

Meanwhile Yuan Shikai had consolidated a northern stronghold, since the troops loyal to him constituted the most efficient fighting force in China. To avoid a civil war, Sun offered to relinquish the presidency to Yuan, provided the latter pledge his support to the Republic. Yuan agreed. In February he persuaded the infant emperor to abdicate, and six weeks later he became president.

But Yuan was too ambitious to be content with his role as chief executive. He took steps to limit the power of Sun's republicans, who were now organized as a political party called the Kuomintang. After dissolving this party in 1914, Yuan promulgated a new constitution that gave him lifetime tenure. The next year he declared his intention to become Emperor. Japan, meanwhile, seeking domination over China, presented a list of 21 peremptory bids for territorial rights and economic privileges. Yuan, hoping to gain Japanese support for his imperial ambitions, accepted most of the demands. But Japan repudiated his claim to the throne, and several Chinese provinces threatened to secede rather than serve a new monarch. Yuan was on the point of being forced out of office when he died suddenly in 1916.

As had happened so often before in its long history, China split up into dozens of small states controlled by local strongmen with private armies. These warlords fought among themselves to extend their territories, although the battles were conducted with a minimum of bloodshed, since no leader wished to endanger the army that was his sole claim to power. Yuan's successors maintained a national government in Peking, but its control did not extend beyond the city limits.

This period of political chaos was also one of social and intellectual ferment, as many people, particularly young students and workers in the cities, repudiated Confucian values and sought to adopt Western mores. In many families, a generation gap developed: the obedience and arranged marriages which the parents demanded as filial piety, the children rejected as medieval tyranny. Many of these young progressives staged strikes to protest what they saw as Chinese collusion with Western attempts to dominate China, especially Japan's 21 Demands of 1915 and the 1919 Versailles Peace Treaty, which awarded Germany's economic concessions in Shandong to Japan.

Marxist historians regard the 1919 demonstrations against the Versailles agreement as the beginning of Communism in China. Indeed, only two years later approximately twelve delegates, all of whom saw a Bolshevik-style revolution as the only solution to China's backwardness, met in a small house in Shanghai to found the Chinese Communist Party. One of these delegates was the Hunanese assistant librarian of Peking University, Mao Tse-tung.

Meanwhile the republican supporters of Sun Yat-sen were attempting to unify the strife-torn country. These set up a provisional government in Canton in 1920 and established the Whampoa Military Academy to train a modern army, headed by a young general named Chiang Kai-shek. Sun espoused a progressive programme of democracy, equal opportunity and land reform. His left-leaning ideas won Soviet support, and the Russians advised the Chinese Communists to join the Kuomintang while retaining their own party organization.

Sun died in 1925, and his successors launched a military expedition, headed by Chiang Kai-shek, to unite the warlord-ruled provinces. Chiang's troops were better motivated and trained than any of the warlord armies, and were to some extent supported by the people. By 1929 they had completed the reunification of the country and set up a government at Nanjing — although through the 1930s more than half of the country remained under the control of local strongmen whose allegiance to the Kuomintang was little more than nominal.

The Kuomintang did not attempt to subdue these warlords because Chiang, the man in control of the party from 1927 on, came to view the Communists as posing a far greater threat. The Communist Party had grown since its humble beginnings in Shanghai. As Chiang's army moved north fighting the warlords, Communist organizers followed in their wake, fomenting strikes and demonstrations. In 1927 Chiang sent his troops to Shanghai and Nanjing with orders to shoot every Communist they could find. Thousands were killed, and Chou En-lai, who was supervising Communist activities in Shanghai, barely escaped. Later that year all Communists were expelled from the Kuomintang.

Meanwhile the Communists were hampered by an important dispute over tactics. The party leaders, headed by Li Li-san, followed the orthodox Marxist strategy of seeking support among urban industrial workers. A dissident group, led by Mao, felt this policy was inappropriate for an overwhelmingly agrarian nation. The Communists could not prevail, Mao argued, unless they were based in the countryside and gained widespread peasant support.

As Li Li-san sponsored a series of unsuccessful urban uprisings, Mao and his supporter Chu Teh organized a small guerilla army at Jinggangshan in southern Jiangxi. In 1931 a ''liberated area'' was established there and an effective program of land redistribution instituted. They organized their peasant supporters into an army efficient enough to resist four assaults by Chiang's soldiers. But

Chiang's fifth capaign, which involved half a million troops, proved successful. The Communist guerillas were forced to move westward in October 1934, pursued by Kuomintang forces. Their 6,000-mile epic retreat across raging rivers and snow-capped mountains became known throughout the world as the Long March. When the Communist forces reached Guizhou, the leaders held a congress to plan strategy. At this meeting Mao became head of the party and his rural-based policies were endorsed; the Congress also decided to head for Shaanxi, in northwest China, where there was a Communist-controlled area.

One year after they left Jiangxi, the Communist forces reached their new base. Of the 80,000 who had set out on the Long March, only 20,000 remained. These proceeded to organize a Soviet Republic at Yan'an.

Chiang's preoccupation with the Communist threat during these years prevented him from devoting his full attention to another menace: Japan. In 1931 Japanese troops occupied Manchuria, which they turned into the "independent" state of Manchukuo. Two years later Japan established another puppet regime in eastern Hebei, and her forces prepared to infiltrate four more northern provinces.

Popular feeling in China turned against Chiang, who was fighting a few thousand Communists as the Japanese took over the country. In Xi'an, Chiang's own troops held him prisoner for two weeks in an effort to force him to make a truce with the Communists and fight the Japanese. A few months later, in early 1937, he complied.

In response to the Kuomintang's decision to fight, the Japanese mounted a full-scale invasion. By 1939 Japan had conquered most of China's densely-populated areas, and the Nationalist government moved west to Chongqing. The battle lines remained more or less unchanged until Japan surrendered to the Allies in 1945 — in part because Chiang was reluctant to commit his troops against the Japanese, knowing they would be needed against the Communists later. Mao's forces, meanwhile, operated in the Japanese-occupied areas, where the invaders held the cities while the Communists controlled large portions of the countryside. Within these regions they won the support of many peasants by a moderate program of rent reduction, establishment of schools, and other similar reforms.

The Kuomintang had long since abandoned Sun Yat-sen's platform of social change, and Chiang relied more and more on the gentry for support. When the Japanese surrendered, these landholders reclaimed their land and charged their tenants the same extortionate rents as before. Those who could not pay were forced to borrow money at 200% interest. Not surprisingly, an ever-increasing number of peasants gave their allegiance to the Communists. In the cities, many Kuomintang supporters were alienated by the corruption of its officials and by its failure to deal with the ruinous inflation that had driven the price of a decent meal from around one dollar in the 1930's to one million dollars in 1949.

Unaware that the country was slipping through his grasp, Chiang spurned the postwar American efforts to arrange a truce between the Kuomintang and the Communists. His army took the offensive in 1946 and, at first, seemed to be winning. The tide turned in late 1947. In Manchuria, the Communist general Lin Biao won a decisive victory over a force of 300,000 nationalist troops. From then on, city after city fell to the Communist armies as the Kuomintang retreated to Canton, Chongqing, and finally Taiwan. On October 1, 1949, at Tiananmen Square in Peking, Mao Tse-tung proclaimed the establishment of the People's Republic of China.

Politics

Since the founding of the People's Republic, China's leaders have consistently approached the task of governing their huge country in one of two basic ways which, without undue distortion, can be labelled "Maoist" and "pragmatic." Neither approach can be understood without reference to China's past.

Nearly all of those in the top echelons of power during the past 30 years joined the Party before 1937, and all were deeply involved in the early struggles to survive the combined onslaught of the Kuomintang and the Japanese. Their ideas of how best to modernize and strengthen China were shaped by their experience during this period. Survival then would not have been possible without an unusual degree of altruism and revolutionary zeal. The Maoists view this attitude as the ideal for China today. China's problems will be solved, they believe, when the spirit of the Long March is instilled in every factory worker and peasant. Continuous propaganda and mass campaigns are considered essential to this task.

Not all of China's rulers have adopted the Maoist outlook, however; some, including Deng Xiaoping and his allies, take a more practical approach. These men think it unrealistic to expect today's proletariat to be motivated by the idealism and zeal of the Liberation movement. Economic progress, in this view, can be fueled by the profit motive without a return to pre-war capitalism; China can trade with and learn from Western countries without becoming dependent on them; more consumer goods can be created without creating a consumer society. At first glance, the pragmatists' flirtation with capitalism seems to be a complete negation of Maoism. But this greatly exaggerates the difference between the two camps.

The competition between Maoists and pragmatists has been swayed by a fundamental difficulty. The success of either group's policies depends on the dedication of those who implement them: revolutionary campaigns and pragmatic modernization programs are equally liable to be sabotaged by a corrupt or inefficient bureaucracy. China since 1949 has had its share of venal, tyrannical and slothful administrators, though their counterparts in other Third World countries are arguably worse. But the problem of administration is especially acute in China: never before in the history of the world has a bureaucracy been given so Herculean a task. Merely to regulate a large, complex economy without recourse to market forces and corporations would be difficult enough; but the Chinese must transform and modernize as well.

The Chinese government has responded by increasing the size of the bureaucracy. In early 1982 the executive branch comprised 127 organizations staffed by over 20 million officials. These agencies have overlapping, sometimes conflicting jurisdictions and unclear responsibilities. Recently, for example, a city wished to erect a building on a vacant plot of land. The municipal authorities had to secure the approval of 35 different government bureaux, a process which took almost two years.

This unreasonable delay, and innumerable others like it, is caused not only by the number of agencies but by the procrastination of their staff. Bureaucrats in China tend to postpone decisions for as long as possible. This is understandable: decisive action leaves one open to criticism or even punishment if the party line later changes. The official who implements pragmatic economic reform today will suffer for it tomorrow if the Maoists regain power.

In 1949 the lines of cleavage between Maoists, pragmatists and bureaucrats that were to permeate later Chinese history were not yet apparent, except to an astute few. The newly-victorious Communists were united by the exhilaration of victory and by the enormity of the tasks facing them. Two decades of war had left the country in a shambles. Industry was wrecked and inflation was rampant. Urban and rural administration had been weakened, and what remained was run by local gentry and Kuomintang bureaucrats.

During the following years, the new government astonished friend and foe alike by its moderation and political expertise. Even those most critical of the Communists look back upon the early 1950s as a golden age whose latent promise was to go unfulfilled. By 1953 inflation had been halted by paying wages in fixed commodity units, and industrial production was restored to prewar levels. Almost all the land owned by landlords and rich farmers had been redistributed to poorer peasants. This was perhaps the Communists' greatest accomplishment, for the unequal land distribution had kept the peasantry at a bare subsistence level for centuries. (The achievement was marred, however, by the 30-year persecution of the landlords' descendants, many of whom were forbidden employment until 1976.)

In the years 1953-7 China moved closer to socialism. Formation of mutual aid teams and co-operatives was encouraged in the countryside; farmers pooled privately-owned land and tools for central, supposedly more efficient management. In the cities, nationalization of industry was completed; where possible, the government used progressive buying-out rather than outright coercion to induce factory owners to surrender control. China's rate of industrial growth was the fastest in Asia at this time.

By 1957, however, the honeymoon was over. Many new party bureaucrats showed signs of becoming high-handed. Those intellectuals who dared to criticize them during the brief period in 1956-7 when the Party invited the intelligentsia to speak freely (''let a hundred flowers bloom, let a hundred schools of thought contend'') soon regretted it. They lost their jobs in the anti-rightist campaigns which followed. The next year, Mao and his supporters decided that the country's economy could make a quantum leap if the people's revolutionary fervour were kindled. China's peasantry, which was seasonally underemployed, was to work on local industrial projects such as small steel furnaces and fertilizer plants, as well as other labour-intensive projects such as dams and irrigation. Moreover, the farmers were to be reorganized into mammoth communes in which the land would be state-owned and centrally managed, work teams would eat in public messhalls, and the children would spend their days in centralized creches.

The idea of creating small-scale labour-intensive rural industries was later to be expounded by the "small-is-beautiful" school of European economists, and centralized management of the land made more efficient use of tools and labour — at least on paper. Put into practice in what was called the Great Leap Forward, however, this policy proved a failure. Inefficient management was a serious problem, because there were simply not enough people qualified to run a 20,000-member agricultural unit. Motivation, the Maoists' main concern, also flagged, for there was no incentive to break one's back on the common fields. Perhaps even more damaging were the droughts and floods that ruined the 1959 and 1960 harvests. By 1961 the country was in the grip of a large-scale famine, and many people starved to death during these bitter years.

Any last hope of industrial progress during this period was dashed by the Soviet Union's 1960 decision to withdraw its technicians from China. Since its founding, the People's Republic had developed close relations with her sister socialist state. After the Korean War of the early 1950s, China's leaders viewed the United States both as the embodiment of the economic system they detested and as the greatest threat to the regime's security. But the Maoists gradually came to perceive the Russians as exhibiting the same petrifaction of revolutionary fervour they themselves were trying to avoid. Moreover, they feared that Krushchev's policy of peaceful co-existence would in practice bring the Soviets too close to the Americans. A war of words soon developed and the Russians halted all aid. Thus began the Sino-Soviet split which soon became complicated by territorial disputes and has continued until the present day.

The immediate effect of Krushchev's aid withdrawal was to exacerbate the schism between Maoists and pragmatists that by then had become open. Mao and his allies lost much of their power as a result of the Great Leap disaster, and Mao himself was forced to relinquish his post as head of state to Liu Shaoqi, although he remained Party Chairman. From 1962 to 1966 the pragmatist leaders — including Premier Chou En-lai and Deng Xiaoping, Liu's leading protégé who became secretary-general of the Party — guided economic policy. The more communal aspects of agricultural organization (public messhalls and nurseries, commune-level agricultural planning) disappeared. Private plots were permitted and greater use was made of economic incentives.

From 1962 onwards Mao and his allies set about regaining their lost power. Disgusted with the upsurge in materialism and cynicism, they feared that the new liberal economic policies were one step away from a return to capitalism. The Maoists launched several mass movements in these years, most notably the Socialist Education Campaign and the movement to emulate Lei Feng. A young soldier killed in an accident, Lei Feng was held up as an example to the country because of his zeal to serve the Party and people. (The Lei Feng cult is still current in China.)

These movements were portents of what was to follow. In 1965 Mao and his supporters launched a full-scale campaign to regain power, purge corrupt bureaucrats, and restore the country's flagging revolutionary ardour. Thus began the Great Proletarian Cultural Revolution. By 1966 the Maoists had organized millions of activist youth into Red Guards who combined with the armed forces to oust the local Party apparatus in regions controlled by the pragmatists and replace them with Revolutionary Committees of workers and soldiers. Deng Xiaoping lost his job and Liu Shaoqi died in disgrace.

The enthusiasm of the Red Guards was perhaps greater than Mao had expected; what fired them was the opportunity to attack and humiliate overweening teachers and overbearing bureaucrats, and to raid the houses of corrupt officials and smash the illicitly acquired luxury goods inside. Unfortunately, their wrath spilled over to those less deserving of it. Artists, writers and intellectuals were publicly criticized, their works destroyed, and many were resettled in remote villages. Any physical remnant of China's past — temples, monuments, works of art — were considered inextricably bound up with exploitation and feudalism, and many were destroyed. Schools were shut down completely for three years. Thousands of people were shot, or died in the mass demonstrations and fighting.

By 1968 the country was fast slipping into chaos and civil war. The Maoists and their main ally, the People's Liberation Army (PLA), headed by Mao's "closest comrade-in-arms," Lin Biao, brought the Red Guards under control, and many millions of youths were exiled to remote communes. The Maoists and army then turned to the task of restoring order and rebuilding the Party, the schools and the shattered bureaucracy, a task which took several years. During this time the power of the PLA became a threat to the Party. It is unclear whether Lin actually tried to unseat Mao or whether the Maoists merely feared that he would; in any event, he was killed, either in a plane crash (the official version) or by a bullet, and the co-architect of the Cultural Revolution was vilified as a right-winger.

The need to establish order, the death of Lin, and the declining health of the Chairman increased the power of the pragmatists vis-a-vis the radicals. Chou En-lai gradually became responsible for most aspects of day-to-day administration, and Deng Xiaoping was brought back to power in 1973. The previous year, President Nixon's visit to China began the process of normalizing Sino-American relations. Mao himself was behind this move; having come to believe that Russia posed a far greater threat to China than did the U.S., he decided to play the "American card."

Feeling their policies threatened, the extreme left, headed by Mao's wife Jiang Qing, struck back. In 1973 they mounted the incongruously-named "Criticize Lin Biao, Criticize Confucius" campaign. Of course, the left secretly admired Lin, and while they hated Confucius, whose ethics to them symbolized feudal ways of thought, the brunt of the campaign was directed against their contemporary adversaries, particularly Deng.

In the midst of this radical resurgence, in January, 1976, Chou En-lai died. He was widely admired by the people, in part because he was perceived as having restrained the worst excesses of the Cultural Revolution. On Qing Ming, a traditional Chinese holiday to honour the dead, many of Peking's citizens left wreaths in Tiananmen Square to commemorate Chou. These were removed during the night and the next day people passing through the square, outraged to see their tributes gone, started scuffles with the police. The crowd's anger turned into violence, and the mob burnt several cars and set fire to a police station. Two days later the Maoists used the riots to gain enough support to dismiss Deng. Hua Guofeng, a protégé of Mao whom both the pragmatists and the radicals considered one of their own, became Premier.

Mao died in September. Jiang Qing and three other radical Maoists were arrested soon after. The rest of the leadership, including Hua, had combined to forestall another Cultural Revolution. Jiang and her cohorts were subsequently vilified in the press under the label of the "Gang of Four." Some Chinese slyly spoke of the "Gang of Five," a reference to the fact that the most prominent radical, now entombed in a huge mausoleum on Tiananmen, was too much of an embarrassment to be named.

At the 11th Party Congress, held in 1977, Hua became Party Chairman and an attempt was made to replace the cult of Mao, the Great Helmsman, with that of the "Wise Leader, Chairman Hua." It soon became apparent that pragmatism was in the ascendant. In 1978 the Four Modernizations — modernized agriculture, industry, defense and technology — were announced as China's principal objectives, and two years later the "wise leader" was demoted to vice-chairman.

As the absence of a personality cult shows, those now in power are agreed that there will be no return to radical Maoism. To underscore their intentions, Mao's historical importance was "re-evaluated" in 1981 and his radical theories were downplayed. Gone are the hysterical campaigns of earlier days. Loudspeakers on trains and in factories no longer blare Mao's Quotations and propaganda. Time devoted in schools and offices to political instruction has decreased. Most of the billboards displaying stirring revolutionary slogans have come down and advertisements for Coca-Cola have gone up. Articles in the press have become more rational. A recent newspaper editorial on the question of whether to stress grain or meat production based its argument on such statistics as the amount of fodder necessary to produce one pound of meat and the number of acres of arable land available. In Mao's day, a similar piece would have rested its case solely on the published writings of the Chairman, such as his injunction to "store grain everywhere."

In late 1978 it seemed as if reasonable dissent would also be permitted. In Peking, posters criticizing Maoist policy were plastered on walls, and underground journals advocating greater democracy appeared. Around "Democracy Wall," the intersection of Chang'an and Xidan in Peking, the atmosphere was electric, as thousands of people gathered to read ideas no-one had dared voice in twenty years. Deng at first gave his tacit support to this experiment in free speech, hoping it would discredit his adversaries. But, by 1979, the last of the high-level Maoists had been purged, and the Wall was no longer needed. The posters were torn down and some dissidents were jailed, one for 15 years.

The government's main concern today is economic progress. This is reflected in its flexible economic policy, the main points of which were laid down by Premier Zhao Ziyang, a Deng protégé noted for his pragmatic economic reform in Sichuan. They included emphasis on consumer goods and raising living standards, reliance on the profit motive to spur growth in industry and especially agriculture, use of market forces to help set levels of industral production and weed out inefficient producers, and a greater reliance on foreign trade and investment.

The pragmatists face many obstacles in their attempt to implement these policies. Those Maoists who remain, and many do, especially in the PLA, view Deng's program as heresy. More likely than a Maoist resurgence, however, is the possibility that modernization will founder in a morass of bureaucratic sluggishness and inertia. The administrators realize that their power will wane in a modern economy regulated in part by market forces. Recognizing this as the greatest threat to his policies and power, Deng mounted a major campaign against bureaucratic inefficiency and corruption in 1982.

In September 1982, the 12th Party Congress upheld these economic and administrative reforms, demonstrating that the pragmatists, for the time being at least, have the upper hand.

Economics

The basic problem: Although China is one of the largest countries on earth, most of its land is inarable. Since the beginning of the Han Dynasty, the combination of limited land and increasing population has caused widespread poverty and starvation, resulting in recurrent cycles of famine, instability, peasant revolt and the fall of dynasties.

Land scarcity and population growth remain China's foremost problem. Less than 15% of China's land area can be cultivated. This works out to about one-quarter acre per person — less land per capita than in densely-populated India. During the Cultural Revolution it was claimed that arable land could be doubled, but such predictions were unrealistically optimistic, since land reclamation was found to entail massive expenditures of both money and manpower.

To make matters worse, what land is available is often vulnerable to flood and drought, caused either by the vagaries of the summer monsoons or by the unruliness of China's rivers. Chinese historical records, carefully kept for over two thousand years, show that there have been, on average, more than one such calamity each year somewhere in China. In 1981 there were devastating floods in the western province of Sichuan and, simultaneously, a serious drought in the Peking area.

Since land area is fixed, China's main problem in recent years has been demographic. The first half of the Qing Dynasty, from about 1660 to 1810, was an era of peace and prosperity, and China's population grew from 60 million to almost 400 million. Rebellion and famines thereafter held the population more or less constant until the establishment of the People's Republic. But the improved health care and more stable food supplies assured by the Communists lowered the death rate and allowed the population to rise from 450 million to one billion. Despite the limited availability of land, the Communists have managed to more than double food production since 1952, but this gain has been eaten up by the increased population, leaving grain production per capita more or less what it was in 1952.

In recent years a vigorous birth control campaign has been started to counteract what was arguably Mao's worst policy error. Propaganda is bolstered by economic incentives, so that couples who agree to have only one child receive wage increases and better housing, while those who have a third child risk punitive measures. These tactics have been far more effective in the cities than in the countryside, where the absence of government old-age pensions means that the traditional desire for large families as a form of life insurance remains as compelling as ever.

Agriculture: Although all of China's farmers used to belong to one of the 54,000 communes, the function of these institutions is much reduced. The main unit in the Chinese countryside is today, as it has been from time immemorial, the village, renamed the "production team." Life at this level has changed far less since 1949 than most outsiders would think, and many traditional practices are followed. The extended family is still, for the majority, the most important social institution in their lives. Despite government disapproval, arranged marriages are common in the countryside, and payment of bride-money is common.

In outward appearance, villages are a medley of old and new. Houses are family-owned, and many are built in the traditional style, from earth bricks or hand-hewn stone. Furnishings usually consist of locally made wooden chairs, beds and tables, and it is the rare dwelling that sports luxuries such as a television. The majority of villages have electricity, however, and bicycles and watches are becoming increasingly common. Most brigades distribute a yearly ration of cotton cloth to each family, which means that peasants usually have some new clothes, and may even buy colorful ready-made shirts and jackets in the nearest town. Most children go to commune-run primary schools financed by the peasants themselves, and literacy has increased dramatically in the last thirty years.

Agricultural production is still largely based on muscle, both animal and human. Some villages and brigades own tractors or diesel-operated water pumps for irrigation. But most of the land is still ploughed by draft animals, and it is not unusual for men and women to draw the plough, pull heavy carts, or run treadmills to pump irrigation water.

In spite of these primitive means of production, the Communists have doubled grain output since 1952. This increase was made possible by massive water supply projects, including canals, dams and reservoirs, and by efficient recycling of manure coupled with increased production of chemical fertilizer. Villages are now assured of a reasonably stable food supply: those whose crops have failed may get state aid, and the government has organized large-scale relief efforts during major disasters, such as the Sichuan floods in 1981.

Within ten years of the Communists' installment private ownership had been replaced by a system of collective farming. Produce was sold to the state and the proceeds, after tax deductions, were distributed to the families on the basis of work points. Each villager was awarded for his daily labour a certain number of work points (usually between four and ten) which depended on his strength, motivation and political attitude as assessed by his peers. The resulting distribution was far from egalitarian, since the highest earners made four times as much as those on the bottom rung.

The work-point system was used throughout China until 1980. In that year the government, believing that production was stagnating because farmers did not have enough material incentive, introduced the individual responsibility system. Under this procedure, households make yearly contracts with their supervisors. The farmers agree to plant an assigned piece of land with an agreed-upon crop, and to turn over a specified number of tons of produce to the team. They may keep and sell anything grown in excess of this quota. Government statistics claim that 90% of all production teams have adopted the new system, though the true figure may be lower. What is almost universal is "sideline production": villagers are allowed to make furniture and other handicrafts and sell them in town.

Industry: Almost all heavy industrial plants and nearly half the light industry factories in China are state-run: three of four urban workers have government jobs. These consider themselves lucky, for although wages are not higher than in other poor Asian countries, the work conditions are in many respects among the best in the Third World. Jobs in the state sector are guaranteed for life, and additional security is usually provided by medical insurance and old-age pension plans. Many factories build large residential complexes and lease apartments to their workers for nominal rents. Many enterprises provide schools and recreational facilities. There are eight wage grades, and advancement up the ladder is more or less automatic. The work day is eight hours excluding the lunch break, and the pace of work is much less hurried than in Hong Kong or Singapore.

While the Chinese government is proud of factory work conditions, it is dissatisfied with the efficiency of its own enterprises. Until recently, factories were totally insulated from market pressures of supply and demand. The State Council Planning Commission and its subordinate ministries would tell the enterprise how much of each product to manufacture. The goods would be sold at fixed prices to state commercial bureaux for distribution, and after wages were paid any surplus would be turned over to the state. There was thus no material incentive to increase profits, because they could not be used to raise wages or expand the factory (which required government permission). The link between what consumers wanted and what the factories offered them was tenuous at best.

In recent years the government has attempted to increase the autonomy of individual enterprises and to augment the role of market forces in regulating the economy. Factories have been given the power to determine price and output, and may keep all profits above a specified amount to reinvest or use as they see fit. They may award wage bonuses to unusually productive workers, and fire those judged grossly incompetent. Inefficient plants are to be closed down or merged.

The state has also begun to foster the growth of collective and private ownership. Collective enterprises are run by a group organization, often a rural commune or urban neighborhood association, sometimes a partnership. These collectives were once restricted mainly to the countryside; but the government, faced with the problem of finding jobs for the millions of urban youths who enter the labour market every year, decided to encourage their growth in the cities as well. The members of each collective set wages, prices and output, and market their own product. After paying taxes, they distribute remaining profits among themselves. In effect private corporations, these collectives have succeeded both in providing employment for many school graduates, and in diversifying the range of consumer goods and services available.

Chinese economic performance: American or European visitors arriving in China direct from their homelands are often shocked by the poverty they find. But those with any experience of the economic situation elsewhere in the Third World will be impressed by China's relative efficiency and growth. Progress is *not* automatic. Indeed, the economic escalator runs downhill, and countries have to run upward just to maintain their place. In Africa, agricultural production declined 10% over the past decade notwithstanding the widespread availability of fertile land. In India, despite a comprehensive land redistribution scheme, widespread government-sponsored social reforms and a massive program of rural development, the percentage of rural poor has increased since 1950 and the average urban real wage has remained constant for two thousand years.

Some free-market Third World countries seem at first glance to be exceptions to this trend. Ivory Coast and Thailand, for example, are widely touted as economic miracles. But their economies are fundamentally unstable in ways which China's is not. Like most of their neighbors, they are under-industrialized, and any manufactured products they use — especially heavy industrial goods such as steel, concrete and motor vehicles — must be imported. The end result is that most poor countries are dependent on the industrialized nations, be it the U.S., Europe or the Soviet Union, for markets, for imports, for loans, for managerial aid, and sometimes even for food.

There is a prominent school of economists who believe that the political, economic and cultural distortions produced by this dependency are the predominant characteristics of most Third World nations. But years before this fundamental theory made its first appearance in the scholarly journals of the West, the Maoists intuitively recognized and avoided the pitfalls of dependency. A full range of heavy and light industry was developed, imports severely limited, and autonomy preserved. Today the Chinese consider their past economic policy too isolated, but they can now enter the world economic arena from a position of relative strength.

Another set of interrelated problems facing most underdeveloped countries — but not China — can be grouped under the rubric of "urban overdevelopment." In most nations, what industrial and other development exists is concentrated in one region, usually the capital city. Skilled professionals, such as doctors and engineers, all seek well-paying jobs in the capital. Few, if any, wish to work in the countryside, where they are urgently needed. In addition, hundreds of thousands of villagers flock to the cities to make their fortune. Most end up unemployed, beggars or worse, eking out a living in the sprawling shantytowns that surround so many booming metropolises.

Although there is a wide gap in living standards between city and country, China has taken measures that seem draconian until one remembers the alternative. Villagers are forbidden to work in urban areas. University graduates are assigned jobs by the state. Industrial development has been encouraged throughout the country, so that it is well-nigh impossible to find a city or even a small town without a fringe of factories.

Culture

Around 550 B.C., three men were born who were to exert as great an influence on Chinese thought as Jesus did on our own: Confucius, the Buddha, and Lao-tzu, the semi-mythical founder of Taoism. Their teachings became the three great religions of China.

Confucianism is less a religion than a system of ethics designed to ensure an orderly, smoothly-functioning society. Such a society, Confucius believed, would come into being if each man and woman fulfilled his or her obligations to fellow-humans. The paramount duties were those of the family: children owed their parents filial piety. Stable families formed a stable nation: the Emperor, like the father, cared for his subjects, in return for which he was respected, and his commands unquestioningly obeyed.

Implicit in this system of obligations is the precedence of society over the individual. Since Confucius' day, the Chinese have usually deemed order and stability more important than personal freedom. Not surprisingly, in view of its conservative bias, Confucianism was made the official state philosophy in the 2nd century B.C. The Confucian Classics, which consist of works written centuries before that date, became the basis of all education and later civil service examinations. Their role was not unlike that of Greek and Latin literature in the West. Many of these Classics were books of history, ancient poems and even folk songs, but all were given moral interpretations, often distorting the meaning of the original.

Taoism, China's other great indigenous philosophy, provided something of a counterweight to the Confucian emphasis on social order. Lao-tzu's teachings stressed personal fulfillment. The follower of Tao seeks communion with nature and harmony with the Way of the

Universe. The Taoist exhortation to surrender one's mind to the flow of nature had a great influence on Chinese art, especially painting. Originally atheistic and profoundly mystical, Taoism was in later centuries transformed into a popular religion complete with a large pantheon of folk deities and spirits that its founders might have ridiculed.

The last of the three great Chinese religions, Buddhism, did not originate in China. Half a millenium after the Buddha's death, Indian monks travelled to China to preach his doctrines of asceticism, reincarnation and nirvana. Over the years, many famous monasteries were founded and some emperors became devout Buddhists. The Ch'an sect, founded in the 6th century, was greatly influenced by Taoism, stressing meditation and mental training to achieve enlightenment. Ch'an was even more influential in Japan, where it was called Zen.

Notwithstanding the zeal of its disciples, undiluted Buddhism was too heady a doctrine to appeal to the Chinese masses. New Buddhist deities had to be created, and the worship of the bodhisattvas, a rank of supernatural beings in their last incarnation before Nirvana, became increasingly important. Temples were filled with images of Maitreya, the future Buddha (portrayed as fat and happy over his coming promotion), of Amitabha, a savior who will reward the faithful with admission to a Christian-like paradise, and, above all, of Guanyin, a Madonna-like goddess of compassion. Lines of demarcation between this Buddhism and the popular form of Taoism became blurred. The great mass of the people worship Confucius, Guanyin, the Taoist immortals, respected figures from ancient history, and their own ancestors with equal vigour.

Besides the introduction of Buddhism and the institutionalization of the Confucian Classics, the other great cultural achievement of the Han Dynasty was the development of historiography. The work of the historian came to be viewed as an adjunct to Confucianism. History was conceived to be a morality play in which wicked rulers were punished by war, rebellion or other calamities. Sima Qian, who lived in the first century A.D., was the founder of this intellectual discipline. From then on, the official history of each dynasty was written by a committee of scholars formed immediately after its fall. The historians were given access to mountains of documents from the imperial archives, and were traditionally not subject to political pressure despite the distortions produced by the Confucian perspective, these works were more comprehensive and accurate than anything produced elsewhere in the world until modern times, and it is to them that we owe our detailed knowledge of ancient China.

Literature in China blossomed under the Tang Dynasty. The 7th and 8th centuries produced several of the greatest Chinese poets, including Li Bai, Du Fu and Bai Juyi. Their poems were written in *shi* form — each line had the same number of characters (usually five or seven). Because the lines are so short, the language is often cryptic and allusive. Some of these poems seek to convey Buddhist and Taoist doctrines of impermanence and flux; Li Bai compared the cosmos to an ocean whose waves follow one another in an eternal chase. Others paint a landscape and all its attendant emotions with a few words: a lake at sunrise, the mountains in winter. Still others — especially those of Du Fu — are political, and portray a populace weary with the endless wars of imperial expansion.

Visual arts were slower in developing, and the Golden Age of Chinese painting came during the Song Dynasty. Most of the brushwork produced during this period can be considered landscape painting, but Chinese artists never placed primary importance on the depiction of pastoral settings with photographic precision. Rather, they believed that nature mirrors man, and that both embody the flow of energy that composes the universe. A painter might spend days wandering in the hills until he believed he had discovered their spiritual essence. He would then return to his studio and attempt to project this intuition on paper.

The Song Dynasty also witnessed the greatest resurgence in philosophical speculation since the age of Confucius and Lao-tzu. Although known in the West as neo-Confucianists, these scholars were influenced as much by Buddhism as by Confucianism and, indeed, attempted to fuse the two doctrines. According to Zhu Xi, the greatest of the neo-Confucianists, the entire universe evolved from a "great void" composed of fundamental energy in a state of flux. The process of evolution was conceived to be everlasting, and was governed by the laws of science, which posited the interaction of Yang, the positive, male, active force in nature, and Yin, the negative, female, passive element. This conception neatly combined the Buddhist belief that the cosmos is a void with the Taoist conception of a world subject to constant change. There was no place for God in the neo-Confucian cosmology. It denied the presence of a "man in heaven" overseeing the universal flux. Instead, change occurred according to laws that were themselves unchanging. Zhu Xi's philosophy eventually became the official doctrine, and any belief in a deity came to be viewed as a superstition appropriate only for the uneducated.

When, in 16th century Europe, a conception of natural law similar to neo-Confucianism was accepted, it sparked a renaissance of scientific inquiry. For reasons which are still being debated, no such thing occurred in China. Nevertheless, practical science advanced under the Song. The compass was invented and used by mariners. Gunpowder was discovered and crude cannons built. Printing also came into use.

The Mongol invasion of the 13th century did not end cultural development in China. The Yuan saw the flowering of Chinese drama and opera, which further evolved under the Ming and became popular with scholars and common people alike. Novels, too, were written under the Ming, including the ever-popular *Romance of the Three Kingdoms,* a historical drama of the period just after the Han Dynasty when China was split up into three states, each contending for supremacy. The *Romance* stressed the Confucian ethic. It favoured the state ruled by descendants of the legitimate Han emperors, and its heroes were loyal and virtuous. The *Water Margin,* on the other hand, chronicles the adventures of a Robin Hood-type band of outlaws fighting government oppression and injustice. *The Dream of the Red Chamber,* which some consider the greatest Chinese novel, was written in the 18th century. It is the story of love between two cousins thwarted by their elders, who arrange other matches for them. Implicit in the novel is a protest against the Confucian injunction to obey one's elders, no matter how harsh or foolish they may be.

The Ming period is also noted for its superb porcelain ware. Porcelain had been manufactured as early as the Tang Dynasty, and beautiful monochrome pieces in crimson, brown and blue were produced under the Song. But the porcelain made under the Ming, in blue-and-white and polychrome, was even more creative. It was exported throughout west Asia, Europe and East Africa and is still widely sought after by collectors. The volume of production and export increased in later centuries, and was so well-known in England and America that the name of the producer, China, became synonymous with that of the product.

During the latter half of the Qing Dynasty, porcelain, painting and philosophy stagnated. The literary field, by contrast, was the scene of radical change. Since the beginning of the 20th century, those who viewed Chinese society as backward and in need of reform looked to literature to show the way. Radical writers, both Communist and non-Communist, believed that novels should be written in *baihua,* the spoken language of the people, and that they should be realistic and should have a social message. During the 1930s, some of these novelists — most notably Lu Xun, Lao She and Mao Dun — produced outstanding works in which the party line occasionaly took second place to the careful portrayal of complex characters. The Communist Party, however, considered artistic merit to be of less importance than propaganda value. Indeed, it feared independent artists as potential critics. In 1942 Mao, in his *Yan'an Talks on Literature and Art*, laid down the principles that have governed the Party approach to culture ever since: all creative artistic work has to serve political ends, and the Party has the right to censor any work whose content or style fails to reflect the Party line.

This policy reached its climax during the Cultural Revolution, when Jiang Qing, Mao's wife, set herself up as arbiter of China's cultural life. She required all artistic works to be "revolutionary" — in other words, to spout Party propaganda as crudely and blatantly as possible. Plots were simple and obvious: heroic Mao-loving workers would battle against and ultimately triumph over the cowardly attempts of villainous counter-revolutionaries to sabotage production. Many artists could not conform to these strictures, and were exiled to labour camps or remote villages. In their absence, creativity came almost to a standstill. Concerts were composed mainly of hymns to Mao, and bookstores sold his works and little else. Only eight operas, six ballets and a handful of films were cleared for production. They were shown over and over again, and tickets were distributed free of charge, perhaps because no-one would buy them. Nor did other, less obviously political arts fare any better. Landscape painters were forced to depict factories and power stations, and ivory carvers laboured to produce minutely detailed models of the house in which the Chairman was born.

The situation has vastly improved since 1978. The Party appears to have abandoned the doctrine that all art must actively champion the Party line, adhering instead to the relatively liberal view that no work may too severely question or criticize Party policy. Peking Opera and other traditional art forms have made a resurgence, and many films and novels with neutral political content have appeared, including love stories and even a paperback translation of *The Day of the Jackal.* Some more worthwhile work has appeared, including Yu Luojin's autobiographical *A New Winter's Tale,* the story of a young woman's quest for personal fulfilment in a world which conspires to stifle her. Many writers, artists and performers persecuted during the fifties and sixties have returned from their place of exile to take up their work anew. Nevertheless, those writers whose ideas or language are considered too "bourgeois" or cynical are still criticized in the press.

More pessimistic commentators contend that the Communist attitude toward culture has always been cyclical, with periods of repression following times of liberation as inevitably as winter follows summer. But the post-1978 policy is not just the same old wine served up in a new bottle. Rather, the Party's view of the role of culture has changed. The Maoists attempted to use art and literature to spur far-reaching changes in traditional Chinese beliefs and attitudes. The Confucian emphasis on obedience was ridiculed, and Ah Q, the selfish, servile, semi-moronic antihero of Lu Xun's famous story, whom the Communists considered the embodiment of the traditional Chinaman, was to be replaced by the dynamic, resolute New Socialist Man.

Today the idea of turning the masses into supermen has quietly been shelved, and the pressure on the artist to be the midwife of a new China has ceased. Obedience to authority, the Communists have come to realize, promotes both social and Party welfare. And the leadership has of late laid considerable stress on traditional Confucian virtues such as courtesy and helping the aged.

Despite radical efforts to alter its history, Communist China is in culture and outlook as much Chinese as it is Communist. In their attempts to create a New China, the Maoists isolated their ancient country from the influence of Western rationalism and consumerism, which has had a corrosive effect on traditional culture in virtually every other corner of the globe. Many young Chinese display an almost touching innocence compared with their streetwise counterparts from Upper Volta to New Guinea, but this state of affairs may soon change. Once they become aware of their existence, movies and motorbikes are what the people crave.

City Life

Confucianism and Communism agree that the state, like a benevolent big brother, must look after the welfare of its subjects. In material terms, the present government has been successful in its task, and the life of the average factory worker is more comfortable and secure than ever before. But at times the kindly Big Brother takes on a more Orwellian aspect. In urban China, everyone belongs to a unit, be it a factory, a retail store, or a university department. The unit's supervisory staff, usually headed by a Party cell, wields an enormous amount of power over the lives of its members. The unit distributes ration coupons for flour, rice and clothing. It determines who is criticized and who is promoted, and who will be allowed to live in the factory's apartment blocks. Without its approval, it is difficult and sometimes impossible to marry, divorce, have a child or transfer to another unit.

Many unit bureaucrats do their jobs conscientiously, while others make a practice of reserving the choicest plums for the most obsequious toadies and penalizing anyone who dares criticize them. There is little that the victim of such unfairness can do. Most workers steer a middle course, try not to offend anybody and to build up a network of *guanxi,* or good relationships, with those above them and around them. This attitude spills over into everyday life. If pork or cigarettes are in scarce supply, those who have an understanding with the store clerks will get the sought-after commodity.

Though few things affect a person's life so much as a unit assignment, this decision is made by negotiations between the middle school and the state employment bureaux, and the prospective employee has little say in it. Usually, this lack of choice is not seen as a hardship. Almost everyone wants the security of a job in a state-owned enterprise, and since these lifetime meal tickets are in short supply, most people will gratefully accept any such position offered. Families are occasionally broken up, and husbands and wives assigned jobs in cities thousands of miles apart, but this practice has become far less common than a decade ago, and according to the media most of the couples separated during the Maoist era have now been reunited.

The 1% of China's youth who go to university have more cause for concern. Their job assignment determines whether they will teach in a remote backwater in Heilongjiang or do graduate work in Peking, and they fear that their lives will be shaped by a combination of chance and bureaucratic whim. One sure way of getting an uncongenial posting is to be controversial, critical or noncomformist, so the wise student will not deviate from the herd. As a result, the stimulating all-night conversations common in European and American colleges are relatively rare in China, and the prevailing atmosphere is one of bland compliance.

Both in university and factory, the unit is responsible for safeguarding the morals of its charges. They are aided in this task by the neighborhood committee that supervises each city ward, and by the police. Often, these organizations do commendable work mediating in quarrels, counselling teenagers and helping the aged They can, however, be unbelievably meddlesome, and the code of morality they enforce is often xenophobic and puritanical. Chinese who have European friends jeopardize their prospects of promotion, and those who dare to dance to disco music court arrest. Sexuality is especially taboo, and fornication calls forth the work unit's severest wrath.

Other forms of passion are also in short supply. Slowly but surely, the millions of young Chinese are evolving into a cynical, streetwise generation. Idealism, especially of the socialist variety, is considered "uncool," and the prevailing ideology is "Serve yourself; only fools try to move mountains." Many cut classes or skip work whenever they feel like it, and smuggle magazines into the weekly political instruction sessions. In the evening they fill the beer halls and retreat into sullenness, or play drinking games with thinly veiled aggresssion.

Many of today's James Deans were formerly devoted Maoists who, during the 1960s, believed that united they could sweep away the inequalities they saw around them and usher in a new Socialist millenium. But it was the Red Guards who were rounded up and packed off to the countryside, and the system went on as before. Today many of these once-committed youths feel betrayed, most feel powerless to change the world around them, and *everyone* is sick of politics.

The disillusioned often turn to new illusions, and faith in Mao has been replaced by an equally naive faith in the West. Many Chinese view America much as some Americans once viewed China — as a trouble-free utopia in which all the problems afflicting their own society have been resolved. They wear blue jeans, sunglasses and gold crosses, see every American film shown, and listen to disco whenever they can. One reason that the Party frowns on Western influences is that it perceives them, quite correctly, as a subtle form of dissent. But, though cassettes and smart clothes can be banned, it is far more difficult to curb the anomie they represent.

Entries

Not so long ago, the gates of the Middle Kingdom were firmly barred against the outside world, and only a few were able to penetrate what outsiders dubbed "the bamboo curtain." Then, in 1977, tourists were welcomed — but only if they joined carefully supervised group tours. In 1981 the situation changed overnight. China began granting individual tourist visas, through both Hong Kong and certain of its embassies and consulates abroad.

Guidelines for issuing these visas vary from place to place. In some cities, such as (at last report) New Delhi and Moscow, the missions grant them fairly routinely; in others, such as Washington and many European capitals, they continue to discourage applicants. Some embassies in Europe will give transit visas to those going by train from Russia to Hong Kong, and these ten-day permits are sometimes extendable in China. In Australia and possibly other countries, two-week entry visas, easily extendable, are given those who buy round-trip air tickets to Peking. The best source of information on these visas are travel agents, student organizations or the embassy itself. Bear in mind, however, that many travel agents offer misleading information in the hope of snaring customers for expensive group tours.

Hong Kong has always been the easiest place to get a Chinese visa. Policy changes without notice, and next year's regulations are as hard to predict as next year's Derby winner. The official China Visa Office usually requires applications to be made through a travel agent, and during the first half of 1982 many supplied visas for fees ranging from HK$50-$200 (HK$5.80 = US$1). In July, some agencies were required to sell a one-day tour of Canton with luxury accommodation along with the visa — total price HK$450 — while others sold the visa alone for HK$200. These are the companies that were able to procure individual visas in 1982 (be sure to try more than one):

- China Tour Centre, Room L1-55, New World Centre, Tsimshatsui, Kowloon, 3-683207.
- Hong Kong Student Travel Bureau, Rm. 1020 Star House, Tsimshatsui, Kowloon, 3-694847.
- Phoenix Services, Room 11, 1st floor, Bowring Centre, 150-164 Woosung St., Tsimshatsui, Kowloon, 3-7227378.

- Traveler's Hostel, Chungking Mansions, 36-44 Nathan Rd., Tsimshatsui, Kowloon, 3-687710.
- Wah Nam Travel Service, Rm. 1003 Eastern Commercial Centre, 397 Hennessey Rd., Wanchai, Hong Kong, 5-8911161.
- United (Tai Shan) Travel, 1st floor, 43D Dundas St., Mongkok, Kowloon 3-849269.

You can also go directly to China Travel Service, the official Chinese travel bureau at 77 Queen's Rd., Central, and 27-33 Nathan Rd., Kowloon, or to the Visa Office at 387 Queen's Rd. East, but it might take several visits and success is not guaranteed.

Visas are generally good for 30 days counting from either the date of entry or the date of issuance (it varies), and may be extended. They are valid for two cities, which are listed on the visa, although you may have more cities added once you are in China. This is discussed in detail under Travel Orientation.

It is also possible to go to China as a student. Many Chinese universities, including Beijing Language Institute, Fudan University in Shanghai, and Nanjing University, offer language courses to foreigners. Although most students attend for a year or more, some courses last only six weeks. Once you are accepted by the University, a visa is automatically yours. You may travel around China after the course ends, and will be eligible for substantial student discounts in lodging and transportation. Contact student organizations in your home country for details.

Getting to Hong Kong

For the traveller in the U.S.A or Britain, the cheapest road to China passes through Hong Kong. (Hong Kong, of course, is a tourist attraction in its own right. See the Appendix for details.) Because Hong Kong is considered part of the U.K., IATA fare regulations do not apply to flights from London to the colony, and several airlines, including British Airways, British Caledonian and Cathay Pacific, offer very cheap fares (about £200) on this route. Inexpensive tickets from the United States are also available. O-C Tours, a California-based travel agent, sells one-way passage on World Airways from San Francisco to Hong Kong for about $300, and Korean Airlines and Singapore Airlines have similar packages at a slightly higher price. Fares from New York by O-C or Korean are about $150 more.

In Asia, the least expensive tickets to Hong Kong are purchaseable in Bangkok, Penang or Singapore. A flight from Bangkok to Hong Kong on Gulf Air or Air Lanka should cost under US$100, and a Korean Airlines ticket from Bangkok to California, including stopovers in Hong Kong, Taipei, Seoul, Tokyo and Honolulu is priced at less than $500. Because these cheap fares are not sanctioned by IATA, they are available only from travel agents. Some are more reliable than others, so ask around before you buy.

You can find similar travel bargains in Hong Kong. Several airlines offer cheap fares to the U.K. As in Bangkok, tickets to other destinations, including North America, must be bought from travel agents, who advertise in the classified section of the newspaper. But beware! Many of the shadier Hong Kong agencies have developed a variety of ingenious routines for bilking the unwary. For example, you might pay a deposit and then be told that the price of the ticket has doubled and the deposit is non-refundable. Those travel agents who are members of either HKTA or HATA are usually reliable. Many of these companies will sell you a flight to California for under US$350, and some include stopovers in Taiwan, Korea and Japan.

From Hong Kong to China

Train: You can make the journey from Hong Kong to Canton in five hours for less than US$5 by local train. There's no need to book in advance — just go. Trains leave Hung Hom Station, Kowloon (bus 5C from Star Ferry) at least hourly for Lo Wu, the border station an hour away. Follow the crowds to the immigration post, then walk over a footbridge into China. There you will be directed to health control (no inoculations required; they merely ask you if you are in good health), passport control, and customs, where you may or may not be searched. You will be asked to declare your valuables (watch, camera, radio, gold, silver and jewelry). Don't lose this paper since it will be examined thoroughly when you leave. If a listed item is found to be missing you will be fined, and any articles not recorded may be confiscated. Money need not be declared. There is a bank to change money (the rate is about the same as in Canton). You then go into the adjoining station to buy your ticket for Canton, 5.50元tourist price, Chinese price unavailable. Four trains a day make the three-hour journey; the last leaves at 3 p.m. There are also daily buses to Fujian Province (see The Coast Road). Allow at least an hour for paperwork, especially on weekends when the border is very crowded.

Reverse the process to go from Canton to Hong Kong, but remember that the last train leaves Canton at 10:20 a.m. (In March 1982 it was announced that the Lowu border would remain open until 9 p.m., so it's possible that later trains will be introduced.) Tickets are sold at the station on the right hand side of the ticket office, and not by CITS, unless you go first class.

Luxury express trains travel twice a day between Kowloon and Canton (book at the station or through an agent). Service is direct, with immigration formalities completed in the train station, but is three times the cost of the local train.

Air: If you want to get to North China in a hurry, you might consider flying. CAAC has frequent flights from Hong Kong to Peking (about US$200), Shanghai (US$130), Nanjing, Hangzhou and Kunming. Three planes a day make the short hop from Hong Kong to Canton ($40).

Boat: One of the most pleasant ways of making the China passage is by boat from Hong Kong. Steamers depart nightly for the half-day trip from Hong Kong to Canton and vice-versa. Dormitory tickets cost HK$45, and are available from Chu Kong Shipping, 15 Connaught Rd. West, 5-487902. Hovercrafts also make the journey, with thrice-daily departures costing HK$100.

Every week a steamer leaves Hong Kong for Shanghai, and its twin leaves Shanghai for Hong Kong. These cruise liners are equipped with bars and swimming pools to help you while away the two-and-a-half day voyage. Dormitory accommodation is HK$260 or 90元. In Hong Kong, tickets are available from China Merchants Steam Navigation Co. Ltd., 152-155 Connaught Rd., Central, 5-430945, while in Shanghai bookings can be made through CITS or at the Shanghai Branch of the China Ocean Shipping Agency, 255 Jiangxi Rd. (Huang Pu Hotel). This is a good way of leaving China in decadent splendour. Similar (though more expensive) liners go from Hong Kong to Shantou and Xiamen.

Via Macau: The charming, tiny Portuguese territory of Macau, more relaxed than Hong Kong but more colourful than China, makes a good intermediate stop between the two (see Appendix). Luxury minibuses make the trip from the Macau border to Canton and vice-versa every morning for HK$20 or 7元, and there is an overnight ferry for the same price. Tickets are available at the dock or bus station. Departure time varies from day to day; check in Canton or Macau.

China Direct

Air: There are direct flights to China from many parts of the globe, though these are usually quite expensive. CAAC flies from Peking to New York, San Fransisco, Tokyo, London, Paris; Karachi, Tehran, Addis Ababa and Moscow, from Shanghai to Los Angeles, San Fransisco, New York, Osaka and Nagasaki, and from Canton to Bangkok and Manila. Many foreign carriers also fly to China, including British Airways, Lufthansa, Pan Am, Air France, Swissair, Pakistan International, Philippine Airlines, JAL, Ethiopian and Aeroflot. One unusual international route is the weekly CAAC flight between Rangoon and Kunming. To leave China this way you must have a Burmese visa, available in Peking but not in Kunming, and your stay in Burma is limited to a week.

Train: The Trans-Siberian express, one of the world's most romanticized trains, crosses the endless Siberian steppe on its way between Moscow and Peking. There are twice-weekly departures in either direction: on Fridays a Chinese train makes the five-day journey via Mongolia, while the Tuesday Russian train takes an extra day to pass through Manchuria. Tickets cost about US$160 in second class, the cheapest seats, roughly equivalent to Chinese soft berth. (The ride from Western Europe to Moscow is much more expensive per mile.) Tickets may be purchased through the CITS main office on Qianmen St. in Peking or, in Moscow, through the railway booking office in the Metropole Hotel building (side entrance). Mongolian, Chinese and Soviet visas may be arranged at their respective embassies in Moscow or Peking; allow up to a week for processing. A Mongolian visa is required for those who go through that country, even if they don't get off the train. Stopovers are permitted in Novgorod, Novosibirsk, Irkutsk and Ulan Bator, and accommodation must usually be arranged through Intourist in Moscow or the Soviet Embassy in Peking. In Europe the visa, ticket and reservations can be handled inexpensively by a travel agent. Near the border the Russian dining car has a tendency to run out of food.

Orientation

Travel in China is unlike travel anywhere else. The newly arrived visitor, even one who has spent years in Asia, will feel as Alice must have felt just after she stepped through her looking-glass into a world in which all the basic rules of living had been changed. Indeed, China goes one better, for often there are *no* set policies and the rules are malleable, ready to be reshaped by the traveller and the bureaucrat with whom he or she is dealing. And however unreasonable the creatures Alice dealt with might have been, they at least understood English. Very few Chinese people do (although this is changing). Even hotel clerks speak English haltingly if at all.

Despite these basic difficulties, travel in China is not only tolerable but pleasant. What makes it so is the kindness and humanity of most of the people you will meet. This includes the majority of policemen and other bureaucrats, and virtually all the ordinary people of China. By and large, a traveller is usually treated as an honoured guest rather than as someone to be exploited or avoided.

One can only hope that in return the Chinese benefit from the recent influx of visitors. The example of other Third World countries does not lead to undue optimism, for most gain little if anything from tourism. These nations have found that most of the hard currency brought in by foreigners is spent to import the fancy food and other luxuries the visitors demand. Any remaining profits are re-invested to maintain the existing hotels or build more of them, or are siphoned off by the (often foreign) businessmen who own the facilities. The tourist industry creates fewer jobs per dollar invested than do other projects, and the waiters and maids often find their employment relatively ill-paid and demeaning. Any economic gain these jobs bring is usually offset by inflation. Not all food is imported, and the heaps of rice lying uneaten on tourists' plates would have found better use on a poor worker's table.

China has a good chance of avoiding some, but not all, of these pitfalls. Because all tourist facilities are government-owned, profits from tourism benefit the entire country rather than a few hotel owners. Also, work conditions in hotels are better than in most under-developed nations. But any economic gain to China may be outweighed by another factor: the explosive impact of hordes of tourists on the culture of a once-closed society. This cultural interchange may not be entirely unhealthy: some of the restrictive aspects of life in China today are tolerated by the people only because they seem as inevitable as cold in winter. Foreigners can show the Chinese that they do not have a monopoly on viable systems of social order. Nevertheless, the effects of tourism are not always so benign, as any visitor to Kathmandu or Bali will testify. There, the "cultural interchange" of tourism has led only to increased prostitution and the emergence of particularly unpleasant hustlers and drug peddlers. Whether the social changes brought by tourism to China will be for good or ill remains to be seen. In part, it's up to you.

Bed and Board

Hotels: Choosing a hotel in China is easy. In most cities, only a few hotels are open to you. The big, dingy, very cheap hostelries where most Chinese travellers stay are usually forbidden to accept foreign tourists, though students and experts with valid Chinese work papers have sometimes succeeded in talking themselves into rooms. Without such identification, however, the clerks at these hotels will almost always turn you away, since they would otherwise get into trouble with the authorities. If by some chance you get a bed in one of these hotels, you may be visited by the police. They will sometimes escort you to the tourist hotel, sometimes merely examine your passport and let you stay.

If selecting a hotel is simple, getting a room is not. Hotels offer a bewildering array of room classes and prices. The standard tourist hotel is a huge complex with hundreds of rooms ranging from luxury suites to cheap dormitories, with many grades of accommodation in between. Some of these are reserved solely for tourists, some are kept for students, and some are restricted to Chinese citizens. Moreover, travellers, students, foreign experts and Chinese each pay a different price for the same room. But in almost every city there is something available to suit the budget traveller — usually dormitory accommodation for 5-9 元. The best double rooms with bath — the sort tour groups are billeted in — cost about 30 元 Single travellers are usually allowed to pay for one bed only; in theory they must share the room, but in practice they are rarely asked to. Foreign students in Chinese universities can in most places get a luxury room for 6 元 ;

42

foreign experts (teachers, engineers, etc. working for the Chinese government) are charged 9元 Students are usually required to show their Chinese university card, a distinctive document bound in bright red plastic, but the receptionist will sometimes accept your word. Some vagabonds have gotten very cheap accommodation this way.

Most travellers prefer to stay in the dormitories. But although these are almost always open to foreigners, the hotel staff would generally rather you took a more expensive room. Thus, on occasion, a sympathetic-looking receptionist will tell you that he is very sorry but there is no dormitory, or the dormitories have been closed for renovation, or (the most usual line) the dorms are full. Do not despair. In nine cases out of ten, the story is untrue. Patience and polite persistence will win the day. Sit down and wait; within an hour or three, a bed will suddenly become vacant, or perhaps a special room will mysteriously be found. Remember, though, that the receptionist will never admit that he made a mistake; he doesn't want to appear a liar or a fool. The most inventive solution to this problem was found by a Shanghai receptionist "Oh," he said with surprise to an irate Frenchman who had been waiting *two days* (an all-China record) for a bed, "you want a place in the *male* dormitory! We thought you wanted a place for a *woman,* and the female dormitory is full." (And where did the Frenchman sleep while he was waiting for a spot in the allegedly full dormitory? In the dormitory, of course. He reasoned, quite correctly, that he would not have to pay to sleep in a bed supposedly occupied by someone else.)

These protracted battles are relatively uncommon and are, thankfully, becoming rarer. In all of the largest tourist cities there is now at least one hotel that routinely offers dormitory accommodation to anyone who wants it, although foreigners must sometimes pay two or three yuan more than Chinese citizens. The further you go off the beaten track, the more likely you are to have difficulties, since many smaller places are unaccustomed to individual travellers. This is where a little vocabulary is useful: a "luguan" or a "fandian" is apt to have cheap rooms, but a "binguan" (Guest House) almost certainly will not. Before you allow someone to direct you to a binguan, try to find out if there is anywhere else that might accept a foreigner. Even if this doesn't succeed, it demonstrates to the binguan staff that you really are attempting to economize, and you can further bolster your case by showing the clerk your old hotel receipts : the fact that other establishments have given you cheap accommodation will weigh heavily in your favour. But don't make the mistake of walking into a hotel with a siege mentality. This will only aggravate people who might otherwise be willing to help you, and makes it more difficult for other single travellers later on.

After negotiations have been concluded, you will be given a short registration form in English which is subsequently sent to the police. You must also show your travel permit; the hotel usually keeps this until you leave, but will return it earlier if you need to take it to Public Security.

In most cities the dormitories are comfortable, and long-time economy travellers will find them almost luxurious. Most have between four and ten beds; there are always separate rooms for men and women. Sometimes there is even a private bath; if not, there's usually a shower down the hall, although some hotels have hot water for only a few hours a day. Many hotels are unheated and/or unairconditioned (if you don't think this is important check under "Climate"). Blankets are provided in abundance, however, and many beds come equipped with a mosquito net.

Restaurants: China has one of the world's most sophisticated *hautes cuisines,* and the best restaurants in Peking, Canton, Shanghai, Suzhou and Chengdu rank among the best Chinese restaurants in the world. Don't believe those running dogs who claim that nothing in China equals Hong Kong's finest! This was true during the Cultural Revolution, when politics was in command in the kitchen and the best chefs were demoted to dishwashers while dishwashers with model political beliefs took over the wok and stove. Happily, those days are gone, and China's restuarants have returned to their former glory.

For the budget traveller, China's chief culinary delight is that you don't have to blow your inheritance to get the best. You can eat a good meal in the finest restaurants in China for under 4元 (which will barely buy you two Big Macs in Hong Kong). Most good restaurants have several sections: posh banquet halls reserved for tourists and high cadres, and more spartanly furnished dining rooms for the masses. These cheap sections, though intended primarily for Chinese, usually welcome travellers. If they tell you to move to the tourist section, remain where you are. As everywhere in China, polite persistence is the key.

At the other end of the scale are the numerous noodle and dumpling houses. The fare is limited, but the prices are right (usually between 10 and 40 fen), and the atmosphere pleasantly noisy and animated. Somewhat more expensive are the smaller restaurants offering meat and vegetable entrees for between 50 fen and 2元. These are often hidden on the second floor of what appears to be a noodle shop. To find the best, look for the most crowded. In most, you must wait in line to buy meal tickets, then wait again for the food. Often, when the cooks spy a foreigner, they will insist on serving him first and will not take no for an answer.

It is best to pay in advance, or at least fix the price. Otherwise, the bill might be shamelessly padded; you will be told that "special ingredients" were used. This has befallen travellers even in small towns not normally visited by tourists. The cheaper sections of the best restaurants, and the cheapest noodle shops, are usually the most honest. Note that tourists are not required, as are Chinese, to carry ration tickets. Your bill might be slightly higher because you do not have a ticket, but you should never pay more than 10% extra.

Finally, a word about hotel restaurants. These come last because the food there is usually bland and boring. But hotel dining halls are often the most convenient, especially if you arrive in a city after 8 p.m., and they do serve Western breakfasts (about 3 元). Lunch and dinner are between 3 元 and 6 元 (students half price), and some hotels offer à la carte dishes for between 1 元 and 3 元. In some smaller areas (Shaoshan, Jinghong, Leshan, etc.) the hotel restaurants are cheaper and are the best in town.

Transport

Trains: China has an extensive network of railways, and express trains are fast, clean and fairly cheap, and usually run on time. There are three main classes: soft bed, hard bed and hard seat. These correspond to first, second and third class — which is what they were called until the Cultural Revolution. Hard seat, the lowest category, is quite comfortable, and travellers fresh from other countries might well think they have blundered into an upper-class carriage. Despite the label, seats are usually padded, although the cushions are not as thick as those in soft class. For daytime trips this section is perfectly adequate; it's also a great place to meet people. But hard seat is very crowded and the lights are on all night; on longer rides, your desire to make new friends might take second place to your need for sleep. In that case, if you can afford it, it's better to go hard bed, which consists of three-tier berths with a thin mattress, sheets, pillow and blanket. At night, the car is darkened and the music stops; there are no standees. Soft bed features four berths in a closed compartment.

Prices, as is usual in China, vary according to who you are.

Foreigners, except for students in China and foreign experts, are required to pay a 70% supplement. The Chinese claim that the normal prices are kept artificially low by government subsidy, and this might well be partly true, although the prices are higher than in many other Asian countries. The price is calculated according to an arcane formula based on the distance and the speed of the train (local, express and fast express). A hard seat journey of 500 kilometers by express will cost 10.20元, by fast express 11.80元, while a hard sleeper, center berth, will run an additional 6.70元. For 1,000 kilometers, the figures are 17.60元, 20.50元 and 11.50元; for 1,500 km, 23.70元, 26.70元 and 15.50元; for 2,000 km, 29.30元, 34.10元 and 19.20元; for 3,000 km, 42.50元, 49.40元 and 27.90元. In sum, a long journey costs somewhat less than several short stops; you can save money by buying one long ticket. A hard seat ticket (but not the sleeper supplement) is good for several days from the date of sale, the exact number being printed on the bottom of the ticket. Any station sells tickets to any other, and you can thus buy a hard seat from, say, Kunming to Harbin or Urumqi to Xiamen, although the sleeper supplement for connecting trains must be paid en route.

Train timetables are easy to find and, once you know the Chinese characters for your destination, easy to read. The complete edition, a large paperback, is sold for 60 fen. The times are altered slightly every few months, so confirm departure times when you buy your ticket.

You can usually buy a ticket at the train station within half an hour, but in some cities, especially Canton and Peking, the lines seem endless. If you don't want to endure this, you can get tickets at your hotel or at CITS, in which case you are more than likely to be stuck with the surcharge. Assuming time is less important to you than money, your best bet is always the station, or, in some cities, the ticket offices in the center of town, easily recognized by the distinctive hammer-and-circle logo. Sometimes the ticket seller will issue a normal-price ticket without question. This is most often the case in towns away from the main tourist routes, and these are usually good places to buy long-distance tickets. Some tourists claim to be students in China, a bluff which, if bolstered by international student cards and used normal-price tickets, often works. Still less scrupulous travellers ask Chinese friends to buy their tickets for them, but this might land the Chinese friend in jail.

Tickets can usually be bought a few days in advance, stamped with the day and train on which you will travel. If you are breaking your journey, you must get your ticket restamped, a procedure which often takes far less time than buying a new ticket. You cannot reserve a seat or a berth except in the town were the train originates or in a few very large cities such as Nanjing and Wuhan. If you don't have a hard seat reservation, you may have to stand or sit in the aisle unless you are willing to pay for a hard bed. Berths are almost always available on the train; you simply go into the hard bed carriage or to the counter set up for this purpose and pay the supplement on the spot. Don't leave your ticket on the train, because it is checked at the station when you disembark.

You don't need to take food supplies along. Every few hours, attendants circulate through the carriages selling food tickets for 30 or 40 fen. The rice-and-veg meals, brought to your seat in a metal bowl, are basic but filling. Better food is available in the dining car. On some trains tickets are sold in advance, while on others you order when you sit down to eat. Main courses usually range between 50 fen and 2元. Between meals samovars in each car provide an endless supply of boiling water (bring your own mug and tea).

Buses: China has a full network of inter-city buses. Most routes are for relatively short distances, and thus are theoretically barred to foreigners since passengers bound for "open" destinations must overnight in "closed" towns. There are a few longer routes, and these are described under the city listings. Though less comfortable than the trains, buses are the best way of seeing the country. They pass through — and stop in — backwater villages that the trains tend to skirt around. Moreover, bus tickets are as cheap as or cheaper than hard seat on trains, and everybody pays the same price.

Planes: Although more susceptible to delay than the trains, planes are the fastest way of getting where you want to go. They are also the most expensive. Tourist price is inescapable, and is double — sometimes triple — the ordinary fare. Sometimes, however, you may feel it is worth paying 40元 or 50元 extra to avoid a particularly circuitous train connection, as from Canton to Guilin or Kunming to Chonqqing. You can buy your ticket at some hotels, at CITS, or at the CAAC office. The price includes a bus from the CAAC office to the airport and vice versa. Note that there is no refund if you miss your flight.

Boats: Ocean liners ply the coastline between Dalian, Qingdao, Shanghai and Fuzhou, and smaller boats steam up the Yangtse and many other rivers besides. The larger, seagoing ships each have four or five classes ranging from luxury double staterooms to plainer eight-berth cabins, spartan 48-berth dormitories or a place on the deck. A restaurant serves plain but palatable meals for under 1 元. Tickets usually go on sale at least two days in advance, and it's best to buy early. If the boat leaves in the early morning, you can sometimes board the night before.

Hitching: Hitching is a mode of transport whose potential has not yet been fully tapped. Of the few travellers who have tried it, some have been brilliantly successful, while others have been arrested. Traditionally tolerant areas such as Hainan Island and the Pearl River Delta south of Canton have proved particularly amenable. Hitching at times offers the only opportunity to penetrate closed regions, which is illegal. The thumbs-up sign is not understood; wave your arm and flag the truck down. And don't be discouraged if hours go by and nobody stops — the next truck might take you where you want to go.

Bikes: This is another form of travel waiting to be pioneered. It is easy to buy a bicycle in China and only slightly more difficult to cross the border with one. You can take the bike with you on the train. Although a separate license is required for each city, in practice few travellers have been stopped. Inter-city bike travel in theory requires police permission, but may be possible, especially in the southern regions. Carry your receipt of purchase or other proof of ownership at all times. You may be able to resell the bike when you leave China, but the law requires such transactions to be made through government-run used bicycle shops.

Local transport: City buses are very crowded, and pushing and shoving one's way on seems to be the national sport. You buy a ticket when you board; the fare is calculated by distance, and is usually between 4 and 10 fen. If you don't know the name of your destination, you can hand the conductor 10 fen, or indicate the number of stops you are travelling, or point to a ticket. Remember that bus service stops quite early; the last bus usually goes around 9:00 p.m., somewhat later in such metropolises as Peking and Shanghai. At hotels, bookstores and most train stations you can get a city map for 20 fen showing every bus route in town.

Taxis do not cruise the streets, but you can normally find them at the hotel or train station. The fare is usually about 80 fen per kilometer. In some cities pedal or motorized trishaws are available, and these are cheaper if you negotiate with the driver.

In Peking, Guilin and a few other cities you can rent bikes, usually for around 1.50 元 per day. You leave your passport as security. This is a great way to explore the town and surrounding countryside. The bike rental shops are small and have a sign outside, often in English.

CITS

Until recently travellers in China were not permitted to make their own travel arrangements. This was done for them by a state organization set up for the purpose, the China International Travel Service (CITS). CITS still exists, bigger than ever, with branch offices in most tourist towns, usually in the largest hotels. Although the individual traveller need never come in contact with its numerous functionaries, they can often make your life easier (though more expensive) by buying train or plane tickets, reserving hotel rooms, organizing city tours, and even getting cinema tickets. They are not, however, geared to the budget traveller, and rare indeed is the CITS clerk who will help you book a dorm bed, or buy a rail ticket at the Chinese price. Quality of service varies widely. Some clerks are friendly, helpful and full of useful information about the city in which they are stationed, while others are rude, incompetent or both. Remember that having CITS do a job is not always a guarantee that it is done right. Hotel reservations occasionally get botched, and a few travellers, issued with incorrectly written rail tickets, have not been allowed to board their train.

China First Class

Many would-be visitors to China want the hassle-free luxury of a group tour but not its regimentation. Those taking a brief vacation from a high-pressure job do not want to fight for a dorm bed, nor to sleep in one. It is for this kind of traveller that CITS is at its best. Once you get your visa, the CITS office in each city — starting with Hong Kong — can reserve a hotel room in the next town on your itinerary, book a soft berth or air ticket to go there, and arrange for a car to meet you when you disembark. CITS can also fix travel permits and arrange city tours and commune visits.

For even more flexibility, you can dispense with the CITS escort. Have CITS book your transport but not your hotel. On arrival, take a taxi from the station to the best hotel in town — listed in our city descriptions — where the receptionist will be delighted to give you the poshest room available. (The only hitch is that, at the height of the season, you may have trouble finding a good room in the most popular tourist cities, in which case a reservation comes in handy.) By travelling in this fashion you can sleep in the same rooms as the group tours, travel in the same soft-berth carriages, and eat much the same food for half the price or less. If you were content to go hard berth and share a hotel room, you could make the tour for one-quarter the group price. Of course, the freedom to go on your own has a value that cannot be measured in dollars and cents.

Officialdom

Public Security: The organ responsible for issuing travel permits and visa extensions is the Foreign Affairs Division of the Public Security Bureau. Public Security is the name given the Chinese police force, both uniformed and plainclothes. It is responsible for a whole gamut of activities from KGB-like suppression of political dissent and crime detection to mediating family quarrels and directing traffic. Those whose image of the Chinese police derives from the sinister characters in James Bond novels will be pleasantly surprised. Public Security people are usually far kinder and more polite to foreigners than their counterparts in other Third World nations. We know of relatively few instances where police have "played the heavy" with tourists. The worst that has happened — and this is quite rare — is for particularly errant travellers to be detained and interrogated before being put on a plane to Hong Kong. Usually if, say, you visit a town not open to tourists, the police will either ignore your violation or put you on a train bound for an open city the next day.

Travel permits: You cannot stop anywhere in China — except for the two cities named on your visa — unless your destination is listed on your Alien's Travel Permit. You can easily obtain this buff-coloured cardboard document in Canton, Shanghai, Peking, the cities granted on your visa, and usually in other cities as well. Problems will arise, though, if you choose a town that doesn't have the official forms in stock — best to apply in Canton if you are coming from Hong Kong. There you can usually get it in an hour or two, even if Canton is not listed on your original visa. (See "Canton" for details.)

You may add cities to your travel permit as many times as you like in any town with a Foreign Affairs Division — that is, in any large town open to tourists. Approximately 120 places are officially open, and you can obtain permission easily for most of them, although some of the more exotic, such as Xishuangbanna, are given only in the capital of their province. If you are refused by one office, shop around; you have scores of Foreign Affairs Divisions to choose from. There is no harm in requesting permission for a closed area, and if you succeed you will probably be allowed to go there, although in theory any Public Security officer may cross the city off your permit.

Remember that you are not allowed to stop even in an open city unless it is listed on your permit, which is always checked by the hotel. In many towns, nobody cares if you don't have permission, but in others you will politely but firmly be evacuated. The police of some railway junctions such as Hengyang, Guiyang and Shijiazhuang will often refuse to let you leave the train station if your papers are not in order.

Visa extensions: Entry visas are usually extended at the Foreign Affairs office, but the policy varies by the city, by the official, and even by the moment. One traveller applied for his first extension at the Foreign Affairs bureau of a large town. Two charming policewomen sat him down to tea, then informed him, through an interpreter, that, though they wanted very much to help him, their city did not have the authority to grant extensions. He would have to go to the provincial capital. Being wise to the ways of the world, the traveller thanked them, left, came back six hours later and asked again, pretending to have forgotten the previous encounter. Apparently, so had they; he had his extension within ten minutes.

Extensions are usually for either two weeks or one month (ask for a month), and cost 5元. You should get your travel permit extended at the same time, which costs an additional 1元. Most (but not all) cities will refuse to give you more time if you have already had two extensions, and a growing number of towns will not give any extensions beyond the first. At any given moment there are a number of cities whose Foreign Affairs offices are more lenient than others, but this is the sort of information best communicated by word of mouth.

Nuts and Bolts

What to take: There is no need for the China-bound to assemble the sort of armada of luggage that Stanley and Baker took to darkest Africa. Pack as you would for a journey anywhere else.

Laundry service in hotels is fast and fairly inexpensive, and detergent is available almost everywhere, so one or two changes of clothes is enough. Functional if dowdy garments can be bought all over China. Good shoes, however, are hard to come by, especially in larger sizes. In summer you can get by with jeans and T-shirts. The Chinese are used to seeing hairy-legged men, and while shorts are less acceptable for women, they will never call forth the unpleasant reaction common in Iran and India. Warmer clothing is required from October to April, when long underwear, heavy sweat shirts and high-quality down jackets are on sale throughout the country.

Chinese-made toiletries are easily purchased, although some items, especially shampoo, tampons, make-up and razor blades, are inferior to the Western variety. Suntan lotion is unavailable, as is mosquito repellent — the Chinese use coils and screens — but strong sun and aggressive insects are usually not a problem. Kodak and Fuji film is available in the major tourist cities, at a price about 50% higher than in Hong Kong. Film processing, however, is not up to international standards, and photographs of controversial subjects are likely to be mislaid. Chinese tea is ubiquitous, but instant coffee is on sale in only a very few cities. Western tableware is unknown in many places: if you must use it, bring your own. Locally-made cigarettes and whiskey are sold at innumerable state-owned outlets, and imported brands may be bought at most of the hotels and Friendship Stores that line the tourist trail. Reading material is a problem. In most large cities, bookstores sell a smattering of Dickens and Hemingway and a few Chinese novels translated into English, as well as copies of the Peking-based China Daily newspaper. At a few of the finest hotels there is a reasonable selection of American and British paperbacks and news magazines.

Some Western medicines, such as tetracycline, Flagyl, aspirin and vitamins are manufactured in China and are available without prescription at prices far below those charged in the West. Chinese remedies are also stocked in pharmacies, and are especially efficacious for head colds and diarrhoea. Bandages, iodine and antibiotic ointments are hard to find, as are any unusual medicines. Take a supply with you, as well as the name written in Chinese. If you need medical advice, a doctor will call at your hotel for under 2元. Cannabis is rare except in Xinjiang, where it is sold covertly, and in Yunnan, where it grows wild in the Stone Forest.

Money: China prints two kinds of money. Foreign Exchange

Certificates (FEC or "tourist money") sports engravings of China's scenic attractions and is issued in exchange for foreign currency. Renminbi (literally "people's money") is adorned with more proletarian scenes — steelworkers, women on tractors — and daily use makes it noticeably more shopworn than its stiff, crisp counterpart.

Most hotels and hotel dining rooms require travellers to settle their accounts with tourist money. You must also use FEC when you buy plane tickets and when you shop in Friendship Stores. Train tickets may usually be bought with either money; Renminbi creates less of a fuss at the train station, although you will not spoil your chances of getting the Chinese price by using FEC. In some less-visited towns, smaller shops and eating places won't take tourist money because they have never seen it before. If you use it in a closed town, this will quickly alert the police to your presence.

In many cities, however, your tourist money is eagerly sought after by all vendors, even farmers selling produce at the market. The explanation for this is in the Friendship Stores. These emporia, which exist in almost every sizeable town, are full of imported or luxury commodities unavailable to the ordinary Chinese, as well as a full range of handicrafts, artwork, bric-a-brac and souvenirs. Good-quality bicycles and televisions, for example, are rationed, and a worker might have to wait a year before his turn comes to buy one. At the same time, dozens of these items might be readily available in the local Friendship Store. In some cities, such as Peking, only foreigners can use the Friendship Store, and detectives guard the entrance to keep them free of local Chinese. In most towns, however, anyone with FEC is welcome, and the only source for this magical currency is tourists. You will receive many offers to trade Renminbi for FEC, and in some places, most notably Guilin, you can even get a premium. This is illegal, although it is permitted to use tourist money in smaller restaurants and food stalls. (In April 1982, in an attempt to curb the black market, it was announced that ten of the most popular commodities, including TV and bicycles, would only be sold on production of a bank receipt showing that the purchaser had changed foreign currency into Renminbi.)

You can change foreign currency, including traveller's checks, at banks in most large towns (usually located at the main tourist hotel). The rate is more or less the same everywhere. Save your bank receipts, because with them you can change your FEC back into dollars at the border or in Canton. Note that the banks are very reluctant to convert Renminbi.

In a few of the major tourist cities you can cash a personal check if you have American Express or Visa credit cards. The American Express check-cashing service is available in Peking, Canton, Shanghai, Xiamen, Nanning, Guilin, Quanzhou, Fuzhou, Qingdao, Hangzhou, Tianjin, Nanjing, Wuxi, Suzhou and Changsha. Don't count on plastic money to settle your hotel bill, although the latest word is that this is imminent.

The basic unit of Chinese currency, both tourist and people's, is the yuan, worth about US60¢. Most people call these "kwai." One yuan is divided into one hundred fen, and ten fen is also called a jiao. Thus, seven jiao is the same as 70 fen. The slang word for jiao is "mao" — the same character that often precedes Tse-tung.

Shopping: Though travellers are no longer greeted with a bargain at every town, there is no shortage of shopping opportunities in China. Most large cities have Friendship Stores which cater primarily to tourists. These emporia offer many products not available in other shops, such as fine silks, crafts, jewelry and so on. Those articles carried by local stores, however, are often sold at less than "Friendship" prices. The cost is fixed and cheating is rare in state-owned stores, though private peddlers may charge what the traffic will bear. You may be unable to buy items such as cotton cloth without a ration coupon unless you go to the Friendship Store. But the local shops' selection of non-rationed items is often bewilderingly vast, especially in larger cities such as Shanghai and Canton where entire stores are devoted to actors' costumes, or musical instruments. If an item catches your fancy, buy it; you may never find its like again.

Some cities have government-licensed antique and art shops, where a red wax seal is affixed to all items over 100 years old. Save the seal and your receipt: all antiques, jewelry and paintings by famous artists not bought in licensed stores may be confiscated when you leave the country. Unfortunately, tariffs in these official shops are often higher than in their counterparts in the U.S. and Europe. Only those with current knowledge of the world market can hope to find bargains.

The most extensive selection of Chinese-made handicrafts and manufactured goods can be found, not in China, but in Hong Kong. At the large, Chinese-owned superstores in Kowloon and elsewhere, many items are available at prices lower than in China. It's advisable to visit these shops before heading north in order to have a standard of comparison later on.

Entertainment: China's theatres offer an almost inexhaustible source of entertainment. The best-known fare is, of course, Chinese opera. Peking opera is only the most popular of the many regional variants. Most provinces have at least one form native to them, and some, such as Jiangsu, have several. All are rigidly stylized, and every gesture has a fixed meaning, but the color, the music and the grace of the actors can be appreciated by all.

In larger cities, operas are staged almost every evening. The theatres are usually in the center of town, and the best seats are rarely more than 40 fen. Seats can be booked at the box office and sometimes also through CITS.

Other possibilities include plays, concerts, ballets, acrobatics and martial arts exhibitions, as well as variety shows that are a potpourri of all of these. And of course, there are movies: revolutionary dramas, love stories, expensively-made historical epics set hundreds of years ago, even comedies. Gone are the days when Chinese films were so boring that tickets could not be sold. Today, many are good enough to play to full houses. Tickets cost about 20 fen. Despite the heavy demand, the box offices often have extra seats reserved for tourists and other VIPs, and scalpers sell tickets up to showtime for a premium of 10 or 20 fen.

Climate: The weather in China can be painfully miserable. Winters are cold, sometimes bitterly cold, as icy Siberian winds sweep over the entire continent. The north is, of course, usually far more frigid than the south; Peking is almost as far north as New York and is even colder. On an average winter's day in the capital, the temperature does not get above the freezing point — although it is almost always sunny and dry. The regions beyond the Great Wall are even more icy, with the mercury at times plummeting to 40 below. In the south you may be pleasantly surprised by warmer spells, even in January. Xi'an and Sichuan, protected by mountains, are noticeably milder than other parts of central China, and Kunming and Canton are even more temperate. The warmest places in winter are Xishuangbanna and the southern coast of Hainan Island.

By contrast, summer in both north and south can be uncomfortably hot and sticky. Temperatures in Peking may soar over 100°F (38°C), while the average minimum between June and September is 75°F (25°C). The temperature in the south is about the same, but the humidity is higher. Most of the year's rainfall in both north and south comes in summer. An excursion to the mountains (Emei Shan, Huang Shan, etc.) is a pleasant respite from the summer heat.

The best times to visit are during spring and autumn. But it's far better to go in January or August than not to go at all.

Crime: Pickpockets, muggers and rapists do exist in China. But there are very few cases of foreigners being assaulted or robbed by force, since the culprits face the firing squad if caught. China is one of the safest places in the world for men or women travelling alone. Though reasonable prudence is advised, the paranoia that is justified in many other countries is out of place here.

Mail: Airmail to anywhere outside China costs 70 fen for postcards and 80 fen for letters weighing 10 grams and under, except for mail to Hong Kong, which costs 10 fen. Mail takes between five and ten days to reach its destination. There are special philatelic shops in hotels and some post offices which sell beautiful sets of stamps for use on your correspondence or as souvenirs. In some cities you may find older stamps showing determined workers increasing production and fierce-looking soldiers defending the motherland; more recent stamps feature traditional landscape paintings and innovative modern designs.

Mail addressed to your embassy in Peking will almost certainly reach you; you will probably also get mail addressed to a hotel. Incoming and outgoing mail may be monitored.

Toilets: Since you probably know how to use the European variety little remains to be said about the Chinese. Except in the posher tourist hotels, they don't have pedestals and paper isn't provided. You can buy the latter in most cities, although it can be hard to find (it often comes in oblong packages) and you might end up "borrowing" some from hotels or buying Chinese newspapers.

Chinese cities probably have more public toilets per capita than any others in the world, and you'll soon learn to recognize these malodorous, barn-like structures. The first Chinese characters most travellers memorize are 男 (men) and 女 (women). They're mostly to be found in the side streets. Partitions are low or non-existent. Nobody minds; higher walls would interfere with the conversation.

By using the facilities, you're helping to boost agricultural production. The wastes are gathered by women pushing wooden wheeled tanks, and shipped to the countryside to fertilize the fields. These workers are relatively well-paid and honoured in the press; in countries such as India, they're paid starvation wages and considered untouchable.

Nightlife: Forget it. China goes to bed by nine.

Itineraries

Planning one's route is always difficult, and China is so vast that the possibilities seem endless. Still, geography makes some routes more feasible than others.

Starting in Canton, as most people do, you can head either north, east or west. To the west, Guilin, reachable by train, plane or bus, is a logical first stop. Those who wish to spend only a short time in China can go from Guilin to Nanning by train, then by bus to Beihai, Zhanjiang and Hainan Island, and finally return to Canton by boat. If, however, you wish to see more of the Southwest, take the train from Guilin to Kunming (perhaps making a detour to sunny Xishuangbanna), then continue north to Chengdu and Chongqing, the departure point for the Yangtse River cruise. (You can go from Guilin to Chongqing more quickly via Guiyang.) Many people take the Yangtse boat only as far as Wuhan, from where they either head north toward Peking or return to Canton, but it is also possible to continue on to Nanjing or Shanghai. Alternatively, disembark at Yichang or Wuhu en route to Luoyang or Huang Shan.

The only part of China not conveniently combined with the Yangtse boat route is the Northwest, which includes the ancient capital of Xi'an. It is possible to start with this region before taking the cruise on your way southwards (Chengdu to Chongqing to Wuhan to Guilin) — but then you will miss Kunming. If you are going north after Xi'an, Peking is accessible by way of either Zhengzhou and Luoyang or Taiyuan and Datong. Xi'an is also a logical jumping-off point for the long trek westwards Urumqi. Those who go this route can vary the return journey by taking the train from Lanzhou to Hohhot, Datong, and finally Peking.

Peking, like ancient Rome, is a magnet. Express trains leave there daily for every provincial capital in China except Lhasa. It is thus possible to go from Peking directly to Xi'an and continue to Chengdu or Urumqi. Or you can head in the opposite direction, and go by train to Tianjin, Beidaihe, Shenyang and Harbin. From here it is an easy drop down to Shanghai by coastal steamer (direct from Dalian or via Yantai and Qingdao). The land route south from Peking passes through Jinan and Nanjing.

Shanghai offers an equally wide range of travel options. Many of China's oldest and most beautiful cities, such as Suzhou and Hangzhou, are close by. There are also trains to Fuzhou and Xiamen, which can be reached in a more leisurely fashion by following the coast road, which continues as far as Canton and beyond. To the west, express trains make the four-day run to Urumqi (stopping in Xi'an), and boats go upriver to Chongqing. Finally, for those who have reached the limit of their money, patience or desire, there's always the weekly boat to Hong Kong.

These itineraries are only the most obvious. Many more exotic routes tempt the trailblazer. Can you go from Nanning to Kunming by bus? Or to Inner Mongolia via Yan'an? Or Tibet...? You won't know until you try. Even if you stick to the roads more travelled by, you are not condemned to follow in the footsteps of your fellow-travellers. Along each of these routes are smaller cities which, though open, are rarely visited. And near these towns are villages that have never seen a foreigner.

For most travellers, the main factor that limits their options is that old *radix malorum,* money. How much will it cost? If you have just arrived from Europe or America, the answer is probably far less than you might think. Hotel and food prices are discussed in detail in the previous section, but US$6-$9 a day for both of them is not an unreasonable estimate. As for transportation, consider: from Hong Kong you could take a series of trains, going hard bed all the way (Chinese price), to Canton, Guilin, Kunming, Chengdu, Xi'an, Luoyang, Peking, Nanjing, Suzhou, Hangzhou and Shanghai *and* take the boat from Shanghai to Hong Kong, all for under US$200! (That would take you about six weeks). If you have to pay the tourist price, try going hard seat. And for those on a really tight budget, there's always a way. Nobody starves in China.

Seeing China

A few years ago, and to some extent even today, a guided tour of China would entail being carted around, day after day, to scruffy parks, ill-maintained zoos, and second-rate museums and temples, with an occasional show factory or Potemkin commune thrown in. Perhaps the Chinese guides genuinely believed that you cannot attract tourists without specific tourist attractions, and failed to recognize that their clients did not travel thousands of miles to see mediocre gardens, ugly neo-Stalinist monuments, and sad-eyed zebras and lions. Or perhaps they feared that if they did not fill every minute of the day with boring excursions, their charges might learn something about China.

Today, visitors to open cities may go more or less wherever they want, without supervision. But the sorry parade of municipal parks, museums, and so forth make a return appearance in the pages of virtually every guidebook on China. Of course, there are some tourist attractions so impressive that it's worth travelling to China just to see them. One thinks at once of the Imperial Palace and Great Wall in Peking. And no trip to the Shanghai region would be complete without a visit to the gardens of Suzhou, the lake at Hangzhou, and the Shanghai Museum of Art and History. But most, and arguably all the tourist sites of China, take second place to the opportunity to see how the Chinese people live.

There are many ways to see and be a part of life in China. Time spent walking around Chinese towns and cities is always worthwhile. Under the city listings we've described the most interesting streets and neighborhoods that we know. With a little effort, you can find many others. Eat at local noodle shops; the food is good and they're jammed with workers. Linger over a cup in a teahouse where older people congregate to play cards, gossip, or just sit. Or try the parks in the early morning, filled with hundreds of people exercising.

You should, at least once, spend a day or two in some smaller, little-visited town that has no tourist attractions. Many of these are open to foreigners, such as Hengyang, Wenzhou or Yangquan. A visit to one of these places is a totally different experience from what you will encounter elsewhere. Expect to be stared at, since you will meet people who have never seen a non-Chinese.

Four-fifths of all Chinese live in villages, but although these are well worth a visit, it takes an effort to reach them because almost all the places where foreigners can spend the night are big cities. There are a few places, such as Shaoshan and Yangshuo, where you can find exciting villages within a few miles of your hotel. In other cities, you can take a local train or bus into the countryside, get off when you see a station with promise and spend the day exploring. Be sure that there is a return train that afternoon; it's illegal to spend a night at a village, and although the consequences are not usually drastic, the police are almost certain to find out.

In the cities you will encounter people who can speak English and, with luck, you might make a friend. Avoid those who lie in wait outside the hotel; usually they only want to practice their English. Visit universities — just walk in as if you belong there, and the gatekeeper will assume you do. Students are likely to approach you as you wander around the campus and invite you to their rooms for some very interesting conversation. This does not always happen, however, because in some schools students face disciplinary action for talking to foreigners.

Another good way of meeting people is to go into the small factories, hospitals and primary schools that you will find as you explore the cities. Not only might you meet English-speaking doctors, teachers and workers, but these places offer insights into the Chinese way of life. Some of these institutions don't want foreign visitors, and a representative will tell you to leave, but others will welcome you, and it costs nothing to try. Riding hard seat on trains provides yet another opportunity for close encounters. The main rule is obvious: be open, make yourself available.

It is all too easy for conversation in China, as everywhere, to degenerate into polite formulas: "You speak English very well;" "No, I speak only a little;" "How old are you?" and so forth. The responsibility for bringing up more interesting topics — politics, work conditions, etc. — is yours. You may feel that pointed questions are rude; that is for you to judge. Your friend may become evasive, or suddenly not understand a question, or may tell you that the subject is complex or that he has forgotten the answer. This is his polite way of indicating that your question is impolite.

Finally, it's important to remember that the authorities often look with suspicion on those Chinese who talk to foreigners. The attitude towards casual discussions fluctuates according to the political mood at the top. In mid-1982 the policy was very restrictive, and there is no way of knowing when or to what extent it is likely to be relaxed again. Usually the Chinese know the situation, and a genuine invitation is tantamount to saying that the risk is minimal. This hospitality is often difficult to reciprocate, however, since the Chinese will usually not be allowed past your hotel gate. They may be stopped, or their names taken and their unit notified. Be discreet.

1. North China

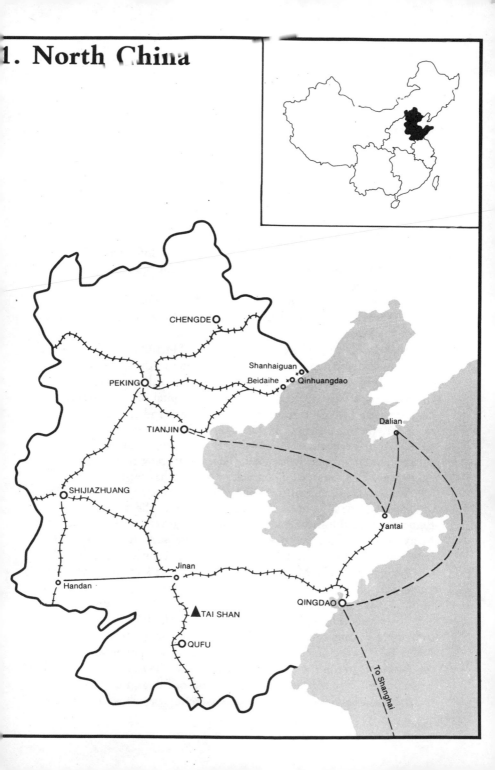

Peking

For almost 800 years, Peking has been the center of the Chinese world. By the time Marco Polo reached it at the end of the 13th century the city, then the capital of **Kublai Khan,** was already one of the world's great metropolises. From his long detailed description, it is clear that Polo was utterly overwhelmed by Peking's size and opulence. "There is so great a number of houses and people," he declared, "that there is no man who could count the number."

Peking's history began long before the explorer's visit. Fragments of the bones of "Peking Man," discovered just outside the present-day city, show that the region has been inhabited for half a million years. Under the Zhou Dynasty and possibly even earlier there was a settlement named Ji, where Peking is today. Sima Qian, writing over two thousand years ago, referred to Ji as "one of the large northern towns." Peking, however, did not assume national importance until a thousand years later. It became a secondary capital of the northern empire of the Liao Dynasty in the 10th century and the capital of its successor, the Jin Dynasty. In 1260, when Kublai became the ruler of all China, he decided to administer it from Peking, and built a huge palace in what is now Beihai Park. The city thereby rose to a pre-eminence which, except for short interludes, it has retained.

When the founder of the Ming Dynasty overthrew the Mongols in 1368 he made his capital Nanjing, but his son, the Yong-le Emperor, re-established Peking as the seat of government in 1421. Many of the landmarks of the city today were built during the next century, including the Imperial Palace and the Temple of Heaven.

Peking under the Ming was divided into four sections. The focal point was the Imperial Palace. The great halls of the palace, with their bright yellow-tiled roofs, were the highest structures allowed in the almost flat settlement. Around the palace was the Imperial City containing various court and governmental buildings. It included Beihai Park in the north and extended as far as the present-day site of the Peking Hotel in the east. This in turn was the center of the much larger Inner City, with its main streets laid out in a grid. The rectangular areas between these streets were intersected — as they are today — by a network of little narrow lanes called *hutong*, containing the grey-walled, grey-tiled domestic courtyards of the common people. To the south, the Outer City was a similar urban area newly developed in the 15th century The northern boundary of this Outer City was Qianmen, just south of what is now Tiananmen Square.

This plan remained basically unchanged until 1949, but Peking has been radically transformed — some would say sterilized — since. The huge city walls and gates were demolished, as were the wooden arches that graced the main thoroughfares, and wide new avenues, most notably Chang'an, were built both to impress and to accommodate increasing road traffic. Hundreds of thousands of workers toiled night and day on monumental — and monumentally ugly — construction projects, including the Great Hall of the People and the Railway Station. Large modern housing blocks with a dozen or more stories are increasingly replacing the urban villages built along the *hutong*. To cope with the perennial housing shortage, construction has been accelerated in the past three years. One of these huge blocks just south of Tiananmen precipitated a scandal two years ago because it was so shoddily built as to be uninhabitable. But the destruction of historical monuments has stopped, and some have recently been restored.

Today more than ever, Peking is the political and cultural heart of China. All clocks in the People's Republic, even those in far-off Xinjiang and Tibet, are set to Peking time, and the standard language, *putonghua*, is based on the Peking dialect. In addition, Peking is a major industrial center, with a population of over eight million, more than half of whom live in the core urban area.

The Town

Peking has many moods and many faces. The Great Hall of the People on a steely grey morning seems worlds removed from the crowded lanes of Qianmen on a warm summer night. But, like any great city, Peking has its distinctive cachet. In its own special fashion, Peking combines the excitement and sophistication of a large metropolis with the unpretentious ambiance of a far smaller town. Some of the low buildings that flank its principal arteries — with the exception of Chang'an and Qianmen — date from Imperial days. The boulevards themselves are jammed with men and women bicycling to work or walking to their neighborhood shops and markets. And if you leave these thoroughfares and plunge into the network of alleys and *hutong*, you will find a series of interlocking urban villages where

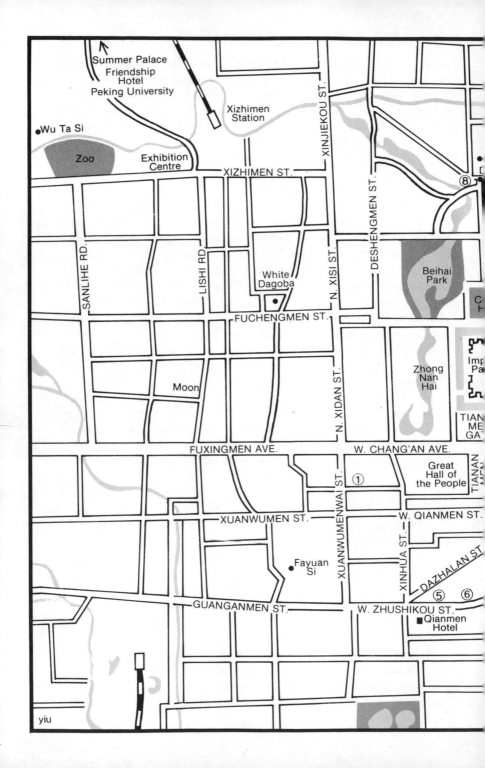

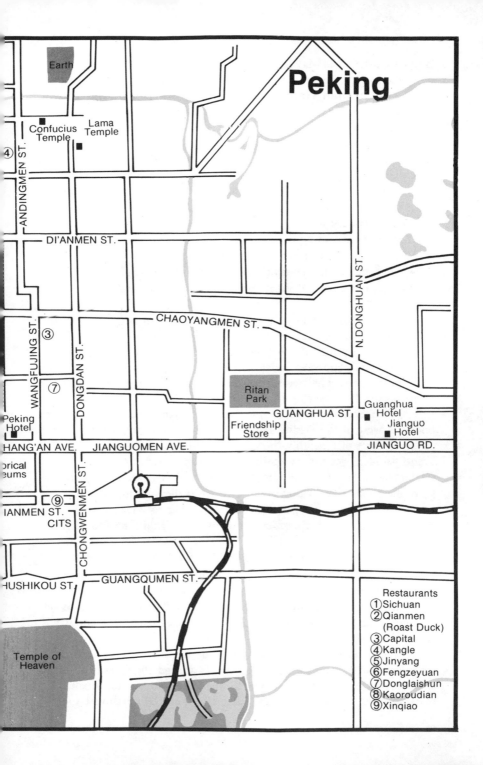

Peking

Earth

Confucius Temple

Lama Temple

ANDINGMEN ST.

④

DI'ANMEN ST.

N. DONGHUAN ST.

WANGFUJING ST.

③

⑦

DONGDAN ST.

CHAOYANGMEN ST.

Ritan Park

GUANGHUA ST.

Guanghua Hotel

Jianguo Hotel

Peking Hotel

Friendship Store

HANG'AN AVE.   JIANGUOMEN AVE.

JIANGUO RD.

orical eums

CHONGWENMEN ST.

⑨

IANMEN ST.
CITS

GUANGQUMEN ST.

HUSHIKOU ST

Temple of Heaven

Restaurants
① Sichuan
② Qianmen
   (Roast Duck)
③ Capital
④ Kangle
⑤ Jinyang
⑥ Fengzeyuan
⑦ Donglaishun
⑧ Kaoroudian
⑨ Xinqiao

families cluster in old-fashioned compounds behind thick grey-brick walls.

One particularly attractive older section of town is located just south of **Qianmen Gate,** which adjoins Tiananmen Square. This recently-restored massive 15th-century structure used to mark the boundary between the Inner and Outer Cities. Qianmen Rd., which runs south from this gate, is a busy shopping street; some of the smaller lanes running west from Qianmen are even more crowded. One of these, Dashalan, about a hundred yards south of the Gate across the road from the Roast Duck Restaurant, has been famous since the 17th century for its shops and theaters. Some of the many stores on this busy lane are hundreds of years old. Opposite Dashalan is a narrow road leading east whose buildings seem to lean against one another. Both Dashalan and its eastern counterpart lead to a maze of *hutong* and on summer evenings the families of the neighborhood move their chairs out onto the street to gossip, play cards, and watch the world pass by.

Another more sedate shopping area is **Wangfujing St.,** just east of the Peking Hotel. Before 1949 this road, then known as Morrison Street, was the principal shopping district for foreigners living in the imperial capital, and even today most of the larger stores in town are to be found here. The tree-shaded boulevard is also a popular place for promenading Pekingese.

Xidan St., the large avenue running north from Chang'an about one mile west of the Peking Hotel, is another good street for walking. Xidan is more of a neighborhood thoroughfare than Wangfujing or even Qianmen, yet the two-mile stretch from Chang'an to Xizhimenwai St. (the road leading to the zoo) is varied enough to hold one's interest all the way. (There are trolleys going back to Chang'an; take no. 105.) Another street similar to Xidan is Andingmennei, the northern continuation of Wangfujing (bus 2 from town).

For early risers, **Ritan Park,** behind the Friendship Store and near the Guang Hua Hotel, is an excellent place to start the day. Go at dawn to see amateur but dedicated opera singers and musicians practicing before an enthusastic audience, as well as the ubiquitous tai chi chuan. Later in the day you can go roller skating at the popular rink.

Other good places for walking include the area around the small lakes just north of Beihai Park, the streets around the Qianmen Hotel, and the village-like roads, lined with one-storey houses and small markets, west of the Friendship Guest House in the northwest suburbs.

One of the best ways of seeing Peking is on a bicycle. You can rent them for 1.50元a day (overnight) from the Limin Bicycle Shop, 2 Chongwenmenwai Rd. (near CITS), or from the Jianguomenwai Bicycle Repair Shop opposite the Friendship Store.

The Main Attractions

Imperial Palace: Between 1420 and the present century the Imperial Palace was the *omphalos* of China; for the Chinese, it was the center of the world. Twenty-four emperors of the Ming and Qing Dynasties lived in the halls, pavilions and courtyards of what was called "the Forbidden City." Only seldom did they emerge into the region beyond the red walls of their 250-acre home.

This impressive history alone would justify ranking the Palace as the foremost tourist attraction in China. It is a masterpiece of architecture as well. The scale is monumental but never oppressive, the design symmetrical but not repetitive. There is an extraordinary sense of balance between the buildings and the open spaces they surround. Like the Parthenon or the Taj Mahal, the Palace calls forth mysterious echoes deep within the soul of the viewer; like those other great monuments, it can be visited again and again.

Between 1406 and 1420, over 200,000 workmen were involved in the building of the complex. Burnt almost to the ground during the Manchu invasion of 1644, the buildings have been restored, repainted and rebuilt many times since. However, the basic design of its founder remains.

You enter the Forbidden City through the famous Tiananmen Gate (see below). Walking north through the Upright Gate, you arrive at the large **Meridian Gate** (1420), from where, each year, the emperor used to announce the calendar. You then cross a small stream, go through another gate, and are faced with the largest and most impressive building in the palace, the **Hall of Supreme Harmony,** previously used for the most solemn of ceremonial occasions such as New Year and the Emperor's birthday. Just beyond this building is the small **Hall of Complete Harmony,** used by the emperor to rest and to dress before entering the Supreme Harmony. The last building in this series, the **Hall of Preserving Harmony,** was used for state banquets, for reception of tribute, and for examinations of the highest rank of scholars.

Behind and to the north, through a gate that is the least-restored in the palace complex, are the three **Rear Palaces** — the Palace of

Heavenly Purity, the Hall of Union, and the Hall of Earthly Peace. In early times the emperor and empress lived in these magnificent large buildings, but later, during the Qing, they moved to smaller, more informal parts of the palace. The Qing emperors nevertheless continued to consummate their marriages in the Hall of Earthly Peace. The last Emperor, Pu Yi, was allowed to use this chamber on his wedding night even though he had been deposed a decade earlier. But, intimidated by the red colour scheme, he fled to his usual quarters at once. Through the gate behind this hall is the attractively landscaped **Imperial Garden.** (There is a public toilet just west of the garden; others are located just outside Tiananmen, and between Tiananmen and the Meridian Gate.)

The main palaces so far described all lie on the central north-south axis of the complex. In the northwestern section are the Hall of Mental Cultivation, where the last three emperors lived, and the six **Western Palaces.** The infamous 19th-century Empress Dowager lived in one of them, the Palace of Eternal Spring.

In the northeastern section are the six **Eastern Palaces,** which now house collections of ceramics and bronzes. A series of three halls exhibiting imperial treasure lies to the extreme northeast; just south is the Palace of Peaceful Old Age, where Qianlong retired after his abdication in 1795.

Tiananmen Square: The Palace Museum houses the ghosts of China's Imperial past, but the spirits that haunt the huge adjacent plaza are of more recent vintage. It was here that, on October 1, 1949, Chairman Mao proclaimed the establishment of the People's Republic of China. During the mass rallies of the late sixties hundreds of thousands of frantic Red Guards brandishing Mao's Red Book jammed the square. A few years later, in 1976, battles between police and people commemorating Chou En-lai's death (the Tiananmen Incident) were a crucial episode in the power struggle between the radical Maoists led by Jiang Qing and the more moderate faction of Deng Xiaoping.

Appropriately enough for a place that has become the symbol of modern China, the square itself, which until this century was filled with office buildings, is new. So are most of the surrounding edifices. The one exception is the massive yet graceful **Tiananmen Gate** (Gate of Heavenly Peace) that joins the square to the palace. It was built in 1650, and Imperial decrees were once read to the populace from its high balcony.

On the west side of the square is the **Great Hall of the People,** which was constructed during the '50s to house the People's Congress. What this monolithic edifice lacks in beauty it makes up for in size, for it is larger than all the buildings of the Imperial Palace combined. Southeast of the Great Hall is **Mao's Memorial Hall,** built in ten months by almost a million volunteers. Inside is the body of the late Chairman. Visits by individual travellers to these two buildings are not encouraged, though some have succeeded. You may have to try several times to get inside and possibly even make arrangements with CITS. It's hardly worth the trouble.

Two buildings you should visit are on the eastern side of the square: **the Museum of Chinese History,** with exhibits from prehistoric times to 1911, and the **Museum of the Chinese Revolution,** which concentrates on the growth of Communism in China, from its birth to its ultimate triumph.

Temple of Heaven: A masterpiece of Ming architecture, the Temple of Heaven is entirely distinct in style from the Imperial Palace. It was built in the early fifteenth century as the setting for important rituals designed to perpetuate the rule of the dynasty. The emperor in China regarded himself as responsible to the celestial power. In the Temple of Heaven he performed biannual rituals to inform heaven of the details of government. Much later it also became customary for the Emperor to pray for good harvests. The temple was last used for prayer in 1914 by Yuan Shikai, president of the Republic, who hoped to become Emperor.

Symbolizing heaven and earth, the temple enclosure is rounded in the north but square in the south. At the southern end is a triple-tiered white marble altar and, immediately beside it, the **Imperial Vault of Heaven,** a round, blue-roofed building. At the end of a long raised walkway is the most imposing building in the complex, the magnificent **Hall of Prayer for Good Harvests.** Constructed in 1420, it was rebuilt on the original plans after being burnt down in 1889. The structure is entirely of wood (no nails) and is supported by 28 huge pillars transported from Yunnan.

The Temple of Heaven is south of Chang'an Ave. Bus 116 goes from Tiananmen Square to the southern entrance. Outside the northeastern wall is a large free market that contains a bewildering variety of goods including orchids, pheasants, crabs, sofas and paintings.

The Great Wall: Snaking 3,700 miles across the mountains of north China, the Great Wall is one of the true wonders of the world. Originally built in small sections by individual feudal states in the 5th century B.C., the wall was linked on the orders of the First Qin Emperor 200 years later. It has been rebuilt and renovated many times since then, most extensively during the Ming Dynasty. The most accessible part of the Wall, at Badaling, 50 miles from Peking, is a recently restored Ming section.

The Wall was built as a defensive line against the warlike horsemen of the north, a function it performed fairly well. It certainly wasn't designed to be beautiful, but beautiful it is, whether covered with snow in winter or surrounded by summer greenery. At Badaling the Wall dips down to traverse a valley between two high hills. One can climb up either to the left or the right; the Wall has been restored for several hundred feet in either direction, but stretches on unrestored beyond this point. Try to make it to the unrestored part; not only is it more interesting, having been untouched for 400 years, but it is also almost deserted, even when the center is jammed with people. Don't be afraid that there won't be room for you to walk on the Wall; it can hold over 100 million tourists at once (although sometimes it may be more convenient to use one of the adjacent paths).

There are several ways to get to the Wall. A train leaves Peking in the early morning for Badaling, returning in the afternoon. It is about a mile from the train station to the wall. Or you can organize a group of four or five to share a taxi and set your own time — for example, sunrise — but this is expensive (about 20元 per person). Perhaps the best way is by tour bus. The all-day tour costs only 6元, including a visit to the Ming Tombs (see below). At least an hour is spent at the Wall, and the guide does not try to shepherd the group around; he tells you what time to be back at the bus and lets you off on your own. Tickets are available from a small booth opposite the CITS office on East Qianmen St., a few minutes' walk west of the train station. Go in the morning at least one day in advance.

Other Sights

Ming Tombs: The Ming imperial necropolis is usually visited on the way to the Great Wall and pales by comparison. There are 13 imperial tombs around the complex, which is dominated by the main hall in front of the oldest, the Chang Ling mausoleum (built for the Yong-le Emperor, who constructed the Imperial City). The only tomb to have been excavated is the Ding Ling, built in the 1580s. Underground is an impressive vaulted marble palace. Although these two tombs are probably not worth a long day's excursion just to see them, the surrounding countryside is a magical place for a picnic, especially if you get away from the main restored tombs. Bus 345 goes there from Deshengmen; take bus 5 from Tiananmen to Deshengmen. If you come on the Great Wall tour bus, ask the driver to stop for a few minutes at the approach avenue, which is flanked by huge stone guardians, animal and human, carved during the 15th century.

The Summer Palace: To avoid the intense heat of summer, the imperial court used to leave the Forbidden City and stay in a series of palaces seven miles northwest around Kunming Lake, landscaped to resemble the West Lake at Hangzhou. In 1860 British and French troops demolished the palaces. They were rebuilt in 1888 by the Dowager Empress, using money intended for the building of a modern navy. Today the Summer Palace is a delightful, rambling park full of curiosities. Much has been restored and repainted, and it is in a fine state of preservation. To get there, take bus 332 from the zoo, and allow an entire day. If you are on a bike or on foot, there is a more scenic route following the irrigation canal to the southwest corner of Kunming Lake; you enter the palace by a small side gate and don't pay admission. Not too far from the Summer Palace is the site of the **Yuanmingyuan,** one of the palaces destroyed by the Allied expedition and not rebuilt. Its ruins — including the remains of Italian-style baroque palaces — make a delightful picnic spot.

Beihai Park: The site of Kublai Khan's great palace is now a park with a large lake, popular with the people of Peking. On a hill dominating the park is a huge white Tibetan dagoba, built in 1651 and similar to the stupas of Ladakh and Nepal. There is a higher hill in nearby Jingshan Park **(Coal Hill)** from the summit of which you can get a good view of the palace below. South of Beihai lake and just west of the Imperial Palace are two other lakes, Zhong Hai and Nan Hai. They were part of the Imperial City, and the Dowager Empress used to live in a palace there. Today, the top Chinese leaders live and work in this part of town. It is reached from a heavily guarded gate on Chang'an Avenue and is, of course, completely off-limits to tourists.

Yonghegong: Also called the Lama Temple, this is one of the biggest (and most beautiful) Tibetan Buddhist temples outside Tibet.

Founded in the 18th century, it became the residence of a "Living Buddha" and had, at one time, 1500 monks in residence. Closed during the Cultural Revolution, it was re-opened in 1980 with a few monks from Inner Mongolia. There are five large halls, the last of which, the three-storeyed Pavilion of 10,000 Happinesses, is considered one of the finest examples of Chinese carpentry. The huge Buddha image inside is said to be made from a single sandalwood tree transported from Tibet. There is a prayer service every morning starting about 7 a.m. and normally closed to non-Buddhists, though you might be able to get special permission the day before from the head lama.

The Lama Temple is in the northeast part of town (bus 2 from Tiananmen). Just beyond it, on the left, is a small street with wooden arches; halfway down it on the right-hand side is the **Confucius Temple,** founded during the Yuan Dynasty and now containing three small museums, one of which presents a photo essay on Peking. In the courtyard stand more than 150 stone tablets — the oldest dating from the Yuan — recording the names and addresses of successful candidates in the civil service examinations.

Altars of the Sun, the Moon and the Earth: At these three temple complexes, the emperor performed yearly rituals designed to pay respect to the celestial bodies. None of these altars can compare with the Temple of Heaven. Perhaps the finest of them is the Altar of the Earth, built in 1530 and set in a wooded park near the Lama Temple. The Hall of Abstinence there has already been renovated. Some of the buildings of the Altar of the Sun, built in 1531, as well as the altar itself, still exist in Ritan Park. Built in the same year, the Altar of the Moon is on the opposite side of the city. It is now rather dilapidated and a large part of it is inaccessible.

White Dagoba Temple: Located west of Beihai Park, the huge white outline of this temple's 150-foot high dagoba can be seen from afar. Completed in 1279 under the supervision of the Nepalese architect Arniko, it was considered one of the gems of Khublai s new capital. The adjacent monastery was destroyed, rebuilt by the Ming, and destroyed again. The four existing halls date from the Qing Dynasty and contain Yuan and Ming Buddhist statues and Tibetan tankas. During the Cultural Revolution these buildings were occupied by factories but have recently been restored. Today, both the dagoba and temple halls can be visited.

Drum and Bell Towers: Drum and Bell Towers are traditional features of a Chinese city. The drums were struck every hour, day and night. Situated some way north of Prospect Hill, Peking's impressive Drum Tower dates from the Ming period (1420), while the Bell Tower is 18th century.

Fa Yuan Si: The Source of the Law Temple, or Fa Yuan Si, is situated off Niu Jie (Cow Street) in the southwest quarter of the city. Built originally by the Tang Emperor Taizong in 654 A.D. in memory of troops killed in a battle with the Koreans — and frequently restored thereafter — it is one of the oldest temples in Peking. Its halls, typical examples of Chinese architecture, are grouped around six courtyards planted with lilac trees. It houses the Chinese Buddhist Theoretical Institute where a number of novice monks attend classes, and is open to visitors (except on Wednesdays).

Wuta Si: Built in 1465, this Indian-style temple has recently been restored. The stone bas-reliefs of figures and flowers are beautiful and varied. Situated just behind the zoo, it can be reached by a small track leading east off the main road to the Summer Palace.

Dazhong Si: Located near the Friendship Hotel, this charming temple houses a giant Ming Dynasty bronze bell weighing over 46 tons and inscribed with Buddhist scriptures. Recently opened, it has been temporarily closed again for further restoration.

Beijing University: Due north of here is "Beida," founded in 1898 near Coal Hill and moved to its present location shortly after Liberation. The distinctively Chinese architecture of its campus belies its revolutionary history: Beida students were at the forefront of the May 4th Movement of 1919 and the Red Guard campaigns of early 1966. This is home to many foreigners who are studying in Peking.

Hotels

Guang Hua Hotel, Dong Huan Rd. North. From the train station, take bus 9 east along the main boulevard for about ten minutes; when the bus turns left, get off. The hotel is 100 feet back on the left. Most budget travellers end up here because it is the cheapest in town: 8元 a bed in a fairly luxurious carpeted double room, or 6元 in the spacious dorms. The hotel is well-maintained and is near the diplomatic quarter and the Friendship Store. The center of town is easily accessible by bus 1 or 4. There is a helpful CITS office and a medical clinic in the hotel, as well as a restaurant that offers palatable if not exceptional food.

There are several other hotels which, although intended primarily for Chinese, might give persistent travellers beds for under 10元: **Xuanwumen Hotel,** Xuanwumen St. (near the western terminus of bus 9 and opposite the huge Southern Cathedral); **Xiangyang No. 1 Hotel,** 2 E Qianmen St. (near Qianmen Gate); **Xiangyang No. 2 Hotel,** 30 W. Qianmen St.; **Beiwei Hotel,** Xijing Rd. (near Taoranting Park).

Peking's other tourist hotels offer first-class rooms at prices to match. The cheapest of these are: **Friendship (Youyi) Hotel,** Baishiqiao Rd.; **Minzu Hotel,** 51 Fuxingmennei Ave.; **Peace (Heping) Hotel,** Jinju Hutong; **Qianmen Hotel,** Yongan Rd.; **Xinqiao Hotel,** Chongwenmen; **Xiyuan Hotel,** Erligou; **Yuandong Hotel,** Xinhua St. South.

The **Peking Hotel** on Chang'an Ave. is very expensive, but is worth a visit to see its many restaurants, shops and bars, as well as the excellent view of the Imperial Palace from the roof of the old wing. The same can be said—except for the view—of the **Jianguo,** located near the Guang Hua, an American-managed hostelry modelled after the Holiday Inn in Palo Alto, California. (Minimum room charge 110元 a night.)

Restaurants

The best restaurants in Peking are the best in China. Almost all of them have, in addition to luxuriously appointed rooms serving expensive banquets, bistro-like cheaper sections. There the decor is sometimes dingier, but the prices one-fifth that of the posher rooms, the food excellent, and the atmosphere so pleasant and lively that many richer tourists and businessmen would prefer to eat there if they only knew. These sections usually welcome travellers, although they are so crowded that you might have to wait an hour or more to be served. (If a waiter asks you to go to the tourist section, it's best politely to remain where you are.) Note that price is determined by ingredients; a boring grilled chicken can cost four times as much as an exquisite pork dish. Here is a selection of Peking's finer restaurants, at all of which you can stuff yourself in style for 3元 or under. Most of them close by 7 p.m.

Sichuan Restaurant, 51 Rongxian Hutong, a few minutes' walk south of the corner of Xidan and Chang'an. This is the best Sichuan restaurant in China and perhaps the finest restaurant in Peking. Craig Claibourne of the *New York Times* considers it one of the best in the world. It is housed in a beautiful mansion that was formerly a residence of Yuan Shih Kai, the infamous president of the Republic who tried to make himself emperor in 1914. The food is excellent, a symphony in spice (although it is not overly hot, because too much pepper would numb the palate). The cheaper dining hall is a long room in the back of the second courtyard with a menu on a blackboard in front. Dishes average 1.50元 each, and servings are large.

Qianmen Roast Duck Restaurant, 24 Qianmen Rd. For hundreds of years, Peking Duck has deservedly been the most famous of Peking dishes. And, for over a hundred years, the Peking Duck Restaurant has been the best place in China to try it. This restaurant has four branches (the newest of which, the Xuanwumen, is so large and impersonal that some call it the "McDonald's Duck"). The Qianmen is the best, and has a cheap section reached through a small door a few yards to the right of the imposing main entrance. There, a whole duck, including pancakes and a second course of duck soup, is 10元. This is enough for four people or two gluttons. You can get half a duck with the trimmings for 6元. Purists may complain because the crispy skin is not separated from the meat, but the duck is nevertheless excellent. The dining room is lively and very crowded; beggars circulate among the diners, taking pancakes off the tables. Open until 9 p.m.

Capital Restaurant, 60 Wangfujing St., near the Peking Hotel. An attractive dining room with some excellent offerings (primarily the less expensive meat dishes; diced meat with well prepared sauce for about 1元). Crowded, especially on weekends.

Kang Le, 259 Andingmennei Ave., bus 2 from Tiananmen This restaurant serves Yunnanese food better than any available in Yunnan. The well-known "across-the-bridge noodles" is expensive and must be ordered in advance for a minimum of four people. The cheap dining room is on the ground floor.

Jinyang, 241 W. Zhushikou Ave. Very good food, with the pleasant atmosphere of a neighborhood restaurant. The kitchens specialize in the cuisine of Shanxi Province, and the food is better than any you'll find in Taiyuan or Datong.

Fengzeyuan, 83 W. Zhushikou St., near Qianmen. Many consider this Shandong restaurant the best in Peking, but the food served in its cheaper downstairs section does not live up to this reputation.

Dong Lai Shun, Dong Feng Market, just east of Wangfujing. Mongolian Hotpot, a sort of meat fondue, is perhaps the most renowned Peking specialty after the duck, and this Islamic restaurant is famous for it. The Hotpot is served upstairs; downstairs is a good dumpling house where a massive serving costs less than 1元.

Kaoroudian, Shishahai. This small, unpretentious (but sometimes expensive) restaurant is just north of Beihai Park in an interesting part of town.

Peking Vegetarian, 74 Xuanwumennei Ave. Vegetarians, starve no more! Large portions, moderately priced. Eat on the friendly, bustling second floor.

The Peking Hotel has a far better dining room than most hotels in China; one section stays open late. There is a lunchtime buffet, all you can eat for under 7元.

Restaurants near the Guang Hua Hotel: The Sun Altar Restaurant, Ritan Park, has good food for under 2元 per person, quiet setting, not very crowded, only foreigners are allowed, open 5-9 p.m., closed Fridays. Another restaurant, the Phoenix, on Dongdaqiao Rd. just south of Guanghua Rd., is somewhat more expensive (and elegant), and attracts high cadres. There is also a small dumpling house at the corner of Donghua and Jianguomenwai.

Western food: The Peking Exhibition Centre Restaurant has a wide European menu that still retains a strong Slavic flavour. Known as the "Moscow" when it first opened in 1954, this is an interesting legacy of the Russian presence in Peking. With its immense dining room and high ceilings, the restaurant's severe decor is evocative of the Russian architecture of the '50s.

The International Club, near the Friendship Store, also offers Western cuisine as well as good Chinese food, as does the Xinqiao Hotel, Chongwenmen, also known for its simple Pakistani curries.

In the Friendship Store, ground floor, you can find such delicacies (when in stock) as cold cuts, cheese, pastries and hamburgers. Sweetened yoghurt in porcelain flasks is sold there and throughout Peking for 25 fen (plus a deposit). Coca-Cola, locally bottled, is equally ubiquitous.

Entertainment

Peking is a cultural center for ballet, drama and Peking Opera. The CITS office in the Guang Hua Hotel will often reserve tickets for you. There are plenty of movie theaters in town, but getting a seat through the box office can be difficult. The best bet is to buy your ticket from a scalper half an hour before the show.

Most of Peking goes to bed by nine. This state of affairs has proved intolerable to the hopelessly decadent Western diplomats and businessmen stationed in the capital, and there are a number of places where they gather after hours. One is the main bar of the **Peking Hotel,** to the left of the lobby in the new wing. Some call it the "Peking Zoo." Another is the **Bell,** the only authentic British pub in China, located in the British Embassy compound, Guanghua Rd. (a 10-minute walk from the Guang Hua Hotel). Since this is in effect a private club, you should check with the Embassy during the day to see if they will welcome you. In April 1982 what promises to be Peking's most chic nightspot opened at the Jianguo Hotel. **Charlie's Bar** has drinks for 6元 and hopes to acquire a Filipino band. The bar at the **International Club** is a cheaper, but far less exciting alternative. There are also disco sessions several nights a week at the **Minzu Club** on the west side of town, but these are expensive and either boring or (reputedly) the scene of brawls. Wherever you go, remember that virtually all bus service ends before midnight, although you can get a taxi after that in front of the Peking Hotel.

Embassies

Most diplomatic personnel are quite friendly. The U.S. Embassy will hold your mail, a service they do not provide in other countries.

Australia, 15 Dongzhimenwai Ave., Sanlitun, tel. 522331;

Britain, 11 Guanghua Rd., 521961; **Canada,** 10 Sanlitun Rd. North, 521475; **France,** 3 Sanlitun No. 3 Street East, 521331; **Italy,** 2 Sanlitun No. 2 Street East, 522131; **Japan,** 7 Ritan Rd., 522361; **New Zealand,** 1 Ritan No. 2 Rd. East, 522731; **Sweden,** 3 Dongzhimenwai Ave., Sanlitun, 521770; **U.S.,** 17 Guanghua Rd., 522033; **West Germany,** 5 Dongzhimenwai Ave., Sanlitun, 522161.

Public Security

In an old mansion on Donghuamen Street in the former Imperial City. They will add cities to your travel permit (or sometimes issue a new permit, if Peking is your first port of call in China), but you must go through CITS, who charge a 5元 "handling fee."

The police in Peking take good care to prevent contact between foreigners and Chinese, so if you make friends during your visit, be especially discreet. The Peking Hotel is surrounded by detectives whose job it is to prevent any Chinese from entering, notwithstanding the poster in the lobby that declares "We have friends all over the world."

Transport

Peking is the rail transport hub of China. From the imposing main station, express trains leave for every provincial capital (except Lhasa), as well as to other large cities such as Chongqing and Qingdao. The main station's booking office is very crowded and will usually require you to pay the tourist price. Tickets to the Shanghai area can also be booked at the less crowded Xizhimen Station, near the zoo. It is easiest to book at the main CITS office, but there you are assured of paying the higher price.

Tianjin

Tianjin lies less than 100 miles from Peking, and its fortunes have always been linked with those of the capital. When Peking was made the seat of government, Tianjin, the nearest harbor, soon became a prosperous entrepôt. In the 19th century the nations of Europe cast covetous eyes on what had become North China's largest seaport, and the Second Opium War was in part fought to open Tianjin to foreign trade. By the beginning of the 20th century the city had been parcelled out between eight powers. West of the Hai River were (from north to south) the Japanese, French, British and German concessions, while to the east lay the Austrian, Italian, Russian and Belgian territories. During the concession era, trade grew and industry was developed.

Expansion continued after 1949. The port, now located 20 miles outside town, was enlarged in 1952 and again in 1976, and many new textile, machine and steel plants were erected. In 1976, a major earthquake devastated much of the city. Two years later, Tianjin was inundated by a flood of youths who had been "resettled" in remote villages during the Cultural Revolution. Instead of sending them away again, the city authorities found them temporary jobs: many were given the task of repairing buildings demolished by the earthquake.

With a population of seven million (including rural suburbs), Tianjin is the nation's third largest city. Like Peking and Shanghai, Tianjin is a municipality, administered directly by the central government.

Though far less exciting than Peking or Shanghai, Tianjin is not visually dull. Many of its streets — like those of any concession city — are a potpourri of incompatible architectural styles. Neo-Grecian temples rub pediments with turreted French chateaux, and Art-deco movie palaces jostle Gothic churches. Futuristic glass and steel structures leaven the mix. This architectural pastiche is most evident in the old French and British sections along Jiefang Bei Rd., and in the small streets around **Quanye Chang,** Tianjin's oldest department store. Near the Quanye Chang are Tianjin's most elegant shopping streets, Heping and Binjiang: visible at the end of Binjiang is a Catholic church with a domed design reminiscent of Sacre Coeur in Montmartre.

Farther north, in the **Old Chinese Town,** narrow alleys thread their way between rambling brick structures and a few scruffy traditional-style houses. One street has a large wooden arch at its entrance just west of Heping Rd. (bus 1 or 24 from the Quanye Chang district). The area south of Nan Ma Rd. and west of Heping, just outside the old city, is another shopping district, more proletarian in character than Quanye Chang and much more lively.

Concealed in one of the rococo mansions of the concession era is the excellent **Tianjin Art Museum,** at 77 Jiefang Bei Rd. On the third floor are displayed a jade burial suit and other objects found in the tomb of a Han princess, while the second floor is devoted to modern handicrafts. The first floor is the best, with an abundance of fine landscapes. Those in the two rooms to the left of the entrance date from the Ming; all the others are Qing Dynasty.

Five **hotels** stand almost in a row on Jiefang Bei Rd. (bus 13 or trolley 96 from station): the Tianjin Hotel, Tianjin No. 1 Hotel, Tianjin No. 2 Hotel, and two Chinese boarding houses. All are loath to give cheap accommodation to foreigners. The Tianjin Hotel has doubles for 24元, as well as dorms that are perpetually full. One way of avoiding the problem is not to spend the night: the sights of Tianjin can be more than adequately covered by a day-trip from Peking.

Around the block from the Quanye Chang is the **Tianjin Roast Duck Restaurant,** a shade inferior to its Peking counterparts but less crowded and with a quarter-duck for 3.50元. In the old German concession (bus 13 one stop south of the Tianjin Hotel), **Kiesling's,** once Austrian-run, has the decor, prices and cuisine of a 1940s New York Automat. Another western restaurant, as well as swimming pool and billiard room, is in the Tianjin Friendship Club (once a British country club) in the southern end of town (bus 13 to terminus). It is used mainly by foreign seamen.

Expresses to Shanghai and Harbin pass through Tianjin, as well as numerous trains to Peking. There are also boats to Shanghai from the harbor at the outskirts of town.

Summer Cities

Peking can be oppressively hot in summer, and several towns in the cooler areas near the capital were first developed as summer resorts for the governing classes. The most famous of these is **Chengde,** which lies on a main rail line 220 miles northeast of Peking and is the site of Jehol, the beautiful 18th-century resort of the Manchu emperors. The sovereigns had palaces and temples built to blend in with their natural surroundings. There are four main palaces, and the throne hall of the largest was built with fragrant wood. North and east of the palaces are seven magnificent temples erected by

Qianlong. Several are copies of the architectural style of newly-annexed provinces; one, the Putuo Zhongsheng, is modelled on the Potala at Lhasa. Many of these monuments are currently being restored. A three-bed room at the Chengde Hotel is 29元.

Another summer resort, but one totally different in character, is **Beidaihe,** a western-style beach town five hours by train from Peking. Originally developed at the turn of the century as a refuge for Europen residents of Peking and Tianjin, it now accommodates workers on holiday and high cadres.

Many of the younger vacationers are quite friendly, and a visit to the beach may be rewarded by stimulating conversation. But the best reason to come to Beidaihe is to forget China entirely, and the **Xishan Guest House** is ideally designed for this. More a neighborhood than a hotel, the Xishan is composed of about 50 bungalows, each with its own yard planted with fir trees. A bed in a double room in one of these villas costs between 12元 and 18元. The Xishan is about a mile west of town, and the reception office is one block back from the beach. In the center of town, opposite the post office, is **Kiesling's,** once Austrian-owned, which features excellent fish entrees and chocolate sundaes. Dining is alfresco and breakfast is served until 10 a.m.

The Beidaihe train station is on the main Peking-Shenyang line, about 10 miles from town. Buses from train to beach run every 90 minutes, with the last bus leaving at 6 p.m. A few buses pass by the Xishan, but most don't, so you will have to walk from the station. Taxis, the only other form of transport, are 9元.

While in Beidaihe you can easily visit **Shanhaiguan,** about 25 miles away on the main rail line. This ancient walled town guards the eastern end of the Great Wall, only a few miles from where it meets the sea. Its main landmark is a massive gate, built in 1639, with the bold inscription "First Pass Under Heaven." Only five years later this gate was opened by an opponent of the rebel regime then in power in Peking, and the Manchu invaders streamed through.

It may be difficult to get permission to sleep at Shanhaiguan, but you can spend the night at nearby **Qinhuangdao,** which, with a population of 300,000, is one of China's main seaports. From there buses run every hour or so back to Beidaihe.

Shandong Province

A few hours after leaving Peking, trains on the main Shanghai line pass through Shandong Province. Tourists who are racing along on a Grand Tour will get a good glimpse of the northern countryside, but those with more time should consider a stopover. Though relatively few foreigners visit it, Shandong has attractions both modern and ancient: the birthplace of China's most revered philosopher, her holiest mountain, and a pair of popular seaside resorts all lie within its boundaries.

Since the dawn of history the Chinese have worshipped mountains as gods, and for thousands of years **Tai Shan** was considered the most powerful of all. The more learned Chinese, who were too scientific to believe in spirits, nevertheless considered Tai Shan a vital source of cosmic energy and an integral part of the great natural cycle that determined, among other things, the success or failure of the harvest. Scores of emperors and countless commoners — the most famous of whom were Confucius and Mao — made the pilgrimage up the peak. Today the mountain is as popular as ever, and though most climbers seek no more than a spectacular sunrise, some villagers still leave expensive offerings on the summit in the hope of ensuring a good harvest.

The Peking-Shanghai line passes by Tai Shan, stopping at the nearby town of **Tai'an.** A mile from the station is a hotel and, close by, a magnificent temple, the **Dai Miao,** built during the Han, Tang and Song dynasties and restored many times since. 500 yards north of the temple, a Ming Dynasty stone arch marks the beginning of the path to the top. The six-mile long trail has over 6,000 steps and takes four to seven hours to climb. Recently a road linking Tai'an with **Zhongtianmen,** the midpoint of the path, was built west of the main trail, and travellers can now take a bus halfway up the mountain. (A cable car to the summit is under construction.) The road to Zhongtianmen bypasses the old temples and pavilions that line the lower half of the trail — including the Lower Temple to the Princess of Coloured Clouds and the Temple of the Goddess of the Big Dipper, both now used as teahouses — and it's a good idea to make either the ascent or the descent on foot.

About half a mile beyond Zhongtianmen is the **Five Pines Pavilion.** The ancestors of the present grove of trees sheltered the first Qin emperor during a rainstorm and were given knighthood in return. From this point on, the path is quite steep. Just before the summit is Nantianmen, a stone gateway, and the Temple of the Princess of Coloured Clouds, the traditional spot for pilgrims to make their offerings to the mountain. Nearby is the **Tai Shan Guest House,** where a double room costs 7元 with meals 2元 each. (There's also a hotel at Zhongtianmen.) From here, with luck, you will be able to see a fiery sunrise the next morning.

A few hours from Tai Shan is **Qufu,** the small, sleepy town where in 551 B.C. Confucius was born. Qufu was protected as a holy place until the fall of the Empire, but its monuments were treated much more cavalierly in the years thereafter, especially during the Cultural Revolution and the subsequent ''Criticize Lin Piao Criticize Confucius'' campaign. The town rejoiced when, in the late 1970s, both the shrines and Confucius' good name were restored; after all, one-fifth of its inhabitants are directly descended from the philosopher.

Qufu is about 10 miles east of the main rail line; get off at **Yanzhou** and proceed by bus. The main attraction is the huge, walled **Temple of Confucius** (Kongmiao), which contains some of China's finest architecture. The first hall is the Great Pavilion of the Constellation of Scholars, a wooden structure dating from 1190. In a courtyard beyond a monumental gateway is the Great Temple, built in 1724. One of the few remaining examples of Imperial Palace-style architecture, its ornate columns support a roof nearly 100 feet high.

East of the temple is the **Residence of the Descendants of Confucius,** a 1,000-foot long compound where, until recently, the philosopher's heirs lived. It is now functioning as a guest house; a double room is 30元. There is another hotel near the railway in Yanzhou, less glamorous but cheaper (6元). Nearby is a cemetery, still in good condition, where most of Confucius' direct descendants were buried.

The eastern part of Shandong is a long peninsula whose rocky coastline is indented with numerous harbors. One of these, **Qingdao,** became a German concession in 1898. Between then and the First World War, the Germans transformed a small village into a modern, well-laid-out city. Most of their stolid buildings remain, and Qingdao still has a distinctly Germanic flavor. Although it's now encircled by factory-filled suburbs, Qingdao is best known as a seaside resort. It is quite popular with high party officials, who have their own private residential area. The beaches, though crowded, are good for swimming. Another attraction is the famous Qingdao **brewery,** China's finest, where a tour includes free samples. The beer is available on tap in town.

At the main hotel, the Huiquan (bus 6 from train station), double rooms are officially 32元, but some travellers have been given a 9元 student rate. The Overseas Chinese Hotel near the station has doubles for 24元 . From Qingdao there are boats to Shanghai three days out of four (9.80元 third class, very comfortable), and trains to Peking. The train passes through **Weifang,** a commercial and industrial center, open to tourists.

On the north coast of the Shandong Peninsula is the port of **Yantai.** Though the city is modern, there is an older section ("Chefoo") and several beaches. Yantai can be reached by train from Peking or boat from Dalian, in the Northeast.

If you are visiting Shandong it's hard to avoid the capital, **Jinan,** a place of little interest to anyone who doesn't live there. The Jinan Hotel on Jingsan Rd., about a mile southwest of the train station, has single rooms with bath for 16元. There is a shopping area northeast of the hotel, in the direction of the train station, and another can be reached by taking a bus about a mile east along Jingsi Rd., one block south of the hotel. Jinan's main tourist attraction is its four natural bubbling springs, set in parks dotted with pavilions and teahouses.

Peking-Canton Railroad

The 1500-mile long railway from Peking to Canton, perhaps the most important line in the nation, is also among the oldest. The British, it is true, built a railroad near Shanghai in 1874, but the storm of protest by superstitious Chinese proved so violent that the government was forced to dismantle it and ship the wreckage to Taiwan for disposal. The track laid south from the capital proved less offensive to public sensibilities. Financed by a Belgian corporation, work was begun in 1897. By 1905 the line extended to Wuhan.

Like a modern Midas, the railway transformed whatever it touched. Settlements that had been little more than villages soon mushroomed into large cities. A classic example of this is **Shijiazhuang,** the first stop, 150 miles south of Peking, whose population jumped from 500 to half a million. The town nevertheless has one section that appears older than the rest, just west of the train terminal. Right outside the station is the main shopping street, Zhongshan Rd.

Shijiazhuang has no ancient monuments, but there are two in nearby towns that may be visited. The graceful, functioning **Zhaozhou Bridge,** built about 600 A.D., is located 25 miles southeast, near the town of Zhaoxiang. At Zhengding, 30 miles to the north, the **Longxing Monastery** is perhaps the oldest in Chinas whose building have been partially preserved. A series of 10th-century Buddhist temples and large courtyards are set amidst verdant fields. Inside the chief temple is a 71-foot high Song Dynasty bronze statue of Guanyin, with 42 arms.

Most visitors to Shijiazhuang stay in the **Hebei Guest House** at the southeastern edge of the city. Take bus 6 from the train station to the end of the line, then walk; ask the conductor to point the way. A double room in the huge, recently-completed new wing is 18元 per person (6元 student rate), and cheaper rooms may be available if you insist.

Eight hours to the south is **Handan.** This city was one of China's largest during the 4th century B.C., and the man-made hillock in Congtai Park is said to date from that period. From the train station, take a motorized rickshaw to the Handan Hotel (8元). Be especially careful that your travel permit is in order; the police are not used to tourists, and it will be checked and rechecked.

The next stop, **Anyang** (see Yellow River map), is built near the site of Yin, the last capital of the Shang Dynasty. Excavations there during the first half of this century uncovered a royal palace, royal tombs, workshops and houses. The tombs contained thousands of bones used for divination and inscribed with the earliest Chinese writing yet discovered. Although there is little to see at the excavation, the town itself might be worth a visit. Nicknamed "Little Peking," it has many old houses surrounded by courtyards planted with trees, and a 1,000-year-old pagoda.

Nearby **Linxian County** is a rural area famous for its irrigation works. The 1,000 miles of canals, all dug by hand over the course of a decade, were used during the Cultural Revolution as an example of what the mobilized masses could accomplish. Objections that a few pipes and pumps could have done the job with far less trouble were dismissed as the carping of the "Liu Shaoqi clique."

The major junctions between here and Canton are Zhengzhou, Wuhan and Changsha, all listed under separate headings. Other possibilities south of Wuhan are discussed under Changsha. Just before entering Zhengzhou the train passes through **Xinxiang,** a large, open industrial town.

2. The Yellow River

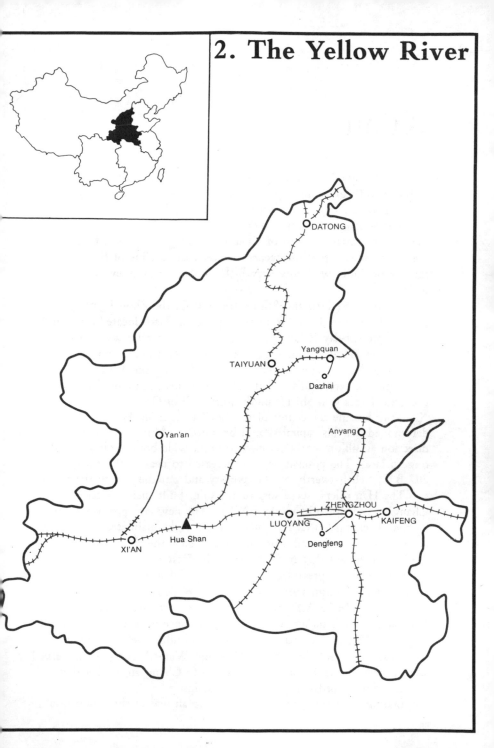

Xi'an

Xi'an, capital of the Empire for almost a thousand years, was one of the world's great metropolises, rivalling and even surpassing its contemporaries: Baghdad, Constantinople and Rome.

It is also one of China's oldest settlements. At Ban Po, just east of the modern town, remains of a neolithic village have been found. Of the three millenia that intervened between the decline of Ban Po and the rise of Zhou, we know very little. Villages slowly evolved into towns.

Between the 11th and 8th centuries B.C. the Zhou Dynasty governed northern China from their palace at Hao, located a few miles west of present-day Xi'an. Although the Zhou capital was moved to Luoyang in 771 B.C., Hao, now known as Xianyang, remained one of the four largest cities in North China. During the 4th century B.C. it became the capital of the state of Qin. When, a hundred years later, the great leader Qin Shi Huangdi unified all of China under his rule, Xianyang became the center of the Empire. Qin Shi Huangdi determined that his capital should be worthy of him, and under his direction a million workers toiled to build wide boulevards and eight huge palaces. The population had increased to nearly 800,000 when, in 207 B.C., rebels overthrew the dynasty and put the city to the torch.

The Han rulers, successors to the Qin, built their capital of Chang'an just north of modern Xi'an. The new city prospered, and by the 1st century B.C. its walls enclosed eight main streets and 160 alleys, and enormous suburbs sprawled outside the ramparts. It was during this period that trade began with West Asia and the Roman Empire. Just as in present-day China, a special street was set aside to accommodate foreign visitors and a protocol department supervised their undertakings. In 25 A.D. the seat of government was moved east to Luoyang, and Chang'an declined in importance until the first Sui emperor, Wen-ti, ordered his engineers to build a new metropolis southeast of the old Han town. Although Wen-ti's successor governed from Luoyang, the Tang rulers returned to Chang'an, which they completed in accordance with the Sui design.

During the next two centuries Chang'an was at the center of a cultural and political renaissance that many historians consider to be China's golden age. The Emperor's writ reigned supreme from the Korean peninsula to the deserts of Turkestan. Painting, literature and music all flourished, as did the more sybaritic art of gracious living. Among the court poets were Li Bai and Du Fu, and many of their most famous compositions describe the elaborate, Versailles-like fetes and revels of the day.

Chang'an provided a worthy foil for this Imperial splendor. Rectangular in shape, it covered 30 square miles, and almost two million people lived within its walls. The Grand Canal connected it with the ports and granaries of South China, and innumerable caravans plied the Silk Road to Persia, Byzantium and the Middle East. Foreigners who settled in the capital brought the fashions and culture of their homelands with them. Mosques and churches dotted the city, while the songs and dances of Central Asia were performed in many of the wineshops that surrounded the huge Western Market. Scholars and students flocked from all over Asia to immerse themselves in Chinese culture. Many came from Japan, and the city of Kyoto was modelled on Chang'an.

In the 10th century the Tang Dynasty fell, the capital moved to Kaifeng, and the city's days of splendor came to an end. It remained a regional center, although the town of Xi'an during the Ming and Qing dynasties was not much larger than the Tang Imperial Palace. Growth, if not glory, began again in 1949; new industries and universities were built, and the population has quadrupled to two million.

The Town

Though the excitement of its golden age has never been recaptured, Xi'an is a pleasant town nonetheless. Its people seem to share the taste for the dolce vita that pervades Chang'an's sister city of Rome. On summer evenings they spill into the streets and plazas to stroll, window-shop or exchange gossip. The most popular promenade is Dongdajie, Xi'an's main avenue, though a close runner-up is Xidajie, on the other side of the Bell Tower that marks Xi'an's center. Here, the big shops and theaters of Dongdajie give way to tiny wood-fronted houses. Similar old neighborhoods are sprinkled throughout the area enclosed by the Ming walls, especially in the region of the Drum Tower, where Xi'an's 30,000 Moslems live. Perhaps the best way of exploring the town is in conjunction with

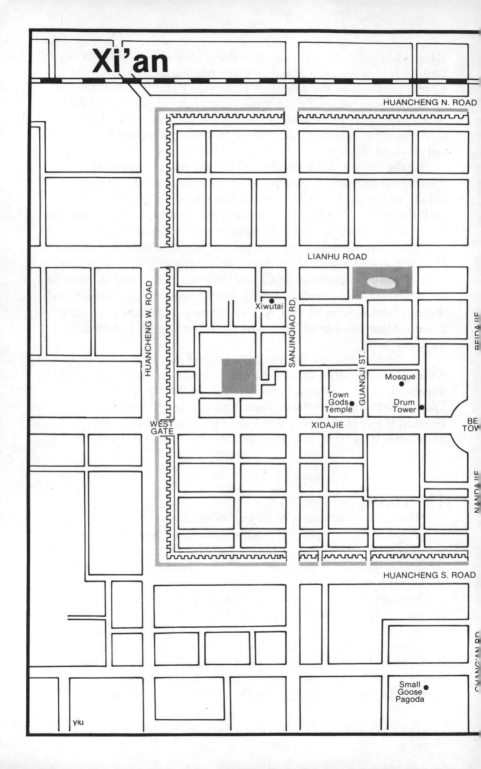

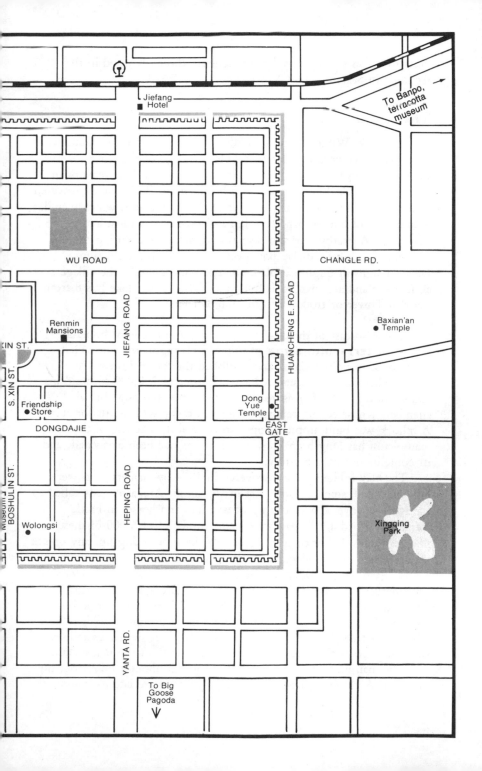

visits to Xi'an's many temples, particularly those discussed in the section "In Search of Old Xi'an."

The Main Attractions

Prehistoric: While all but a handful of Chang'an's many monuments have long since been reduced to rubble, just east of the city is one of the best-preserved neolithic settlement in the world. The remains of **Ban Po,** which flourished in the 5th millenium B.C., were excavated in the 1950s. A building has been erected over the site, which includes foundations of houses, a pottery kiln, storage pits, a moat and a graveyard. A nearby museum displays artifacts found during the dig, including beautiful red-clay pots decorated with abstract designs. Detailed signs in English explain the relics and describe the village's agriculture and art. Ban Po is five miles from Xi'an; take bus 8 from the Bell Tower or trolley 5 from Dongwu Rd.

Qin: Also east of the city is the most ancient relic of Imperial times, the **terracotta army** of Qin Shi Huangdi, the great First Emperor who united China and abolished the feudal system. A ruthless dictator, he conscripted a work force of 700,000 to build his mausoleum. Heaps of treasure were piled inside the huge burial chamber, whose ceiling reportedly formed a sky with pearls for stars. A hillock was built atop the tomb to conceal it. The site of the mausoleum has long been known, but it has not been excavated, and its contents remain a mystery.

The clay soldiers were discovered in 1974 by farmers who were digging a well some distance east of the tomb. Archaeologists called to the scene uncovered a vast army of warriors and horses in battle formation guarding the east face of the tomb. Over 6,000 of these lifesize figures lie buried in the area. 500 have been dug up, any one of which would be considered a major acquisition by any museum in the world. Each has individually moulded features, hairstyles and clothing, with posture and expressions reminiscent of Greek archaic statuary. They are on view inside a large pavilion built over the excavation site. Meanwhile, the digging continues. Two more groups of soldiers have been located nearby, and it is not improbable that similar battalions slumber beneath the fields north, west and south of the mausoleum.

The man-made hill that covers the tomb is about a mile from the museum. A climb to the top will help you to appreciate its mammoth size.

The Qin tomb and army is 20 miles east of Xi'an but easily accessible. Every hour until noon public buses leave from a side street near the railway, stopping in Ban Po to pick up passengers. A few buses leave from the large square west of the Renmin Hotel, but with these you must change buses halfway. Air-conditioned tour buses charge 6元 roundtrip including pickup at your hotel. To book a seat, walk east from the Bell Tower and take the first right. The tour office is about 100 yards down on the left. Another company offering a similar itinerary has a kiosk at the Jiefang Hotel. These tours also stop at Ban Po and — a definite drawback — spend three hours at the boring Huaqing Hot Springs. One traveller who made this detour — and soon regretted it — was Chiang Kai-shek. It was here, in 1936, that he was taken prisoner by his own troops, who wanted him to fight Japanese instead of Communists.

Tang: Two of Xi'an's most famous Tang landmarks are the **Big and Little Goose Pagodas** (the origin of their unusual names is unknown). The Big Goose tower (Dayanta) is far to the south of the modern town, although when it was built in 652 it was two miles north of the city limits. Take bus 5 from the train station (from the Renmin or Little Goose, take bus 3 to reach the 5). Walking from the bus stop you will see the huge, sable-colored pagoda rising out of the wheatfields. One is reminded of the similarly massive ruins of Mycenae, which later generations believed to have been built by a race of superhuman beings.

Next to the pagoda is the **Temple of Great Goodwill** (Daciensi). Founded in the 7th century, this was one of the largest in Chang'an. Its 300 monks included, upon his return from India, the famous pilgrim Xuanzang. The present complex dates from the 15th century, and is the best-preserved Buddhist temple in the city. The buildings are usually locked. Ask to be let in by the custodian, who also sells tickets to climb the 240-foot pagoda.

Behind the temple compound (turn right at the entrance) is an underground air raid shelter whose cool, labyrinthine tunnels have been turned into a popular cafe and amusement arcade (entry 50 fen).

The Little Goose Pagoda (Xiaoyanta) is somewhat closer to town. Take bus 3, then walk a few hundred yards west from the bus stop. Built in 706, this 13-storey tower is all that remains of a once-flourishing temple. The pagoda's design is severe, even fortress-like. Surrounding it is a landscaped garden where fir and banana trees grow side by side.

Two interesting Tang monasteries lie in the hills and valleys south of Xi'an. The **Xiang Ji** has a central pagoda built in 706 over the ashes of the monk Shandao, one of the patriarchs of Pure Land Buddhism, which preached salvation through faith rather than meditation. With luck, the Xiang Ji can be reached in two hours from the center of town. Bus 15 services a small village, four miles from the temple, that has dared to call itself Chang'an. To cover the remaining distance take another bus (irregular), hitch or walk. Head south from the bus depot and bear right at the fork, then right again at the second fork a mile farther on. Three miles out, the dirt road that leads to the temple is on the right (ask for directions). The Xiang Ji, with one monk in residence, stands in the center of a large, very rural village. The main hall was restored in 1980, the 1,300th anniversary of Shandao's death. Inside is a large Buddha brought from a Peking museum, as well as a statue of Shandao donated by a Japanese delegation. Nearby is the 10-storey brick pagoda that marks the monk's grave.

Farther away from Xi'an, but somewhat easier to get to, is the **Xing Jiao Si;** infrequent country buses ply the route between the South Gate and the temple. Here, under a tall pagoda built in 669, is the grave of the monk Xuanzang, whose famous pilgrimage to India was immortalized in the novel *Monkey,* otherwise known as the *Journey to the West.* The two pagodas that flank the principal one date from the Tang and Song periods, but the other buildings are 20th century.

Outside the city are several tombs of Tang rulers. The same companies that run the tours to the Qin army also sponsor daily outings to the Zhaoling, the mausoleum of Li Shimin, 40 miles from town. In the necropolis is a museum with many terracotta figurines, murals and stone inscriptions.

Ming: Most of the elegant landmarks that grace Xi'an today were built during the 14th century, when the city was the capital of a principality governed by the Emperor's second son. The most prominent is the **Bell Tower** that marks the center of town (bus 3). Its huge bell, once sounded daily at dawn, is today mercifully silent. This and the nearby **Drum Tower** are both ornate, multicolored buildings set on high pedestals of grey brick. The four huge **city gates,** built in a more utilitarian variant of the same style, are all in fair condition, though only the East and West Gates have retained both the archer's tower and the gate tower intact. The Bell Tower and the West Gate can be climbed.

It was also during the 14th century that the **Great Mosque** of Xi'an was built, though it was restored in the 16th, 17th and 18th centuries. Most of the grounds are taken up by a peaceful garden with wooden pavilions, stone arches and cobbled walkways. There is some very richly carved woodwork in the prayer hall. The Mosque is still very active and holds five prayer services a day. 2,000 men attend on Fridays. Prayers are not normally open to non-Muslims, who are welcome to enter the hall at other times (shoeless). But the muezzin's haunting call to prayer can be heard from the courtyard outside. To get there, walk north along the street that passes under the Drum Tower, and then take the first left. A sign in English points the way.

Museum: Another very old religious monument, the former Temple of Confucius, now houses the **Shaanxi Provincial Museum,** one of China's finest. The exhibits are arranged chronologically, beginning with the building to the left of the garden, which houses artifacts of the Zhou, Qin and Han dynasties. The objects on display, many of which are labelled in English, include bronze vessels, tools, weapons and other implements, some richly decorated. There are also Han and Qin pottery burial sculptures. Across the garden is a second hall containing artifacts from the Sui and Tang periods. Notice the small sculptures in terracotta and porcelain, far more detailed and lifelike than their Han counterparts.

At the far end of the garden are the buildings containing the famous **Forest of Steles.** This collection of over 1,000 inscribed stone tablets was begun in 1090 and grew slowly thereafter. The stelae, the majority of which date from the Tang Dynasty, have provided historians with a wealth of information about ancient China. All explanatory signs are in Chinese, but tour groups with interpreters pass by frequently.

At the entrance to the collection stands a huge monolith cut in 745 with the Confucian Classic of Filial Piety, written in the calligraphy of the great Emperor Xuanzong. Just beyond, in the first building, is the nucleus of the collection, a set of 114 stelae engraved in 837 with the definitive text of the Confucian Classics.

Behind the Classics hall is a second building whose large Tang steles rest on sculptured turtles. Immediately to the left of the entrance is the most famous. Surmounted by a cross, this stele, engraved in 781, records the history of the Nestorian Christian community at Chang'an from its founding in the 7th century by a Syrian missionary.

In the third hall, to the left of the door, is a series of exemplars written by master calligraphers, including some in the aptly named "wild cursive script" by the Tang artist Huai Su and Zhang Xu. In the fourth building are several Qing steles engraved with landscapes and one, in the center aisle, with a huge portrait of Confucius cut in 1734.

In Search of Old Xi'an

Visitors to Xi'an thirty years ago found a town which, though materially poorer than today, was far richer in architectural heritage. But for much of the period since then, China's history has been viewed as something to be repudiated, and Xi'an's relics were an obvious target. A few temples and pagodas were damaged irreparably, while others were converted into schools and storehouses. Like the unpersons in Orwell's famous novel, these have disappeared from city maps and other publications. But despite their official non-existence, the buildings remain, some in surprisingly good condition.

The search for these monuments is itself an adventure. The surrounding neighborhoods are often as old as the temples themselves, and the residents, especially the older ones, remain proud of their neglected heritage. A request for directions can turn suspicious stares into welcoming smiles. A temple hunt also offers a chance to meet the students and factory workers who have replaced the priests and devotees. (The gatekeeper is liable to admit visitors once he realizes their primary interest is architectural.)

One of the finest of these "lost" relics, the **Town Gods Temple** (Cheng Huang Miao), is within walking distance of the Bell Tower. Go along Xidajie to no. 257, then take the small lane running north through the Muslim quarter, past an active mosque on the left. Turn right at the T-intersection, then right again, down a cobbled alley: a final right at the foot of this lane opens onto the temple gates. Now a school and warehouse, the structure's wooden pavilions are in fairly good condition. The main hall, built in 1723 with materials taken from a Ming palace, has richly carved doors and a roof of bright blue tile. Fairly close by, on the east side of Guangji Bei Rd., is another small temple with an elaborately carved wooden pagoda.

Another Taoist complex within the city walls is the **East Peak Temple** (Dong Yue Miao), founded in the 12th century and much restored under the Qing. Located about 50 yards from the northwest corner of the East Gate, it is now a primary school. Inside, the altars to the holy mountain Tai Shan are gone, but traces of the once-famous frescoes remain. In the rear of the compound is a small Qing pavilion, also in bad condition, with additional murals.

Near the museum is the site of the **Temple of the Recumbent Dragon** (Wolongsi), one of Xi'an's oldest and most famous. Virtually demolished during the Cultural Revolution, only a small portion of one hall has survived: it now houses a particularly noisome factory. Should you wish to go there, turn left at the museum entrance and walk north along Boshulin St. Between nos. 25 and 27 is a dirt path; the factory entrance is a few yards down, on the left.

Close by is the 10th-century **Bao Qing Pagoda.** Walking west along the small road south of the museum, the slender brick spire is just before the South Gate.

The **Five Western Terraces** (Xi Wu Tai), built at the same time as the Bao Qing, were until recently one of Xi'an's most renowned attractions. Red Guards levelled all but one of the man-made hillocks and the graceful pavilions that crowned them. The sole survivor stands "bloody but unbowed" amidst the factories south of Lianhu Rd. Take trolley 3 two stops beyond the North Gate, walk down Sanjinqiao Rd. and turn into the first lane on the right.

Outside the Ming walls are several temples that are in far better shape; some have even been spruced up since 1980. One, the **Daxingshan,** was once Chang'an's greatest monastery, a center of Buddhist art and learning. Its later history is checkered: it was badly damaged during the 9th century, razed during the next, later rebuilt, restored, and pulled down again at the end of the Qing, to be reconstructed once more in 1956. Today the buildings have been newly painted, but the main courtyard is locked. Its grounds have been converted into a somewhat sterile public park. Take bus 3 to the stop nearest the Big Goose Pagoda and walk back along Chang'an Rd. until you come to a large market. The park is down the narrow street just beyond.

A short distance east of the city wall lies the **Temple of the Eight Immortals** (Ba Xian An). Once Xi'an's largest Taoist establishment, it housed 100 monks as recently as twenty years ago. In 1966 half the buildings were demolished, and what remained was converted into a machine plant. One of the halls has recently been restored, and the Ba Xian An, with little fanfare, has become Xi'an's only functioning Taoist temple. Take trolley 5 one stop beyond the wall, walk back along Changle Rd. and take the first left. When that road ends, bear right, and then left. The compound is on the right, concealed behind high walls but with one small gate left open. The one newly-painted pavilion is locked, but votive offerings can be seen through the window. Outside, in a small courtyard, a small knot of aged worshippers burn incense and recite their prayers.

Ruins: The whimsies of Time, whose taste in humor always leans towards the ironic, are nowhere more apparent than in Xi'an. Greece has its Parthenon, Rome its Forum and Egypt its Pyramids, but only a few relatively minor pagodas bear witness to Chang'an's glory. Though the frail spire of the Little Goose is unscathed, the huge Imperial Palaces, built to stand 10,000 years, failed to outlast the dynasties that erected them. Traces of the foundations remain, and upon them you may build your dreams.

Several miles west of the walls is the site of the never-completed **Afang Palace,** which the first Qin Emperor intended to be the finest ever built. Today, all that is left is a small mound about 30 feet high. The remains of several other Qin palaces are currently being excavated near the modern town of Xianyang.

In the wheat fields northwest of present-day Xi'an is the site of the **Han capital.** Some of the walls can be seen, as well as a terrace on which stood the audience hall of the Weiyang Palace.

A short distance northeast of the railway station is the site of the **Daming Palace,** which was the grandest of the Tang Emperor's many retreats. The terraces on which the two principal buildings stood are still visible, together with a depression that was once an ornamental pool. During the 1950s the site was excavated and foundations of 20 buildings uncovered, but the diggings have since been filled in.

Practical Information

The **Jiefang Hotel** is across the square from the train station, on the left. Dorm, 2元per bed. Double rooms are 3.50元per bed or 6元for the room. This hotel is one of China's sleaziest, but the attendants are helpful and the price is right.

Another possibility is the **Renmin Dasha,** bus 3 (not trolley 3) from train station. One bed in a luxurious two-room suite with three beds and private bath costs 10元. Cheaper dorms may be available. This is New China's answer to the Daming Palace.

Shaanxi is one of the few regions of China not renowned for its cuisine, and the reason is obvious when you dine in Xi'an. But try the

Dongya, near the Bell Tower.

There are seven trains daily to Peking, two to Shanghai, four to Urumqi, six to Chengdu, two to Taiyuan, and one each to Hefei, Qingdao and Wuhan.

Nearby

One of the traditional five sacred mountains of China, **Hua Shan** rises nearly 7,000 feet above the confluence of the Luo, the Wei and the Yellow Rivers. It is 70 miles east of Xi'an and trains go from there to the nearby town of Huayin. Pilgrims, poets and painters used to come to see Hua Shan's magnificent scenery of sheer peaks, waterfalls and venerable pine trees, as well as old Taoist temples and monasteries. Although experienced hikers can make the ascent in less than a day, it is not an easy climb. There is a guest house in town near the railway, and a lodge on the summit where a bed is 4.50元 It may be difficult to get permission to visit Hua Shan, especially in Xi'an.

In the far north of Shaanxi Province is **Yan'an,** from 1936 to 1947 the headquarters of the Communists. Mao, Chu Teh, Chou En-lai and their comrades lived in caves cut out of the loess cliffs, some of which are now museums. Yan'an is accessible by bus from Xi'an, an interesting ride through the sandy, eroded landscape typical of northwest China. You can overnight halfway in the town of Huangling, traditionally revered as the "tomb" of the Yellow Emperor, the mythical ancestor of the Chinese race.

Luoyang

For the two thousand years that preceded the fall of the Tang Dynasty, Luoyang was one of China's two great cities, rivalled only by Xi'an. A settlement since neolithic times, Luoyang developed into a small city by the end of the 2nd millenium B.C. The Zhou emperors resided there from 770 B.C. onwards, and although the sovereign's power declined over the centuries, Luoyang did not. Its population by the end of the 3rd century B.C. approached half a million.

Under the Qin and Western Han dynasties Luoyang ceded center stage to Xi'an, but in 25 A.D. the Han Emperors returned to Luoyang and greatly enlarged the town. The Han city, located east of the White Horse Temple, soon became a center of learning as well as commerce, and tens of thousands of students flocked to the huge Central University. But in the decades following the fall of the Han in 220, hordes of nomadic invaders brought chaos to northern China and Luoyang was a primary target. The city was sacked in 311 and again five years later, and contemporary accounts of its devastation likened it to a vast garbage dump. The Toba armies eventually brought peace and established the Northern Wei Dynasty; in 494 they moved their capital from Datong to a rejuvenated Luoyang. It was the Wei who initiated the famous rock carvings on the cliffs near the city. Luoyang continued to prosper, and according to a contemporary account had 1,367 Buddhist temples and 10,000 households of foreign traders. When the Wei Dynasty fell, however, their city was completely destroyed.

In the early 7th century, under the direction of the Sui emperor Yang-ti, a new metropolis was laid out that surpassed the old in grandeur. Its perimeter, which encompassed what is now called the Old Town together with much of the land to the south, was over 16 miles in length and contained nearly a million inhabitants. There were three main markets, one of which sprawled over several square miles and contained 3,000 shops. Many of the merchants who traded here came from abroad, and 400 inns were built to accommodate them.

Although Chang'an was the seat of empire for most of the Tang, Luoyang continued to flourish until the dynasty ended, after which it rapidly declined. By the 1920s it had only 20,000 inhabitants. Since 1949 it has become a heavy industrial base, best known for its tractor factory, with a burgeoning population currently estimated at 900,000.

Apart from the Longmen Caves, few traces remain of Luoyang's past glories. The authorities seem reluctant to disturb the wheatfields south and east of town to lay bare the archaeological treasures that doubtless lie beneath. Most of present-day Luoyang is a sprawling, singularly unattractive array of regimented apartment blocks, factories and farmland. The area known as the **Old Town,** which comprised the entire city in Ming and Qing times, is somewhat less sterile, though it pales by comparison with nearby Zhengzhou and Kaifeng. Much of the Old Town is modern, but there are a few streets of whitewashed houses. One of the most attractive of these is Beidajie, which runs north from the main street, Zhongzhou Rd. The Old

Town is far from the hotel but easy to get to; take bus 8 to its terminus at Xiguan, on the district's western edge.

At Xiguan are buses (line 6) to the **White Horse Temple** (Baimasi), one of the oldest Buddhist temples in China, which lies six miles east of town, in the vicinity of a large village. It was founded in the 1st century, though the present buildings date from the Ming era. They are well-preserved stone halls whose ornately crafted roofs have detailed scenes painted on their multicolored beams. Behind is a staircase to the Cool Terrace, where pavilions surround a cobbled courtyard with fir trees and a tiny lotus pond. A few minutes' walk away — turn left as you exit the temple — is an attractive 1,000-year-old pagoda.

South of the town, on the way to the caves (bus 10), is another temple that now houses the **Luoyang City Museum.** This Ming Dynasty complex is dedicated to Guan Yu, the heroic general of the Three Kingdoms period who was later worshipped as God of War.

Luoyang's sole hostelry for foreigners, the **Friendship Hotel,** is in the western part of town. (Bus 2 from main train station and bus station. If you arrive at the eastern station, you must first take a bus to the main station or to Xiguan.) Beds in a six-bed dorm 4元, in a triple 5元, in a double 6元. All rooms are air-conditioned, even the dorm. Huge suppers for 3.50元. To get to Public Security, take bus 8 from the hotel.

There are daily trains to Peking, Xi'an, Chengdu, Urumqi, Kaifeng and Shanghai from the main station. From Luoyang East, trains to Chongqing via Xiangfan, where you can catch a train to Yichang. Hourly buses from the depot opposite the main station to Zhengzhou. Also a small ticket office for tour buses to the Shaolin Monastery.

Longmen Caves

The rock carvings and cave temples of Longmen are among the finest works of religious art to be seen in China. When the Wei moved to Luoyang in 494 they chose the sandstone cliffs on either side of the Yi River as the site for a series of Buddhist temple grottoes, the successors to those at the previous capital, Datong. Work on the caves continued long after the dynasty had ended, and 1352 grottoes with over 100,000 Buddha images were cut into the rock. Unfortunately, many of the sculptures — especially the heads — were stolen by 19th- and 20th-century tourists and now grace museums and private collections in Europe and America.

The major caves are on the west bank of the river, with the three **Pingyang Caves** closest to the entrance. All were begun under the Wei, and although the northern and southern were finished by Sui and Tang artisans, the statues in all three evince the other-worldliness so typical of Wei religious art. In the central cave, the best of the three, the facial expressions of the Buddha and his acolytes are benevolent, almost saccharine. There are eleven large statues, and bas-reliefs cover the walls, roof and even the floor.

The next major temple, the Tang Dynasty **10,000 Buddha Cave,** is several minutes' walk farther south. In addition to the legions of tiny Buddhas that give the cave its name, there is a fine big Buddha and noteworthy bas-reliefs of celestial musicians. Beyond is the **Lotus Flower Cave,** with a large standing Buddha, now faceless. The ceiling should be noticed; sinuous figures drift around a central lotus.

The next group of statues — "cave" is almost a misnomer since the roof has gone — is by far the largest at Longmen. This **Juxiansi Cave,** cut between 672 and 675, represents a high point of Tang Buddhist sculpture, and its statues are among the most expressive and best preserved at Longmen. The powerful central Buddha, 56 feet high, is believed to be Vairocana, the supreme, omnipresent divinity. Beside him are disciples, bodhisattvas, and two fierce demon defenders. Put your arms around the leg of the left-hand guardian: if your fingers meet, it is considered lucky.

South of the Juxiansi is the tiny **Medical Prescription Cave,** whose entrance is filled with stelae documenting 6th-century cures for common ailments. Adjacent is the much larger **Guyang Cave,** sculpted between 495 and 575. Its high ceiling, narrow width and profusion of fine sculpture, including a central Buddha elongated like the cave, give this dimly-lit grotto the atmostphere of a chapel. But the carved heads in the niches, praised by guidebooks published 20 years ago, have disappeared. A short walk farther on is the last major cave, the **Shikusi,** where friezes depicting religious processions have been carved below the side niches.

If you have time, you can also visit the three large Tang Dynasty grottoes on the other side of the river. There is another series of rock temples, from the 6th century, near **Gongxian,** which is also the site of several Song Dynasty tombs. Gongxian is a small town with a tourist guesthouse halfway between Luoyang and Zhengzhou. Its red brick buildings house shops patronized by farmers from the many villages in the area.

Zhengzhou

During the Shang Dynasty Zhengzhou was one of the most important cities in China. The town was surrounded by earthen ramparts four miles long, with numerous pottery kilns and bronze foundries lying outside the walls. In later centuries Zhengzhou was eclipsed by its neighbor Luoyang, and later by Kaifeng. It was not until the building of the railway that Zhengzhou covered as large an area as it had 3,500 years before. Many of its inhabitants were railwaymen who became politicized and went on strike several times during the 1920s. Since 1950 its population has grown tenfold and now approaches the one million mark. The capital of Henan Province, Zhengzhou is also an industrial center specializing in textiles.

The main streets in the area east of the train station are crowded and colorful. The squat, brightly-painted buildings, the throngs of shoppers, and the profusion of street vendors would not be out of place in a far smaller town on market day. In a plaza in the old part of town stands a large, pagoda-like structure built to commemorate the first of the great railway strikes. Dehua Rd., running south from this monument, has the biggest crowds and the largest stores. Beyond the shopping area and past the massive Stalinist movie theater is a neighborhood of ramshackle houses and enormous markets where villagers congregate to sell their produce. One particularly good walking street, flanked by old, wood-fronted houses, is Jiefang, the road that intersects the February 7 monument square from the east. Others are Datong St. near the station and the tiny alley behind the monument, jammed with Muslim food vendors and sidewalk restaurants.

Near the eastern end of Jiefang is a section of the **Shang ramparts.** All that remains today is a tall mound of earth snaking through the cornfields — but this may be the oldest trace of urban life to be seen in China. The walls are quite far from town; take bus 3 from the monument. Get off when the bus turns right and walk back along Jiefang, turning left into the first small alley. You will see the wall after walking about 50 yards.

An extensive collection of tools and artifacts from the Shang and later dynasties is on view in the **Provincial Museum,** located in the ugly northern part of town (bus 2 or 9).

Near the tall building opposite the station is a men's public **bathhouse.** For 20 fen, you can plunge into a huge tile tank of steaming hot water and rinse off afterwards in a cold shower. This is an instructive exercise in communal living and a good way to get clean.

Most tourists stay at the **Zheongzhou Hotel,** which is far from the center of town (bus 2). The **February 7 Hotel,** opposite the monument, has occasionally taken foreigners, charging 4-8元. A far more convenient location, if you can get in. Or try **Zhongyuan Mansions,** the skyscraper opposite the train station. The Public Security office is on Erqi St., near the February 7 Hotel.

Zhengzhou is one of the busiest rail junctions in the nation. All the fast expresses that link Peking with the south and west stop here and, on some, berths can be reserved. There are over 15 trains a day to Peking. With the same number of expresses headed for Xi'an, this is a good place to begin a journey west. Of special interest is an express to Urumqi that originates in Zhengzhou.

There are frequent buses to Luoyang and Kaifeng leaving from the main bus terminal, near the train station. Outside the depot is a ticket office for daily tour buses to the Shaolin Monastery.

Shaolin Monastery

South of Luoyang and Zhengzhou, nestled in the foothills of Song Shan, lies the Shaolin Monastery. According to a 1,000-year-old tradition, it was at Shaolin that the founder of Zen Buddhism, the 6th-century monk Boddhidharma, preached and meditated until his death. The monastery grew larger and richer during the Sui, Tang and later dynasties. Its monks, threatened by bandits and other enemies, developed a system of self-defense that became known throughout the world as kung fu. The tradition of meditation and martial arts has continued; at this writing it is being forwarded by nine aged monks and three young novices. A recent film based on the monastery inspired hundreds of young Chinese to apply there for kung fu training, but all were predictably turned away.

The Shaolin complex is currently undergoing extensive restoration and several buildings are closed, though you can peek in from outside.

The first main hall is a library containing Zen texts. Beyond this is a small chapel dedicated to Boddhidharma. At the back is the **1,000 Buddha Temple,** used as a martial arts practice hall. Inside are ancient but lively frescoes of Buddha's disciples and the stone lingam in front of which Boddhidharma is said to have sat motionless for nine years. The depressions in the stone floor were allegedly made by kung fu blows. On the right of the gymnasium is a smaller temple whose wall paintings depict incidents from the history of the monastery. Kung fu battles are so realistically portrayed that experts can recognize the different holds. In the small hall opposite, a monk will bless a souvenir amulet for 50 fen. Outside the monastery (turn right when leaving) is a forest of 200 stone cenotaphs to early abbots.

Shaolin can be visited on a day's outing from either Luoyang or Zhengzhou. Both those cities have ticket offices outside the main train station from where tour buses leave at 6:30 a.m. and return the same afternoon. Alternatively, you can take a public bus to the town of **Dengfeng,** walk or hitch to Shaolin, about 10 miles away, and ride back on a tour bus. If you are lucky enough to get Dengfeng on your travel permit, you can spend the night.

Many other temples and monasteries, most dating from the Wei, lie in the area around Dengfeng. Perhaps the best-known is the **Zhong Yue Miao,** also visited by the tour bus. Song Shan is one of China's five sacred Taoist mountains, and it was in this temple that the holy peak was worshipped. The complex was laid out in the 8th century and was extensively restored in later years. Although most of the 850 pavilions have disappeared, many large halls remain. Inside, a few old Taoist priests, their hair in braids, burn incense to honor the mountain.

Kaifeng

The town of Kaifeng has a long and proud history. Capital of one of the Warring States during the 3rd century B.C. and seat of four of the five dynasties that ruled the nation between 907 and 960, it was chosen by the Song Emperors to be the site of their court. Kaifeng remained the capital until 1127, and was thus at the center of the renaissance in thought and culture that made this period one of the most glorious in China's history. The pioneering experiments in landscape painting, the philosophic controversy out of which evolved neo-Confucianism, and the heated debates between the reformer Wang An-Shih and his conservative opponents — all were going on more or less simultaneously in 11th-century Kaifeng. The city itself was an apt foil for this cultural brilliance. Its main thoroughfare, the Imperial Way, was reportedly almost 1,000 feet wide and was flanked with market arcades, rows of plum, peach and apricot trees, and ornamental canals filled with lotus blossoms.

In 1127 invaders from Manchuria brought the city's days of greatness to a sudden end. The Song fled to Hangzhou, while the Jin ruled from Peking. Kaifeng sank to the status of a regional center of commerce. Even today, Kaifeng still seems wrapped up in its past glories. There has been relatively little industrial development, and its population has remained static over the past sixty years.

Kaifeng, least visited of all Imperial capitals, is also the least changed in modern times. Many of its streets are lined with ramshackle Qing houses, built of brick but fronted with wood panelling. Some also sport rickety wooden balconies and elegantly latticed windows. The main street, Zhongshan, is good for its entire length, both within and outside the city walls. Unfortunately, the narrow alleys, or hutong, that are the liveliest part of many Chinese cities are almost all of little interest in Kaifeng.

The sole exceptions to this rule are the lanes east of Beitujie, once the site of Kaifeng's Jewish, Christian and Muslim quarters. Beitujie is the name given a section of the first major street east of the hotel (turn left from the entrance, then left again). Two long blocks up is Dongdajie, just south of which was the old **Jewish area.** During the 12th century many Jewish families, descendants of merchants who had migrated to China hundreds of years before, came to Kaifeng. By the 15th century the Jewish community numbered about a thousand, and many of its members held important posts in the local government.

Today a hospital stands at 59 Beitujie, on the site where its synagogue was located. Until a few years ago three very old stelae recording the history of this unusual community could be seen in the hospital grounds. The first lane south of the hospital, helpfully marked with a "W.C." sign, is Nan Jiao Jing (South Teaching Religion), which used to be the center of the Jewish neighborhood. A few blocks southeast of Nan Jiao Jing is the Dongdasi, an active if somewhat dilapidated **mosque,** built in Chinese style with a bright turquoise tile roof. Ask permission from the attendants before going in. Close by is a **Catholic church** with a Gothic steeple and a full-time priest. These two religious monuments are best approached by going east along Sihojie, the first main street south of the Jewish area. Turn left down the lane with the market to get to the church, and along the next alleyway for the mosque.

Of the many magnificent structures erected during the Song period, only two remain, but both are superb. One is the **Iron Pagoda** (Tieta), set in a rather scruffy park at the northern end of Beitujie. It is somewhat far from the religious area, and is best reached by taking bus 1 or 3 to the last stop. Built in 1049, the pagoda was badly damaged by Japanese bombs in 1938 and has since been restored. Each glazed brick is decorated with bas-reliefs of Buddhas and abstract designs.

On the opposite side of town is the other Song pagoda, the **Pota.** Built in 977, this huge, squat structure recalls the massive temples of Pagan, in Burma. Its bricks are decorated with tiny bas-reliefs of Buddha, similar to those of the Iron Pagoda but unrestored and more finely executed. The Pota is a 10-minute walk southeast of the train station through a gritty worker's district. Also in this area is the **Old Music Terrace,** a park once frequented by the great Tang poets Li Bai and Du Fu.

Another of Kaifeng's old monuments, the **Dragon Pavilion** (Longting), stands at the northern end of Zhongshan Rd. (bus 1) on the site of the Song Imperial Palace. A wide stone staircase with sculpted dragons leads to the 17th-century pavilion, bright red with a double roof of yellow tile. At the foot of the stairs is a large statue of Sun Yat-sen, perhaps put here to exorcise the ghosts of the former residents. The pavilion was used as the villains' headquarters in an immensely popular kung fu film based on the history of the Shaolin Temple.

Closer to the center of town, just west of the hotel, is the **Xiangguo Monastery.** Founded in the 6th century, this became one of the most prominent in China. The present buildings date from the time of the 18th-century emperor Qianlong. The central hall, with an unusual circular design, now houses a many-armed gilt Guanyin statue and an amusing collection of funhouse mirrors. Five minutes' walk away, near (and visible from) the western end of the guesthouse street, is a small pagoda with intricate decoration in blue, green and yellow faience. This is all that remains of the 13th-century

Yanqing Taoist Temple; the rest is now a factory.

One final attraction that certainly deserves a visit is the huge public **bathhouse,** with separate sections for men and women, on Sihojie, a few yards east of Zhongshan. Your 20 fen ticket entitles you to dip into a series of tile tanks, each heated to a different temperature, and then take a nap on a wooden pallet. The male section is full of older men come to bathe, gossip and drink tea.

The leading hotel is the **Kaifeng Guest House,** bus 3, 5 or 9 from train station (bus 1 also passes fairly close by). A bed in a triple is about 9元, but expect protracted negotiations before you get it. Six-bed dorms also exist. Some travellers have stayed at the large hotel on Zhongshan near the station, where a spartan double room is 8元.

Of the few restaurants in town, Youyixin on Sihojie is the best. On the same street is the Diyilou, which has been known for its dumplings for over 70 years. The Public Security Bureau is on Sihojie about 100 yards west of Zhongshan.

Kaifeng is on the Shanghai-Xi'an line, and there are several trains a day in both directions. To go north or south you must change at Zhengzhou, and it might be best to go there by bus. There are about 20 buses a day to Zhengzhou, the last being at 5:30, with stands in front of the train station and opposite Public Security, as well as at the main depot.

Taiyuan

Today a tranquil provincial capital, Taiyuan, located at the northern entrance to the fertile Shanxi plain, has had a long and turbulent history. Founded over 2,500 years ago, it was the scene of a major military engagement during the Warring States era and of several important battles with nomadic invaders between that time and the 10th century. A wealthy commercial entrepôt under the Tang, it became an independent city-state during the Five Dynasties period.

With the advent of Song Dynasty rule in 980, the Emperor himself led an army that invaded the rebel kingdom and razed the town. But a new town grew up on the site of the old. Once again

Taiyuan became a thriving commercial and cultural center, but it remained too tempting a target for invaders, and was besieged by the Jin and later by the Mongols. A few hundred years later the peasant rebels who had overthrown the Ming Dynasty retreated to Taiyuan when they in turn were ousted from Peking by the Manchus. The Manchus pursued them, and Taiyuan was once more assaulted and captured.

A more peaceful epoch of commercial development began after the completion of the railway line to Shijiazhuang at the beginning of this century. Taiyuan today is a heavy industrial city with a prominent steel works and a population of almost two million.

There is a well-preserved older section just north of (behind) the Yingze Hotel. To reach it, go out of the hotel's main gate, turn left and left again. Walk north along (or through the alleys west of) this road until you reach the main shopping street on the left. This area is somewhat reminiscent of Dazhalan in Peking, with several covered shopping arcades. Both north and south of here is a maze of muddy lanes and old grey single-storey houses.

There are many fine old temples in the suburbs of Taiyuan, including the 14th-century **Jindaifusi** (Temple of the Jin Minister) three miles northwest of town, and the earlier **Guandi Miao** (Old War God Temple) west of the city in the village of Xiaoweiying. Ancient scrolls and artwork from these and other temples can be viewed at the **Shanxi Museum.**

The most famous temple complex in Taiyuan, the **Jin Si,** is also one of China's largest, oldest and most beautiful. It is located in a wooded setting 15 miles southeast of the city (bus 8: there is a hotel at the site). The principal building, the Hall of the Sacred Mother, was built between 1023 and 1031 and is one of the best surviving examples of Song architecture. Inside, 43 remarkable statues, contemporaneous with the hall, represent the Sacred Mother and her attendants.

The **Yingzi Hotel** is a ten-minute walk down the broad boulevard leading from the train station. A room with bath in the new building is 9 元 per person; you must bargain. Cheaper dorm accommodation might be available.

There are a few eateries in town, but no good ones. The Shanghai Restaurant, on the main shopping street, is the best of a bad lot.

A few hours east of Taiyuan by train is **Yangquan,** a small, gritty coal-mining town. It has an old section a few minutes' walk from the train station. The Guoji Guest House (take a bus from the station) across the river has beds in a three-bed room for 6元. Near Yangquan is **Dazhai,** the famous (or infamous) farming village that was held up as an agricultural model to the nation during the Cultural Revolution. So great was its prestige that the village head became a Vice-Premier. Today it is claimed that its high agricultural output was made possible by secret state aid and by grossly inflated statistics (although most of the impressive irrigation gullies were built during the 1950s with little more than shovels and sweat). There is a hotel at Dazhai, though it is seldom visited nowadays.

Datong

Datong was founded over 2,000 years ago during the Warring States period. It remained a small town until 386 A.D., when the Tobas, a non-Han people who had conquered North China, made it their capital. For the century that followed Datong was the political and cultural center of the Northern Wei Dynasty. The Yungang caves, carved during this period, bear witness to its sophistication. In 494 the capital was moved to Luoyang, and Datong declined in importance. 500 years later the city underwent a minor renaissance; it served as a secondary capital under the Liao and Jin Dynasties. Under the Ming it was no more than a frontier garrison town. Today, with a population of 300,000, Datong is a center of industry and coal mining, and has one of the last steam locomotive factories in the world.

The older section of Datong is fascinating. Narrow streets clogged with horse-drawn carts are flanked by rows of one-storey houses with grass growing on the roof. There are several very old pagodas and temples scattered about. On the main street fairly close to the bus depot is the **Upper Huayan Monastery,** with a huge red prayer hall that dates from 1140 and is one of the biggest Buddhist temples in China. The interior is richly decorated, as is the adjacent Lower Huayan Temple. Farther east along the same street is the **Nine Dragon Screen,** a 50-yard long Ming Dynasty mosaic of glazed tiles.

To get to this part of town, turn right outside the entrance to the main depot and walk down the street past the main department store, the exhibition hall and other large shops until the modern buildings give way to one-storey houses. You can also take bus 4.

Asian religious art has always been faced with the difficult task of representing in material form people who have transcended the material world. The severe yet graceful Buddhist figures of the **Yungang Caves,** personifying a detachment from the realm of the senses, embody so masterful a solution to this problem that some commentators rank them among the greatest religious art of all time.

Over 50,000 figures are contained in the 21 major and 32 smaller caves. The most impressive are the cathedral-like caves 5 and 6 (numbering is from right to left). Many of the other caves are disappointingly small and badly preserved, due in part to the depredations of art thieves during the first half of the 20th century. (European tourists would mark the carving of their choice with chalk; that night Chinese "businessmen" would cut it out of the rock.)

The caves are accessible by bus 3 from the main depot. The driver will tell you where to get off, after which there is a mile walk.

All foreigners are housed in the Friendship Hotel. From the train station, take bus 2 to the end of the line, the main depot, then take bus 1 for two stops and walk to the hotel, a few hundred yards down the road on the left. (The last bus leaves about 9 p.m.). Dorms on the top floor 6元. Students in China can get a room with bath for 9元 each. Old, cold in winter, and if you get hot water you're lucky — but it's the only place in town.

Food in Datong is to be endured rather than appreciated. The hotel dining hall is passable, and there is a slightly better restaurant just outside the hotel, but beware of overcharging.

The Public Security Bureau is near the main bus depot. Turn right, then take the first left (at the department store) and walk a few hundred feet.

Express trains leave Datong daily for Peking, Hohhot, Lanzhou and Taiyuan.

3. The Yangtse Basin

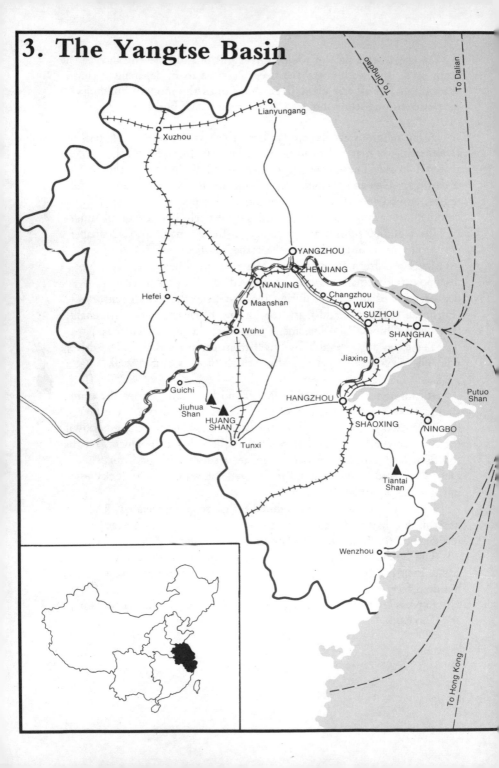

Shanghai

Shanghai. To the armchair travellers of 1940s Europe and
America, the name conjured up visions of mystery and intrigue, of
glamorous romance and shady conspiracies. To the Chinese, however,
Shanghai came to symbolize the darker side of foreign influence and
intervention: the battalions of deformed beggars and teenage street-
walkers, the terrible factories run with forced child-labour, the hundreds
of frozen corpses in the backalleys each winter, the infamous notice at the
entrance of the central parks stating dogs and Chinese were not allowed.

Although Shanghai was founded a thousand years ago, it remained
a small, though prosperous, town until 1842, when it was opened to
European traders by the Treaty of Nanjing. The combination of a
good port, Western technology and commerce, and a limitless local
work force soon made Shanghai one of the leading trading centers in
the East, and grandiose stone buildings were put up along the central
waterfront, or Bund, to house the great banks, trading houses and
consulates of the day. The city was divided into the huge British-
dominated International Settlement around Nanjing Rd., the French
Concession in the southwest, the Chinese City to the southeast and
the Japanese Concession in the north. With the exception of the
Chinese City, all of these zones were autonomous, being governed by
their foreign residents. For most of the Chinese people, living standards
were poor and squalid, and they were treated with contempt by the
foreigners. The resentment this bred made Shanghai a hotbed of
revolutionaries and anarchists. The Chinese Communist Party was founded
here in 1921, and, six years later, a wave of strikes and demonstrations it
organized was brutally suppressed by Chiang Kai-shek. This was the
beginning of the long battle between Nationalists and Communists that
was to last until the founding of the People's Republic in 1949.

The Communists made Shanghai a focal point for their
program of social and economic development. The worst slum areas
were cleared, and modern apartment buildings erected in their place.
Formerly limited to commerce and light industry, the city became a
thriving center for heavy industry as well, including huge steel plants,
automobile factories and shipyards. Shanghai has been transformed

from a consumer mecca into a production center. Over 80% of its industrial products are sent to other parts of China or are exported. And, unlike other major metropolises, Shanghai grows most of its own food: its highly mechanized and prosperous suburban communes have China's highest crop yield per acre.

Shanghai has remained a center of intellectual ferment. It was both the first and last bastion of the Cultural Revolution. Partly as an attempt to defuse this potentially disruptive radicalism, over a million young Shanghainese were resettled in remote villages during the late 1960s. Ten years later, many thousands of these youths, fed up with the cultural and material poverty of village life, sneaked back to their native city. Since they were no longer Shanghai residents, they could not find employment. Most were supported by their families, but some became beggars, pickpockets and muggers, while others organized protest marches.

Many writers have called Shanghai the largest city in the world. But the population figure of 11 million they cite includes the inhabitants of 2,000 square miles of rural suburbs. Nevertheless, the population of the urban core, currently approaching six million, makes it easily China's largest city. It is also its most sophisticated and cosmopolitan. Like New Yorkers or Londoners, the Shanghainese are a race apart who consider themselves superior to the rest of their countrymen. The city pulses with activity, albeit without the brash neon commercialism usually associated with urban life.

City Center

The premier downtown showcase of China is a treasurehouse of European architecture. Most of central Shanghai's buildings date from the International Settlement days, and visitors exploring its highways and byways often feel they have somehow wandered into a European or American metropolis of the 1930s. It is hard to get lost in the city center, since it forms a rectangular grid, with north-south streets named after Chinese provinces and east-west avenues after cities. The most imposing buildings are found along the sole exception to this rule, Zhongshan Rd. East. This beautiful tree-lined waterfront boulevard used to be called **the Bund** and was probably the best known street in the Orient. In the days of the foreign concessions, the Bund was the focal point of the city. Beggars, hawkers and black marketeers mingled with coolies, seamen and the businessmen from the great trading houses and banks that lined the avenue. The road was constantly jammed with trucks, mule carts, trams, motor cars and rickshaws. Today, though the frenetic street life is gone, the buildings remain. They now house state corporations and government offices. Starting at the bridge over Suzhou Creek, you pass the former British Consulate (now the Friendship Store), as well as the buildings that once housed the offices of Glenn Line, Jardine Matheson, the Bank of Indo-China and the Yokohama Specie Bank. On either side of Nanjing Road were the elegant Cathay Hotel, built in 1928, and the Palace Hotel, which dates from 1906; today both these buildings form part of the Peace Hotel. Moving south, the buildings once were the *North China Daily News* offices; the Chartered Bank; the Lyceum Theatre; the Shanghai Club, once considered the best men's club in town, now the Dongfeng Hotel; the Customs House with its tall clock tower; and the massive Hong Kong and Shanghai Bank, now the city government headquarters. The Bund is especially interesting in the early morning — between 5 and 7 a.m. — when the parks by the river are filled with hundreds of people practising tai chi chuan. Early risers can meet many English speakers there. In the evening it becomes a lovers' lane, as hundreds of couples throng the boulevard.

Nanjing Rd., the wide thoroughfare that intersects the Bund at the Peace Hotel, is the most elegant shopping street in China and perhaps the most crowded as well. Over 400 stores line this famous avenue which sells just about every consumer item that China produces. You can find a toy shop at 98, a musical instruments store at 118, a camera shop at 180, a martial arts store at 259, a Chinese flag and banner shop at 309, a huge bookstore at 345 and, at no. 422, an art store with a wide selection of prints and scrolls. There are also several department stores, including the No. 10 Department Store, which used to be the Wing On store, China's largest shopping emporium in the '30s. The No. 1 Department Store, at 800 Nanjing Rd., is the biggest in China.

Another main shopping and strolling area is in the heart of the old French Concession around Huaihai Rd., southwest of Nanjing Rd.

Other Sights

Those seeking a quarter with a slightly more Chinese flavor should head for the circular area bounded by Renmin and Zhonghua Rds. This district, a few minutes' walk south of Nanjing Rd., was the old **Chinese City.** Exploration of the northern area is in general more rewarding, since the south is pockmarked with newer buildings,

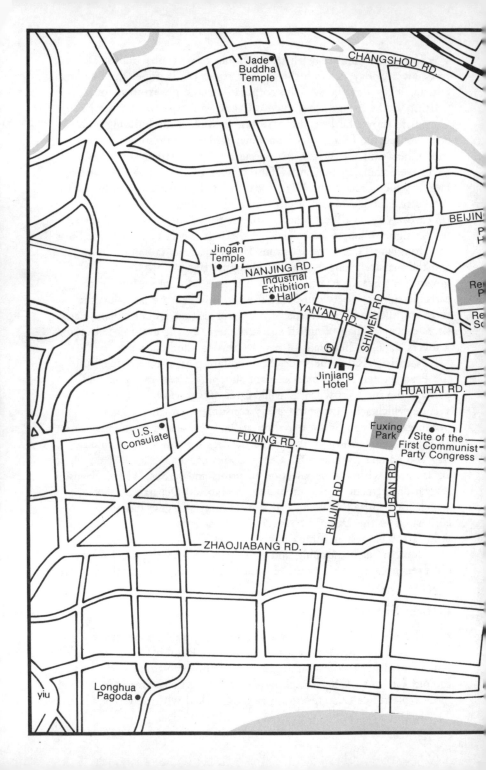

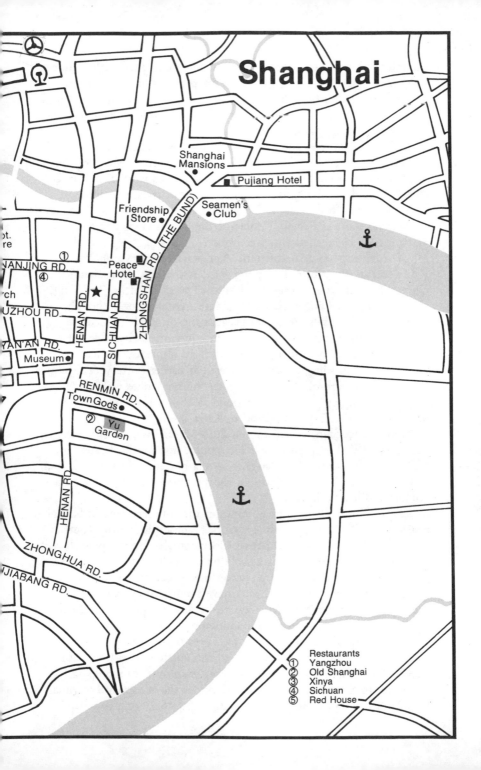

Shanghai

Shanghai
Mansions

Pujiang Hotel

Friendship
Store

Seamen's
Club

① NANJING RD.

④

Peace
Hotel

UZHOU RD.

HENAN RD.

SICHUAN RD.

ZHONGSHAN RD. (THE BUND)

ot.
re

rch

YAN'AN RD.

Museum

RENMIN RD.

Town Gods

② Yu
Garden

HENAN RD.

ZHONGHUA RD.

JIABANG RD.

Restaurants
① Yangzhou
② Old Shanghai
③ Xinya
④ Sichuan
⑤ Red House

though there is a dilapidated Confucian temple in the southwestern part. In the northeast, the **Yu Garden** provides an escape from urban architecture, though not from urban overcrowding. This 16th-century park is similar to many of the famous gardens of Suzhou and contains small hills, lotus ponds, winding paths and over 30 pavilions in addition to its trees and shrubs. On an island in a small lake at the entrance is the famous old **Wuxinting Teahouse.** Much of the neighborhood around the Yu Garden has been converted into an "Olde Shanghai" shopping district where tourists are let loose to experience the "real" China. Despite its artificiality, the architecture is lovely, and there is a small Temple of the Town Gods north of the garden, now being used as a warehouse.

The **Shanghai Museum of Art and History,** on Yan'an Rd. a few blocks south of Nanjing Rd., is the best art museum in China. The top floor contains a wealth of paintings from the Song, Yuan, Ming and Qing periods. Many are masterpieces, although several of the exhibits are copies because the originals, which are sensitive to light, must be stored in the museum vaults. The entire second floor is devoted to ceramics, with an impressive collection of Song, Yuan and Ming porcelain, as well as earlier pottery. The simple but graceful design of some of the older monochrome pieces is particularly impressive. On the ground floor is a fine collection of bronzes from the first and second millenia B.C.

Lu Xun, China's best-known 20th-century writer, spent the last ten years of his life in Shanghai. His house, just south of Hongkou Park in the far north of the city, is now a museum. In the park itself is his tomb, marked by the sort of showy statue that the living Lu Xun would have ridiculed.

At 76 Xingye Rd., a small street in the southern part of Shanghai near Fuxing Park, is the small grey-brick house (now a museum) where, in July 1921, the **Chinese Communist Party** was officially born. On the ground floor is a table with 12 chairs where the meeting supposedly took place, although according to contemporary accounts the delegates met upstairs and may have numbered as many as 15. (Perhaps the number has been reduced because four of the original delegates later defected to the Kuomintang.)

The **Yufo Temple,** famous for its two jade images of the Buddha, stands amidst the factories to the northwest, below Suzhou Creek. The temple is now in active use, with over 20 monks in residence. In the far southwest of the city is the attractive Longhua Pagoda, a 120-foot Song Dynasty edifice. Another Song pagoda is located in Songjian, a small town 12 miles southeast of Shanghai on the railway line to Hangzhou.

Hotels

Pujiang Hotel. Next to Shanghai Mansions along Suzhou Creek; bus 65 from the railway station. Bed in dorm 5元. (They might say that the dorms are for Chinese only, but they are not.) This slightly run down guest house was once the Astor House Hotel and still retains traces of its former elegance.

Peace Hotel. At the corner of Nanjing Rd. and the Bund. Bus 65 from train station. Dorm, for students in China only, 6元(with color TV and videotape!). Built in 1928 and formerly known as the Cathay, this was the most magnificent of the pre-1949 hotels, and everyone of note who visited Shanghai stayed there, or, at least, was seen dancing at the rooftop Tower Restaurant. Its glorious art deco lobby rates a visit even if you aren't a guest.

Jin Jiang Hotel. Bus 41 from train station. Dorm in West Wing 6元. Built in 1931, this posh hotel was originally a private guest house for French residents in Shanghai. Many travellers have been refused admission to these dorms, and we list them only as a last resort.

Park Hotel. 170 Nanjing Rd. West. This is the cheapest of the luxury hotels, for those who do not want or cannot get a dorm space. Rooms here are about 30元. Built in 1934, it is the tallest building in Shanghai.

Restaurants

Not surprisingly, Shanghai has a wide selection of fine restaurants, many of which can be found along Nanjing Road. For the best Shanghai cuisine, rich in oil and elegant in presentation, you can try the **Yangzhou Restaurant** at 308 Nanjing Rd. (1) or the **Old Shanghai Restaurant,** housed in an ugly new building at 242 Fuyou Rd. near the Yu Gardens (2). The **Xinya,** 719 Nanjing Rd. (3), is a famous Cantonese eating place remembered with affection by those who lived in Shanghai before 1949. The second floor of the **Sichuan Restaurant,** 457 Nanjing Rd. (4), offers Sichuanese food as good as any you will find in that province. The **Red House,** at

37 Shaanxi Rd. near the Jin Jiang Hotel (5), offers vaguely European cuisine — before 1949 this was the chic Chez Louis, staffed with French chefs. Finally, the **Gongdelin Shushichu,** 43 Huanghe Rd., is the best-known vegetarian restaurant in Shanghai. Except at the friendly Sichuan, you might have difficulty eating in the cheaper sections of these restaurants, in part because, the Shanghainese being ardent diners, they are usually packed.

Less crowded is the **Sailor's Club,** across the street from the Pujiang in a building that was once part of the British Consulate. Cheap Western chow and even cheaper drinks are available here, but beware of overcharging. For between-meal snacks, try the two **cafes** on Nanjing Rd. just west of the Peace Hotel. They serve coffee, iced or hot, and good lemon meringue and chocolate cream pies. They are crowded with animated students. As in the infamous pie shops of Kathmandu, it is all too easy to linger and eat pie after pie after pie.

Entertainment

Shanghai has 40 theaters and 65 cinemas; you can see opera, acrobatics and plays for about 50 fen each. There is a theater booking office at 660 Nanjing Rd. East.

For those who want to resurrect the flamboyant lifestyle of the International Settlement days, the formerly exclusive French Club, near the Jinjiang Hotel, has bowling alley and billiard rooms, and a huge ballroom. Temporary membership is 2元, with an additional 3元 charge to use the pool (a bathing suit is provided). And, every night at the Peace Hotel, the surprisingly good resident jazz band plays the big band numbers they learned in the forties. Admission is 1元.

Transport

Daily express trains leave Shanghai for most destinations in China, including Peking, Canton, Urumqi, Kunming, Xi'an, Shenyang, Qingdao and Fuzhou. There are several trains each day to Suzhou, Hangzhou and Nanjing.

Passenger boats to Qingdao, Tianjin and Dalian leave from a dock about a mile east of the confluence of Suzhou Creek and the Huangpu River. Ships to Ningbo, Wenzhou and Fuzhou depart from a pier due east of the Yu Garden. Most of these routes are bi- or tri-weekly; the ticket offices are near the docks. There are also daily boats up the Yangtse to Wuhan and weekly liners to Hong Kong.

Nanjing

Nanjing was the first of China's capitals to be situated away from the northern plains. After the Han Dynasty fell and China split into three warring principalities, one king whose land embraced the whole of southern China ruled from there. In the next centuries, while the North was occupied by barbarians, the South was ruled by a succession of Chinese dynasties, none of whom elected to leave Nanjing. Jiankang, as it was then known, was a flourishing economic and cultural center. By the 6th century there were 10 steel foundries and 14 markets where one could find anything from draft animals to ivory and pearls. During the Tang and Song dynasties it was no longer the seat of government — except for a 40-year period in the 10th century — although it remained an important entrepôt.

In 1368 the first Ming emperor, Hongwu, made the city his capital and named it Yingtianfu. He compelled 20,000 rich families to settle there and contribute to the ambitious building projects he undertook. Under Hongwu's direction, massive city walls were constructed, broad boulevards laid out, and a huge palace built. Hongwu's successor, however, moved the capital back to Peking, and gave Yingtianfu its present name of Southern Capital: Nanjing.

In 1853 the Taiping rebels captured Nanjing and made it their headquarters. An Englishman who visited it during Taiping rule was impressed by the city's cleanliness and large public buildings. Unfortunately, the imperial armies destroyed much of the town when they took it in 1864.

In 1911 Sun Yat-sen established the first Republican government in Nanjing, although it was moved to Peking a few months later. Under Chiang Kai-shek the Kuomintang made Nanjing the capital once more in 1928. During the war with Japan, Nanjing fell to the invaders. In the sack of the abandoned capital, 100,000 citizens were massacred by Japanese soldiers, some of whom even organized competitions to see who could catch and kill the most Chinese in one day.

Although no longer a political center, Nanjing today, with a population of three million, is one of China's largest cities and remains a hub of commerce and education. The industrial sector has been

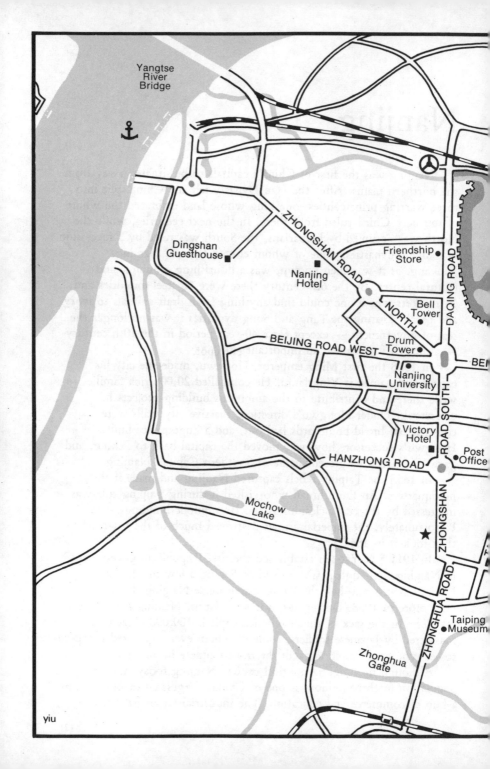

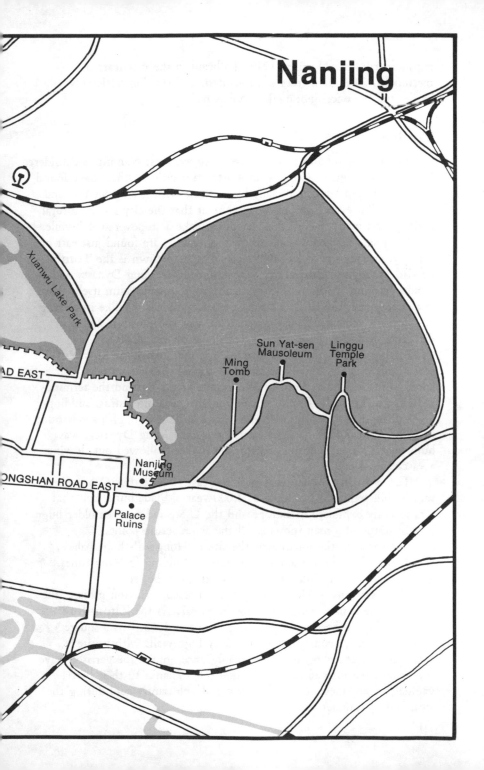

Nanjing

Xuanwu Lake Park

AD EAST

ONGSHAN ROAD EAST

Nanjing Museum

Palace Ruins

Ming Tomb

Sun Yat-sen Mausoleum

Linggu Temple Park

expanded considerably since 1949. To beautify the war-scarred metropolis, 24 million trees were planted, and this has noticeably moderated the once-unbearable summer heat.

To See

With its broad and gracious tree-lined avenues, Nanjing is considered by some to be one of China's most attractive cities. Others have found it disappointingly dull, especially by contrast with nearby Suzhou and Shanghai. But even these are in agreement that the city's rich cultural heritage and many historical associations make a stopover worthwhile.

Nanjing's best-known historical monuments are found just east of the city, an area served by bus 9. The closest to town is the **Tomb of the Hongwu Emperor,** who founded the Ming Dynasty and rebuilt Nanjing. Although little remains of the mausoleum itself, there is a sacred way flanked by 12 pairs of stone animals. Unlike its Peking counterpart, which is a busy paved road, this spirit way is a narrow dirt path shaded by huge trees, especially haunting at dusk.

Farther east, at the bus 9 terminus, is the **Tomb of Sun Yat-sen.** Built in 1929, this impressive tile-roofed mausoleum is approached by a wide flight of 392 granite steps. Beyond the terminus is **Linggu Temple Park,** which contains two interesting buildings — Wuliangdian ("Without Beams") and a 200-foot high pagoda built in 1929. Wuliangdian, a brick structure of the Ming Dynasty, was built over a huge mud mound which was then hollowed out, leaving a vast vaulted hall.

The **Nanjing Museum,** near the eastern gate (bus 6) has some worthwhile exhibits, including a 2,000-year-old jade burial suit that was recently exhibited in Europe and the U.S., and an even older huge bronze statue of a man showing all the acupuncture points.

Just south of the museum is the site of Hongwu's huge palace, which must have been the most impressive building in Ming times. Today, a few scanty foundations are all that can be seen.

Many sections of Hongwu's other major construction project, the city walls, remain. Perhaps the most impressive is the **Zhonghua Gate** at the southern end of the city. Built in 1368, it is a square structure of three courtyards enclosed by high walls with vaulted gates. Several chambers that presumably once housed the garrison have been converted into an art exhibit *cum* cafe. Thanks to their barrel-vaulted design, these stone galleries remain pleasantly cool during the steamiest of summer days.

Immediately north of the gate is a narrow V-shaped canal, clustered around which are some of Nanjing's few remaining neighborhoods, of older houses. One of these areas is east of the gate, on the southern bank. Here the canal is traversed by tow ferries, which provide a good view of it. On the other side, housed in the palatial former residence of a Ming mandarin, is the **Museum of the Taiping Heavenly Kingdom,** whose exhibits show a detailed history of that period.

In central Nanjing — the neighborhood around Zhongshan Road and the Xinjiekou traffic circle — few traces of the city's past remain, though two fine Ming buildings, the **Drum and Bell Towers,** lie near the first roundabout north of the circle. The primary attraction of the Xinjiekou area is the people who patronize its many shops and cafes: the people of Nanjing rank among the most cosmopolitan of China's city dwellers.

Northwest of Xinjiekou is the campus of **Nanjing University** which, with its enormous library (on the right as you enter), is one of the most modern in China.

About a mile northeast of the university is the huge **Xuanwu Lake Park.** It's not unattractive as municipal parks go, and you may be able to climb onto the Ming walls that fringe it to the south. If you haven't yet made the obligatory panda trip, you can find a few grumpy specimens residing in the park zoo.

The **Yangtse River Bridge,** a symbol of China's economic progress, lies at the city's northwestern edge. The Chinese not only designed the four-mile span themselves, but also revamped the domestic steel industry to produce the required 100,000 tons. One of the towers at the end of the bridge has an observation deck.

Across the river, an hour's drive north of the city, is the **Qixia Temple.** Founded in the fifth century, it boasts a large library of Buddhist texts and a Sui Dynasty pagoda. Nearby is the Thousand Buddha Cliff, some of whose sculpted niches are as old as the temple. There are daily bus tours, mainly patronized by Chinese, to these monuments. It's worth investigating if you are spending a long time in Nanjing.

Practical Information

Victory Hotel, Zhongshan Rd. Bus 33 from train station. Dorms 4 or 5元, double rooms for 18元. Centrally located a few paces from Xinjiekou, this small hotel dates from the 1920s. Only 45 rooms, so it's sometimes full.

Dingshan Guest House, Qahar Rd. Bus 32 from station; you must walk the last half mile. Dorms, about 8元. A huge, modern tourist complex on a hill overlooking the city. The dorms here come in many shapes and sizes. Some are unusually comfortable, some are not. The price depends on the receptionist's whim as much as anything else.

Nanjing Hotel, Zhongshan Rd. North. Bus 32 from station. If you can't find a place in the other two hotels, you can get a double room here for 30元; you may get a discount if you are alone.

There are many eateries along Zhongshan Rd., including a **Moslem Restaurant** and, at no. 45, a **Cantonese Restaurant.** On nearby Taiping Rd. South is a **Sichuanese Restaurant** (no. 171) and, at 246, the **Luliyu Vegetarian Restaurant.** If you're stuck in the remote Dingshan, you can get a la carte dishes in the dining room for under 3元. Across the street from the Victory and a few paces north is a cafe notable for its ambience.

There are several trains daily to Peking and Shanghai, and you can reserve seats on some of them even though they don't originate in Nanjing. Trains to Kunming, Fuzhou and Urumqi also stop at Nanjing. Express runs leave Nanjing West Station bound for Xi'an and Lanzhou. The Victory Hotel has bought train tickets for travellers at the Chinese price. Frequent buses reach Huang Shan and Yangzhou. There is also a daily boat to Shanghai and Wuhan.

Canal Towns

Built in the 7th century by the Emperor Yang-ti, the Grand Canal is, with the Great Wall, one of the most impressive construction projects of the ancient world. Still the largest man-made waterway on earth, it significantly improved trade and commerce between the far-flung regions of China, linking the rich ricelands of southern Jiangsu with the food-deficient northern capitals of Peking and Luoyang. Huge grain junks, each carrying several hundred tons, plied the waterways; imperial processions of boats sometimes stretched 50 miles behind the emperor's luxury flagship. Today the pomp and ceremony are gone, but the canal is still a living thoroughfare, crowded with wooden ships transporting produce from communes and villages to the cities.

The Grand Canal brought prosperity to the towns whose walls it washed, and many soon developed into flourishing entrepôts. **Yangzhou,** the most northerly of these, also became known for its beauty, and it was there that Yang-ti retired after he was deposed. But, in a scene straight out of Gibbon, he was strangled by his bodyguard after being spattered with the blood of his favorite son. The sanguinary episode was soon forgotten, and Yangzhou became renowned as a pleasant town whose storytellers were the most skilled and whose women the most beautiful in all China. Today the storytellers that enthralled audiences until a few years ago have disappeared and so, it seems, have the women. In their place, the town has acquired an especially noisome fringe of factories. But, in the center of town, the charm that attracted poets and scholars through the ages can still be felt. The main street, Guoqing, is a low-key, tree-lined avenue, less developed than Guanleng St., the major east-west thoroughfare that intersects it. The best neighborhoods for walking lie northeast of this crossroads. Two streets south of Guanleng is a public bathhouse, cavernous and clean, with an impressive granite facade.

Around Yangzhou are several famous temples to which most tourists dutifully make pilgrimages. But these monuments are in poor condition and are all situated in unattractive surroundings. Visit them only if you have time to spare. In the west of town, two large pavilions similar in appearance to Peking's Temple of Heaven stand in the middle of dusty traffic circles. The one to the south, the Pavilion of Prospering Culture, dates from the 16th century. One block west is the tiny **Stone Pagoda** (Shi Ta), built under the Tang: all but half a dozen faces of its threescore Buddha images have been hacked away. Another, larger pagoda in the southern part of town is climbable (bus 1). Northwest of the city is the scruffy Slender West Lake Park (bus 5), dominated by a large white stupa. Farther north (bus 5 terminus) lies the **Fajingsi,** a functioning Buddhist monastery. Although it was founded some 1,500 years ago, the present buildings are only 50 years old. Inside is a particularly fine stone Buddha and a teahouse for tourists.

Yangzhou's main **hotel,** the Xiyuan, is, like its temples, far from the best neighborhoods. Take bus 3 from the bus station to the end of Guoqian, turn left, and walk 100 yards; the hotel is on your right. (Bus 3 stops running at 5:40 p.m.). With a bit of dickering a double room can be had for 8元. There are dorms (room 212, for example), but the receptionist seems unaware of the fact. A far nicer place to stay, if you can get in, is the Luyang Hotel, a European anomaly in the heart of town. There are two good **restaurants:** the Caijinxiang, on the west side of Guoqing, and the Luchinshashi, on a bustling side street just east. Nearby, on Guangleng St., is a cafe. From Yangzhou buses go to Nanjing and Zhenjiang.

Like Yangzhou, **Zhenjiang** lived by trade. Marco Polo noted its rich merchants, and in the 19th century British and French consulates were established. Zhenjiang was always known for commerce rather than charm, and though there are still a large number of old houses, the face of the city has been pitted by a pox of hideously designed housing projects. The downtown area has wide streets and modern buildings, and the small-town atmosphere of Yangzhou is totally absent. West of the city (bus 2) is the **Jinshan Temple.** Its famous Cizhou Pagoda is quite attractive and worth the climb, but the newly-decorated halls beneath it are marred by insipid murals depicting scenes from the White Snake Legend. (The White Snake was born in the caves of Jinshan before she left to wreak her mischief in Hangzhou.) A more interesting destination is **Beigushan** (bus 4). The Ganluosi Temple on the slope of the hill was wrecked by Red Guards, as were most of its inscriptions, though the walls still stand and now house a coffee-house. But, try as they might, they couldn't destroy the magnificent Song Dynasty Iron Pagoda to the right of the entrance.

Zhenjiang is best visited on a daytrip from Nanjing or Yangzhou. Both of the hotels now open to foreigners are ill-suited for budget travellers. The cheapest room at the centrally located Jingkou (bus 1 from station) is supposedly 22元; the Australian-built Jinshan has nothing but luxury 40元 doubles (20元 for individuals). You may be able to lower the price, but count on a protracted struggle.

Farther south along the Nanjing-Shanghai train line is **Changzhou,** larger than Zhenjiang but more attractive. Waterways web this ancient town, and there are three boat docks, marked with anchors on the city map. The neighborhoods around these piers are excellent places for observing canal traffic. One, in the eastern suburbs (bus 7 terminus), has an interesting commercial area on the waterfront. Another is near the end of West Boulevard, with an ancient bridge and a fabulous teahouse overlooking the canal.

In between these two dock areas and easily reached from either (bus 3 or 7) is a large park containing a pagoda and Qu Qiubai's old house (now a museum), both of which pale by comparison with the nearby **Temple of Heavenly Tranquillity** (Tianningsi). Founded 1,300 years ago and levelled in the time of the Taiping, it was subsequently rebuilt but was wrecked again during the Cultural Revolution. The elegantly-roofed main pavilion is now being restored, piece by piece, and is worth a visit if only to observe the craftsmen. (Enter through a side door in the southern wall.)

Changzhou, unlike its neighbors, has relegated its modern housing developments to the outskirts of town. Some are well-designed enough to be worth a special trip, such as Flower Garden New Village, at the western terminus of bus 3. As a result, the harmony of the city center has been preserved. Many of the side streets are lined with rows of old whitewashed houses, especially in the neighborhood of the charming Changzhou **Guest House.** (Bus 2 two stops west from station, then take the second right, the hotel is on the right.) Low, tiled walls encircle a pretty rock garden. No cheap rooms, unfortunately — doubles are 15元 per bed.

A short train ride southeast of Changzhou is **Wuxi,** included in many tour group itineraries. Over two thousand years ago tin was discovered here, but around 25 A.D. the deposits ran out and the town received its present name, which means "without tin." For the next 1,900 years Wuxi remained a quiet and rather poor market town. But, in the 1930s, Shanghainese businessmen invested large sums in Wuxi's silk mills and the population grew to half a million. After Liberation Wuxi's production was diversified, and today its industrial output ranks among the nation's highest.

As might be expected, most of the city has taken on what is euphemistically called a "new look." Nevertheless, there are still a few older streets, especially Chaoyang Rd. (east of Zhongshan Rd.), and the large park just west of the city, Xihui, is worth a visit. Hidden among the lush foliage in the northwest corner is an enormous old temple complex with a tall pagoda. Best of all is the part of town right outside the train station, in the direction of Jiefang Rd. Several waterways pass through this neighborhood, and the boat traffic is as lively and varied as any on the Canal.

Wuxi's principal drawing card is **Tai Hu,** the vast lake southwest of town. Several uninspired parks have been laid out around the lake, including the Liyuan, a Disney World imitation of a traditional Chinese garden. Unfortunately, most of Wuxi's hotels are grouped around these parks. The price of a room varies. Some travellers have found 6元 dorms in the Taihu Hotel (bus 2, then walk), or have been admitted to the CITS-run 4元 dorms adjacent to the train station, while others have been forced to settle for 15元 beds — discounted — at the Shuixiu (bus 1).

On the west side of Taihu is the ancient town of **Yixing.** It has long been famous for its beautiful pottery, which is still produced today. East of Wuxi is another small town, **Changshu,** known for its lace, a cottage industry in which 15,000 of its 100,000 inhabitants are engaged. The town is quite old and boasts a well-preserved Ming pagoda, the top stories of which are made of bronze.

Suzhou

Of all the cities between Nanjing and Shanghai, Suzhou is the oldest and most interesting. It was built around 600 B.C. by King He Lu to be capital of the kingdom of Wu, and even then was large enough to have eight gates and eight water gates. The historian Sima Qian was impressed by the beauty of Suzhou's buildings when he visited in the 2nd century B.C., as was Marco Polo over a thousand years later. During the interim the area prospered: the opening of the Grand Canal in 605 freed an important trade route to the north for Suzhou's already thriving silk industry, and by the time of Polo's visit in 1276 his "very noble city and great" was the size it is today.

During the Ming Dynasty Suzhou became one of the leading cities in the nation. Its mainstay was silk production, which by the 16th century had developed characteristics that were to appear in the cities of Europe over two centuries later. Weavers toiling in large workshops were paid low wages, job tenure was insecure, and there was a bad unemployment problem. Some merchants became very rich, and Suzhou's "smart set" became the trend-setters of the Qing Dynasty. In the 19th century the operation was taken over by foreign industrialists from Shanghai. The modern era brought new changes in ownership, but Suzhou's reliance on the silk industry has remained.

The Town

Suzhou retains much of the flavor of old China, and many enjoyable hours can be spent wandering along its tree-lined streets and cobbled alleys. There are innumerable compounds of old, whitewashed buildings grouped around series of private courtyards. The red-painted wooden gates that lead to the street are often open, and the wanderer can catch many glimpses of life inside.

The center of town, **Guanqian St.,** is a narrow, crowded, tree-lined thoroughfare fronted by most of Suzhou's larger shops. On the north side of Guanqian, close to Lindin Rd., is a plaza with rows of tailors and food vendors plying their trade in the open air. On the far side of the square is the large Taoist **Temple of Mystery,** founded in the 3rd century B.C. and rebuilt under the Qing. The small east-west street just south of Guanqian has a very crowded square at its western end with a large department store and several theaters. In the evening these feature Chinese opera or comedy variety shows, and tickets can usually be bought up to curtain time.

West of the Guanqian district, across the hectic Renmin Rd., Zhongshi and Jingde Rds. are both lined with old double-storey buildings whitewashed with wood trim and housing small shops and apartments. These lead to a pair of bridges that make a convenient vantage point from which to observe the lively boat traffic of the Grand Canal. There is a well-preserved city gate, the **Jin Men,** close by.

About a mile farther south, near Daoqian St. (bus 2), is another pair of busy harbor bridges. The narrow cobbled lane that hugs the western bank of the river is thronged with porters unloading sacks of rice, vegetable and other produce sent by barge from nearby villages. Near the second bridge is a dock for pasenger boats serving Suzhou's western suburbs, where several temples are to be found. Foreigners are not in theory permitted to visit the large island.

If you are combining both sets of bridges into one excursion, Yangyuxiang Rd. is a recommended route. The continuation of Yangyuxiang Rd. beyond Daoqian St. is far duller than the stretch farther north. But, if you persist until the end, you will be rewarded by a scene that would have delighted Piranesi: the Song Dynasty **Ruiguang Pagoda,** now almost in ruins but majestic nonetheless, looking out onto a romantic fragment of the old earthen ramparts, with two rows of trees growing on its verdant slopes. Also in the area is an extensive, well-preserved fortification, the **Pan Men.**

Although most of Suzhou's colorful neighborhoods lie west of Renmin, a few are in the eastern half of town. These include the stretch of Ganjiang Rd. between Renmin and Fenghuan, and all of Youyi Rd., which, happily, is right outside the Suzhou Hotel. Behind Youyi is a tranquil side canal with ancient houses that seem to grow out of its banks.

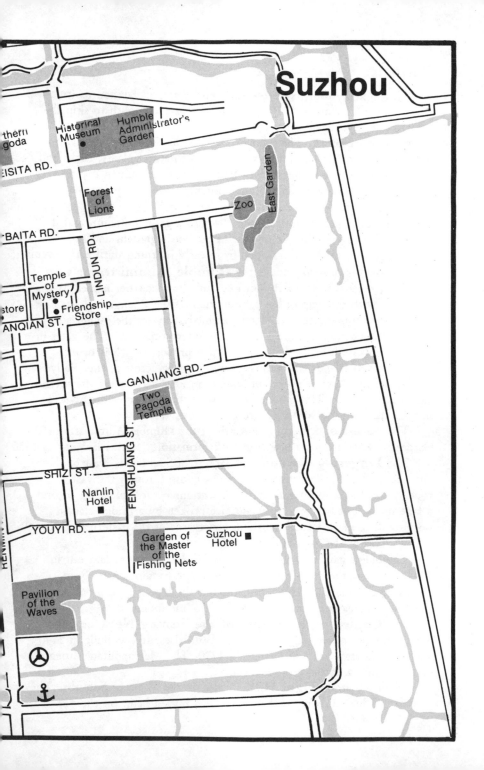

Gardens

All too many tourists devote their entire stay in Suzhou to its gardens. This is a mistake. But it would be just as foolish to skip the gardens entirely, for they are not mere collections of shrubbery: each is a genuine work of art. The Chinese believed in the unity and harmony of man and nature. A skillful arrangement of natural plants, rocks and water could therefore express deep truths about the human psyche, and contemplation of a garden, like contemplation of a poem, novel or painting, provided a way to "nourish the heart."

One would not attempt to run through a great museum, and it might be best to choose one or two of Suzhou's gardens and spend several hours there. Most are open from early morning until early evening.

Perhaps the most famous is the **Humble Administrator's Garden,** created in the early 16th century by a courtier named Wang Xianchen with the help of his painter friend Wen Zhengming. It took 16 years to complete and was later gambled away by the owner's son. The garden's eastern section is a large uninteresting park. The gates in the park's western wall lead to the garden proper, which is broken into a series of islands and pathways zig-zagging across a lake. Fully half of the total area is water, providing an ideal setting for the several beautiful pavilions. This garden is in the northeast corner of town, a short walk from the corner where bus 4 turns west.

The **Forest of Lions,** just south of the Humble Administrator's Garden, is known for its beautiful rock formations. It was laid out in 1350.

The **Lingering Garden,** the largest in Suzhou, is west of the city center (bus 5). The visitor is led clockwise through the vast rockeries of the western and northern sections before emerging to find a lake spread out before him, its surface broken by a bridge clad in wisteria. The more formal halls and courtyards of the eastern section follow. This garden was built in 1525.

The oldest garden is the **Pavilion of the Waves,** laid out in 1044 in the southeastern part of the city. The pavilions have been destroyed and rebuilt many times, though the layout is original. One third of the area is taken up by an artificial mountain.

The **Garden of the Master of the Fishing Nets,** near the Suzhou Hotel, is very small, but full of surprises. It was built in 1140 and restored after years of neglect in 1770. The Metropolitan Museum of Art houses a partial reproduction.

Finally, there is **Tiger Hill,** located in the Western Suburbs. The founder of Suzhou is reputed to have been buried here; on the top is a thousand-year pagoda. Tiger Hill is included on most tourist itineraries. It is not wholly devoid of interest, but isn't worth the long trip (bus 5).

Hotels

Suzhou Hotel, 115 Youyi Rd. Turn left outside station, take bus 2 to center of town, then bus 4. Dorms on second floor of old wing, 5元 a bed. The ultramodern new wing offers a full range of shops and a rooftop bar. There is another bar with music at night in the adjacent Gusu Hotel.

Nanlin Hotel, Youyi Rd. A few minutes' walk west of the Suzhou Hotel. Beds in a three-bed room, 8元. Nice rooms with private bath.

Lexiang Hotel, Dajing Lane (near Renmin Road) has doubles for 22元.

Restaurants

You would have to go to a culinary mecca like Peking to find cooking that surpasses that of Suzhou; even Shanghainese are reputed to visit Suzhou for the food. The best restaurants are found on the small east-west street just south of Guanqian Rd., a short distance west of the Temple of Mystery. The most renowned, and oldest, is the **Songhelou,** where the Emperor Qianlong reputedly ate two hundred years ago. Nearby is the **Suzhou Restaurant,** where fish is a specialty: a whole fish should cost about 4元. On Guanqian, near the temple, is the **Huangtianyuan Cake Shop,** making sweets since 1838 (and apparently not cleaned since then). There are also many good noodle shops — one, for example, is on Renmin Rd. near Guanqian — where you can eat your fill for 20-30 fen.

Transport

Frequent express trains to Shanghai, Nanjing and Wuxi, and a few to Hangzhou. Suzhou is on the main line from Shanghai north, and express trains to Peking, Urumqi and Xi'an stop here, but seats (or berths) cannot be reserved. The ticket office is in a building across the street from and a little east of the station.

Twice a day, boats leave for Hangzhou via the Grand Canal. An overnight trip costs 4元 including a berth but visibility is limited. To see more of this historic waterway, you might consider taking the tiny, hard-seat-only 2元 daytime ferry, which leaves at 5:50 a.m. Though the scenery is not always stimulating, at about noon the boat passes through the fascinating canal houses of **Jiaxing,** a closed town on the Shanghai-Hangzhou railway. Some may wish to disembark and take an afternoon train after exploring for a few hours.

Both day and night boats leave from a dock just east of the main bridge south of the hotel (note that bus 4 does not begin running until 5:30). Tickets are available from an office at the pier or, for the night ferry, from the hotel. Your permit must be valid for travel by boat.

Hangzhou

The magical scenery of Hangzhou has drawn visitors for hundreds of years. The beauty of the West Lake was already famous during the Tang Dynasty and by the 16th century printed tourist guides had become commonplace.

Hangzhou's history is as glorious and romantic as its setting. After the Grand Canal reached the city in 610, a spectacular development began. This culminated in Hangzhou's most brilliant period as the capital of the Southern Song Dynasty from 1138 to 1279. By the 13th century, with a population of about one million, it was the largest and most prosperous city on earth. Marco Polo, whose writings are studded with superlatives, nevertheless gave Hangzhou his highest rating, calling it "the greatest city which may be found in the world, where so many pleasures may be found that one fancies himself to be in Paradise."

Although no smaller in population than its Tang counterpart, Chang'an, Hangzhou covered only ¼ the area and was infinitely more crowded. Five-storey tenements were common, especially around the Imperial Way, the huge north-south boulevard that was the city's central thoroughfare. There were many markets at which one could buy products from all over the Orient. The Imperial Palace and the mansions of the rich were located on Phoenix Hill south of the city, and the shores of the West Lake were studded with summer houses and pleasure domes.

In succeeding centuries, Hangzhou remained a thriving

commercial center, whose silk industry developed along the lines of Suzhou's. But the city was laid waste during the Taiping Rebellion. Perhaps half of the population died during the rebels' siege in 1861, and the recapture of the city two years later by the imperial forces is said to have been even more destructive. When they finally entered Hangzhou, the troops found less than 10% of the population still living there, and three-quarters of the buildings destroyed, including most of the temples and pavilions around the lake.

Hangzhou was slowly rebuilt in later years, when it had a foreign concession. Today, with a population of 750,000, the city has a broad industrial base ranging from the production of iron, steel, petroleum products and chemicals to textiles and electronics.

The West Lake

The West Lake is Hangzhou's foremost attraction. Its exquisitely landscaped paths and gardens have inspired the Song Dynasty's greatest artists; walking around it one sometimes feels as if one had left the real world and entered a Chinese painting. The tranquility of the lake (despite the inevitable crowds of tourists) make Hangzhou a superb place to rest for a few days. One should add that if you travel hundreds of miles, as some do, just to see the lake, you will probably be disappointed.

The lake is of relatively recent origin. Until two thousand years ago it was a shallow bay in the estuary of the Qiantang River. Over the centuries, silt brought by the river formed a barrier between the lake and sea. The lake was further modified, beautified and expanded by a succession of emperors and officials between 800 and 1800 A.D. During this period it became customary for travellers to visit the "Ten Prospects," the ten most famous views of the lake. At least four of these continue to live up to their reputation, and are as romantic as their traditional names:

"Autumn View on the Still Lake." At the southeastern corner of **Solitary Hill Island,** near the Hangzhou Hotel, is a teahouse famous for its view. The pavilion cluster was first built in the 18th century by the Qianlong emperor, who so loved this part of the lake that he also had a large palace erected nearby, the remaining part of which houses the Zhejiang Museum. Near this island is the large Tomb of Yue Fei, the Song Dynasty patriot.

"Observing the Fish at Flower Harbour." A pavilion and a fish pond

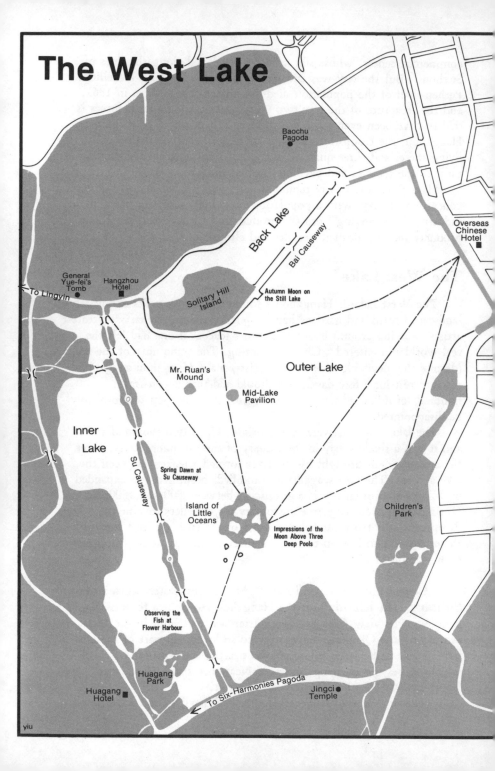

were built in the southwest corner of the lake during the Qing period. Over the past 30 years it has been developed into **Huagang Park,** with some 55 landscaped acres full of trees, flowers and a large pond well stocked with goldfish who grow fat on the bread thrown them by tourists. (Sweet bread is sold here at 20 fen a loaf and makes a good breakfast for humans, too!)

"Impressions of the Moon Above Three Deep Pools." In the middle of the West Lake is the **Island of Little Oceans.** This beautiful island, with four (not three) lakes, was constructed in the 17th century. It can be reached by public boat from either Solitary Hill Island or Huagang Park. Tickets are 40 fen (save your ticket, it's good for a return or onward boat trip).

"Spring Dawn at Su Causeway." The tree-shaded **Su Causeway,** which joins the Hangzhou Hotel to Huagang park, is a beautiful place for a promenade any time of the day or night. Built in the 11th century by the poet-governor Su Dongpo, the two-mile stretch has six hump-backed bridges.

Other sights

Besides the lake, there are several other worthwhile attractions in Hangzhou. Foremost among these is the **Lingyin,** a beautiful functioning Buddhist temple set amidst woods and streams west of the city (take bus 7 to the last stop). It was reputedly founded in the 4th century, and was certainly in existence by the 8th, for several Tang inscriptions speak of it. Unfortunately, the temple was destroyed during the Taiping rebellion, and all of the present buildings are 20th-century. Extensively restored between 1953 and 1958, the complex was preserved during the Cultural Revolution by order of Chou En-lai. On the cliff-face near the temple are carved over 300 Yuan Dynasty statues of Buddhas and Boddhisattvas.

Behind Lingyin is the **Northern Peak.** Cable cars climb to the summit of the 1,000-foot hill whence a spectacular flight of steps swoops down to the temples below. The view of the lake from the summit is equally rewarding — far better than that from Yu Huang Shan, where the tour buses go.

One building that survived the Taiping destruction is the sturdy 200-foot **Pagoda of the Six Harmonies** on Yuelun Hill (bus 4 from the city center). The brick interior dates from the 12th century,

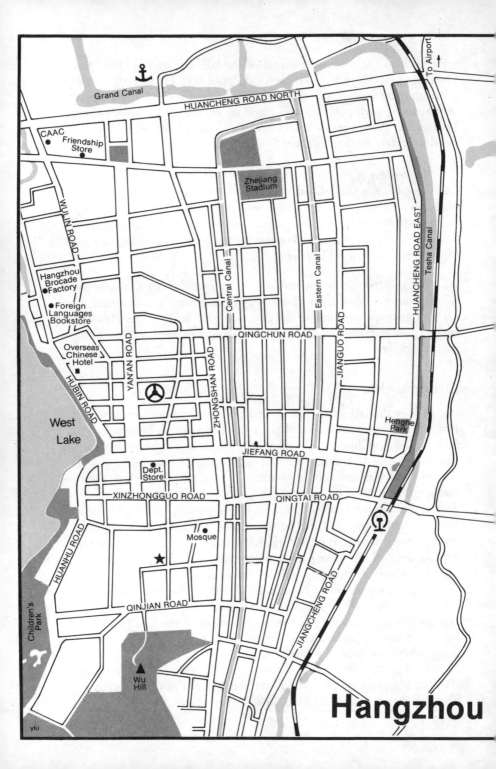

although the wooden exterior was reconstructed in 1900. Bells hang from the eight corners of each of its 13 roofs.

Hangzhou is famous for **its tea brigades,** notably Longjing (Dragon Well) and Meijian, both west of the city. The tea of the former is more famous, but the latter is more interesting, if only because it is farther out and fewer tourists go there. Take bus 4 to the last stop, then bus 18. The driver will tell you where to get off, after which you walk a mile. It is possible to go on foot from Meijian to Lingyin. The five-hour walk is recommended, although the path may be hard to find. There are many other walking trails west of the lake, several of which are clearly indicated on the largest of the Chinese maps on sale in town.

While very few pre-Taiping buildings remain in the town proper, there are nonetheless areas worth exploring. Many smaller thoroughfares are lined with 19th-century shops and houses, including Zhongshan Rd. (once the Imperial Way), Qingtai Rd., Qinjian Rd. and, best of all, Qingchun Rd. Qingchun, a lively but far from modern commercial artery, is a hive of activity for virtually its entire length. Those who prefer to wander through quieter residential neighborhoods should head for the area bounded by Jiefang and Qinjian Rds. Or try the long and narrow lane hugging the length of the central canal. Yan'an Rd., the city's hectic main street, has a few interesting shops and restaurants.

37 miles north of Hangzhou by road is **Mogan Mountain,** known for its springs, waterfalls and dense blue-green bamboo forests. Pleasantly cool at the height of summer, it was developed as a resort for Europeans living in Shanghai during the International Settlement days.

Practical Information

Hangzhou Hotel, Yuefan St. Bus 7 from train station. (From the canal dock, begin by taking bus 54 to the lake.) Dorm 6元. Hangzhou's most luxurious hotel, beautifully situated on the north shore of the lake.

Huagang Hotel, Xishan Rd., opposite Huagang Park. Bus 7 from train station to the lake, then bus 4 to the park. Air-conditioned triple for 18元; cheap dorms also available. In a less convenient (though attractive) location; note that bus 4 does not run in the evening.

Overseas Chinese Hotel, 92 Hubin Rd., on the eastern side of the lake. Bus 7 from station. Double room 22元. Dorms 5元, but usually impossible to get into.

Hangzhou's hotels are sometimes full, especially in mid-September when many people come to town to see the **"bore"**, a huge tidal wave that thunders up the Qiantang River at the autumnal equinox.

Hangzhou has several very fine restaurants. The most famous is the **Louwailou,** on Solitary Hill Island, which offers good food in a beautiful setting; in the huge downstairs dining hall you can eat well for under 3元. Other restaurants serving equally good meals are located along Yan'an Rd. and Jiefang Rd. in the center of town near the lake. These include the Hangzhou and the Zhiweiguan, famous for its dumplings.

There are frequent trains to Shanghai, as well as direct services to Canton and Peking. There are also two boats a day to Suzhou along the Grand Canal (see the Suzhou section for details). Daily buses leave for Huang Shan and Shanghai, and a small rail line runs east to Shaoxing and Ningbo.

Zhejiang Province

Southeast of Hangzhou are several towns that may be visited in a loop without backtracking. One could go from Ningbo to Tiantai and Shaoxing using Shanghai and Hangzhou as endpoints. It is also possible, and more exciting, to drop down to Wenzhou and from there to Fujian Province, picking up the route described in *The Coast Road*.

The charming canal town of **Shaoxing** lies 40 miles from Hangzhou. Founded over two thousand years ago, it is one of the oldest towns in the region. A flourishing trade center under the Song, Shaoxing never attained the heights of prosperity reached by its newer neighbors, Hangzhou and Ningbo. Lu Xun was born here, and the world in which his stories are set — a world of wineshops, rustics and pompous mandarins — was based on his remembrance of the town where he spent his youth. Shaoxing has remained relatively sheltered from the changes that have swept the continent since then, and Lu Xun's readers may feel they are revisiting a familiar town after a long absence. The neighborhoods, the teahouses, the surrounding villages are all there, and the populace remains as pleasantly unsophisticated as ever.

The northeast part of town is the best for wandering. A few canals are flanked by flagstone walkways, and one is spanned by a graceful 13th-century bridge, the **Baziqiao.** There are several teahouses in the side streets, at least one of which features evening storytelling. The upper and lower reaches of Jiefang Rd., the main street, are also rewarding — noisy hawkers to the north, quiet teahouses to the south — and you can bypass the boring center section by using the tiny residential lane that runs parallel to Jiefang for its entire length.

Just west of Jiefang is the **Dashansi,** a slender Song Dynasty pagoda. Another Song Pagoda, the **Yingtiansi,** crowns a hillock towards the southwest. In the countryside southeast of town is the **Temple of Yu the Great,** founder of the mythical Xia Dynasty. Though the complex of gutted 18th-century buildings is not worth the trip, the pleasant rural setting is. If you take bus 2, you must walk a mile to the temple. It's more fun to go by canal: charter a foot-powered boat and driver at the southern end of Jiefang Rd. (roundtrip about 1元). Also on the outskirts is the East Lake (bus 1), but this is recommended only for those who find Shaoxing itself too uncontrived.

The **Shaoxing Hotel** is to the west at the base of a hillock. From the train station walk along Jiefang to the first clear perpendicular right turn above the pagoda — not an intersection — and watch for an arch-bridge combination a quarter mile farther, on your left. The hotel is close by, triple with bath 5元. (Shaoxing has no city buses except to the suburbs). In addition to the rail spur from Hangzhou to Ningbo, there is bus service to Tiantai and Wenzhou.

Ningbo, to the east, was founded in the 11th century and soon became a bustling seaport, exporting silk to Japan and receiving gold in return. In 1842 it became one of five treaty ports opened to European merchants after the Opium War. Church spires and other relics from this era still dot the town, as do older Chinese houses whose walls are made of recycled roof tiles. Near the train station is Moon Lake, with a pretty waterside boulevard along its western bank. The first road east of the lake, Zhanming St., is the liveliest in the city: pass under the fine old drum tower at its northern end (just across the wide East is Red Blvd.) and continue up to Zhongshan Park. The semicircle outside the park is full of street vendors; inside older men play chess or give impromptu opera performances.

Half a block from the lake's northwestern edge is the **Tianyige Library,** founded by a Ming mandarin. The books are gone, but the old buildings are in superb condition, as is the rock garden just outside. In the south of town, near Jiefang St. (bus 6) is the **Tianfeng Pagoda,** built in the 14th century though much restored in later years. There are also several old temples in the suburbs, including the Boguosi to the northwest and the still-functioning Yuwongsi due east of the city. Both can be reached by country bus; allow plenty of time. The conditon of the Tianhougongsi, once the finest in Ningbo, is unknown.

Ningbo's **Overseas Chinese Hotel** is west of Moon Lake (bus 1 from dock or bus depot to the train station, then walk). The hotel makes a practice of charging foreigners 20元 although they have cheaper rooms hidden away. From Ningbo there are frequent trains to Hangzhou and Shaoxing and daily buses to Tiantai and Wenzhou, as well as boats to Shanghai and **Putuo Island**. This holy sanctuary, which was once inhabited by over 1,000 Buddhist monks, is closed to foreigners.

The monasteries of **Tiantai Shan,** however, can be visited. Here, in the 6th century, the Tiantai sect of Buddhism was founded. Its adherents, much influenced by Taoism, taught that enlightenment could be achieved by apprehending the constant essence that underlies the perpetually changing universe. The Tiantai monasteries have remained unusually active, and in mid-1982 150 monks and as many disciples attended a three-month seminar there.

The temples are accessible via Tiantai town, linked by bus to Ningbo, Hangzhou, Wenzhou and Shaoxing. Infrequent buses go from town to the temples, and hitching is also possible. Foreigners are requested to stay at the Shijie Hotel, on the main shopping street, where spacious single rooms are 2元, but the town is too dull to merit an overnight. If you are stranded there for any length of time, try exploring the long, narrow shop-filled lane running perpendicular to the foot of the main drag.

Three of the temples of Tiantai Shan are still inhabited by monks. The largest is the **Guoqingsi,** founded in the 6th century, restored in the 18th, and in excellent condition today, with many fine halls, a Sui Dynasty pagoda, and an ancient plum tree. Five miles up the mountain is the **Gaomingsi,** small, peaceful and off the main road; another six miles brings you to the **Fanguangsi** (more a rest house than a monastery), which overlooks an enormous waterfall. Two of the three Fanguang temples were damaged recently, though one is being restored. Near the turnoff to the Gaomingsi is the **Zhi Zhe Pagoda,** where the founder of the Tiantai sect was buried.

The Guoqing offers bed and board for 5元 ; at the Fanguang, two meals and a bed are 2.50元. Both temples are mobbed with Chinese vacationers during the day, but are tranquil at night. The atmosphere of the Gaomingsi is by far the most conducive to meditation, but try to give its small community advance notice if you plan to stay.

Enjoy the tranquillity of Tiantai while you can; in **Wenzhou,** peace is an impossible dream. Wenzhou is a city of disturbing contrasts — porters pulling enormous loads are sideswiped by Toyotas, and young punks in bluejeans laugh at old men in traditional costume. These are the sorts of sights usually associated with other, more boisterous regions of the Third World. Perhaps a partial explanation of their presence here is Wenzhou's former status as a treaty port. There are plenty of traces of British architecture, but most of the old buildings are in terrible condition and much of the city is in ruins.

Wenzhou is a small city, easily explored on foot: the most interesting steets are along the bus lines. In the park on the town's eastern edge storytellers perform to enormous audiences, accompanied by drums and xylophones. Ferries run regularly to an island just north of the city with two pagodas and a few gutted temples now being restored (slowly). The Overseas Chinese Hotel is in the southwest corner of the city, within walking distance from the bus station: from the boat dock take a cycle rickshaw (1元).

Wenzhou is only a few hours' ride from the Fujian border. There is, however, no direct bus to Fuzhou. You must spend the night at an intermediate point — usually Fuan — and take a second bus the next day. For the continuation of this route, see The *The Coast Road.*

Huang Shan

One of the oddest aspects of travel in China is the hectic profusion of Chinese tourists who flock to the farthest regions of their enormous country, and nowhere are they more apparent than in Huang Shan. Westerners drawn by tales of rugged scenery may be slightly nonplussed by the resort atmosphere of the base camp (with pricey restaurants and a pair of Friendship Stores), or by the ugly concrete walkways that connect the officially designated scenic spots. Still, the beauty is there, for those who don't mind enjoying it en masse. From the peaks, the highest of which is 6,000 feet, there are spectacular views over pine-clad slopes, seas of cloud with floating islands of rock, and streams winding through precipitous valleys.

Though there are many hotels at the foot of the mountain, foreigners must stay at the CITS guest house overlooking the bus station, where a bed in a triple is 8元. Dorms are available in the Beihai Hotel at the summit for 4元. Two trails snake up the slopes between Beihai and the base camp. The western route is longer, but not as steep as the eastern and is therefore more crowded. Old men and women, determined to see Huang Shan before they die, dodder up the slopes. Those in better shape can sprint to the top in three hours, but in doing so will miss the many side paths leading to panoramic views. There are two hotels, both former temples, at the halfway point, the Yupinglou and the Bansansi. From Beihai you can descend by the eastern route to Wingkusi, where there is another hotel, as well as buses back to the base camp. There is also a trail down the back of the mountain with a guest house at the foot, in Songohan, close to the motor road back to town. At one time there was a walking trail heading west from Songohan around the mountains (still shown on the map), but this path is reportedly closed.

One way of escaping the Huang Shan hordes is to head northwest to **Jiuhua Shan** (Nine Flowers Mountain), so named by the peripatetic Li Bai, who compared its nine peaks to beautiful lotus blossoms. It is one of the holiest of Buddhist mountains, and the path to Tiantai, the summit, was once lined with innumerable temples and pavilions.

A spiderweb of transport routes connects Huang Shan to Hangzhou, Jiangxi and the Yangtse River, making it a convenient stepping stone between, say, Nanjing and Zhejiang Province. There is also an express bus from Shanghai. Most of the driving time is spent in Anhui Province, and its small towns and villages are not without charm.

The roads from east and west pass through **Tunxi,** which is connected by plane with Hangzhou and by bus with Jingdezhen. For over a thousand years Tunxi has prospered from trade in tea and wood, and its traditional products are still in evidence today. Many tea plantations lie west of town, and raft after raft of lumber can be seen drifting down the Xin River. During the Ming Dynasty Tunxi's retired merchants built palatial homes in the area: some of these were reportedly intact 20 years ago and may still stand in the villages surrounding the nearby town of **Shexian.** Tunxi itself has a charming older section with flagged lanes and houses fronted with richly burnished wood, by the river; turn left as you leave the bus station. It might be possible to get permission to spend the night in this theoretically closed town.

The nearest open city to Huang Shan is **Wuhu,** a port on the Yangtse. The riverboat stops here, and there are rail spurs to Tunxi and Hefei, as well as a line to Shanghai that passes through Nanjing. Wuhu, founded under the Han, became a treaty port in 1877 and still earns its livelihood by trade. The main street, Zhongshan Rd., is quite lively, as is the area between there and the river. The most interesting side streets are those just north of the canal, where porters unload logs and animal skins. At the confluence of the canal and the Yangtse is the ancient **Mid-River Pagoda,** which appears to date from the Song. North of here a large cathedral, now a shell, serves as a reminder of the treaty port days.

Slightly inland are two small lakes surrounded by parkland, a favorite haunt of chessplayers and other idlers. Snake wrestlers sometimes perform by the lakeside, while an opera house opposite the island in the northern lake stages more conventional entertainment. There is an excellent restaurant on the island, and another one (second floor) on Zhongshan Rd. East of the lake is the **Wuhu Hotel** (bus 4 from bus, train and boat), where a bed in a triple costs 6.50元.

Southwest of Wuhu is **Guichi,** another riverboat stop which, though officially closed, is becoming increasingly accustomed to foreigners since it is the closest point between the Yangtse and Huang Shan.

To the north is **Hefei,** the capital of Anhui Province. A small market town thirty years ago, it is now an industrial center with a population of half a million. A moat encloses the older part of the town. Hefei is linked by bus with Jiujiang and Huangshan and by rail with Nanjing and Wuhu. There is also a direct train service from Peking and Chengdu.

Farther north the line to Peking passes through **Xuzhou,** an industrial town of 500,000 surrounded by scenic hills. From here, a branch line runs east to **Lianyungang,** a remote town near which Buddhist caves were recently discovered. Lianyungang is divided into two parts: a large inland city and a tiny seaport.

4. South China

Canton

Canton is unlike anywhere else in China. Time spent in the center of town will make other Chinese cities seem bland and boring by comparison. And yet, it is not, as some claim, merely a second-rate carbon copy of Hong Kong. Canton is far less mechanized, modern and money-minded. Hong Kong streets at night blaze with neon and swarm with cars full of people hurrying to discos, cinemas and ultra-modern shopping centers. In Canton, warm summer nights on dimly lit tree-shaded avenues are alive with the talk and laughter of families sitting outside their houses, taking the air, or strolling.

Canton is a city famous for rebellion. The Cantonese have a tradition of thinking for themselves, and their capital was one of the birthplaces of both the Republican and Communist movements. Sun Yat-sen made Canton the base of his campaign against the Manchus, and later of his fight against the warlords. Mao Tse-tung and Chou En-lai spent several years in Canton in the 1920s promoting revolution. It is, however, important to remember that Canton has developed as an integral part of the Chinese empire since it was founded over two thousand years ago. (Hong Kong is scarcely older than a century.)

One of the few reliable myths about Canton is that it has always been the most outward-lookng city in China. Under the Tang it was one of the greatest seaports of the Empire. Its community of thousands of foreign traders, most of whom were Arab or Persian, made their fortunes by exporting silk, porcelain and tea. With the arrival of the Portuguese in the 16th century, Canton began trading with the nations of Europe. From then until 1842, when the Treaty of Nanjing was signed, Canton was the only Chinese port open to Europeans, and the city was settled by western traders and missionaries who continued to exert great influence over its life until 1949.

Nevertheless, in many ways, Canton remains the most Chinese of cities; traditional votive offerings to the dead, unavailable elsewhere in China, are openly sold on the streets. Moreover, it was the Cantonese who spearheaded the migration of Chinese abroad. Thus, the stock image a visitor to New York or San Francisco has of an animated, bustling Chinatown is essentially based on Canton.

The Town

Most travellers spend far too little time in Canton. They confine their visit to the area around the Dongfang Hotel and the train station, with perhaps a quick jaunt to the semi-deserted Shamian Island. This is a mistake. Many pleasant days can be spent exploring the huge central section of town, between Zhongshan Rd. and the river. This area seems to have changed very little in the past 50 years (although the notorious slums have disappeared, cleared both by the Communists and the Nationalists before them). The main streets are flanked by· rows of dilapidated four- and five-storey buildings with ornate facades; the upper stories of these buildings jut over the sidewalk to form busy pillared shopping arcades.

Most of these former mansions and office buildings have been divided into apartments, but some have been converted into tiny factories that turn out an extraordinary variety of articles ranging from cardboard boxes, clothes and playing cards to nails, bolts and unidentifiable machine parts. Equally interesting are the many schools dotted throughout the city. The primary schools are easily identifiable by the raucous din of shouting and laughing students.

Many side alleys lead off the main thoroughfares. Entering one, you will find yourself in another, quieter world of small, clean white-washed houses whose occupants are likely to be sitting on stools in the cobbled sidewalk, cleaning chickens, washing clothes, or talking.

One particularly interesting area is just north of Shamian Island. Take bus 31 to the end of Renmin Rd., or trolley 3 to its terminus, and follow the river west along **Liuersan Rd.** Here, rows of formerly imposing four-storey mansions face a waterfront shaded by leafy trees some of which are as old as the houses. In a few minutes you will reach a graceful, stone-arched bridge linking the center of Shamian Island with the mainland.

The **Qingping Market,** one of the world's most unforgettable food emporia, is in the narrow north-south street opposite the bridge. Near the entrance to the market is a large selection of rare spices and medicinal herbs, including dried starfish, snakes, lizards and deer antlers. Beyond this is a somewhat more gruesome section, featuring such delicacies as live owls, pangolins (a scaly anteater considered an endangered species), monkeys, civets, turtles and housecats; freshly butchered dogs are also available, spilling over into the east-west street just beyond.

Crossing this street and continuing north is another market area supplying fresh vegetables, flowers, potted plants, goldfish and the original pet rocks. This is a neighborhood of smaller houses, somewhat less pretentious and more ramshackle than those of Liuersan. Wander through these quiet streets in a northerly direction until you reach Xiuli Rd., a major shopping thoroughfare leading back to Renmin Rd. and the 31 bus. Alternatively, continue north to **Shuguang Rd.,** which also intersects with Renmin. Shuguang is far less flashy than Xiuli and features another large market, this one covered, on the north side of the street, and, a block or so beyond, a tiny coffee shop where you can replenish flagging energy reserves.

Yanjiang Rd., the tree-lined riverside boulevard in the center of town, is another attractive promenade. Although the buildings are of less architectural interest than those along Liuersan, the views of the river more than compensate. The liveliest of the main streets, all lined with shops both big and small, are Zhongshan, Beijing, Xiuli and Renmin. The southern end of **Renmin Rd.** is also noteworthy for its huge European buildings with impressive colonnaded facades. Running east from Renmin a few yards north of the river (near the overpass) is a small street lined with restaurants and movie houses, which is very animated at night.

Sightseeing

There are several tourist attractions in Canton. Some of these are overrated, but deserve mention in tribute to the thousands of tourists forced to see them by their Chinese guides.

One that is definitely worth a visit is the **Huaishang Mosque** on Guangta Rd. (one block south of Zhongshan and a few blocks east of Renmin Rd.) Most guidebooks claim that this mosque was built during the lifetime of Mohammed; while this is not likely, it may well date from as early as the 9th century, when Canton's Arab community flourished. The interior is not very impressive, but the stark fortress-like minaret, visible from the street, is.

Nearby is the **Temple of the Six Banyan Trees,** best known for its Decorated Pagoda, built in the 6th century and much restored since then. With its nine storeys, each with a tiled roof, the pagoda is 180 feet high.

In the center of town near the river is the neo-Gothic Roman **Catholic Cathedral,** built in 1863. It is 80 feet high with twin spires rising 160 feet. For many years used as a warehouse, the cathedral is once again open to worshippers. (Many of Canton's

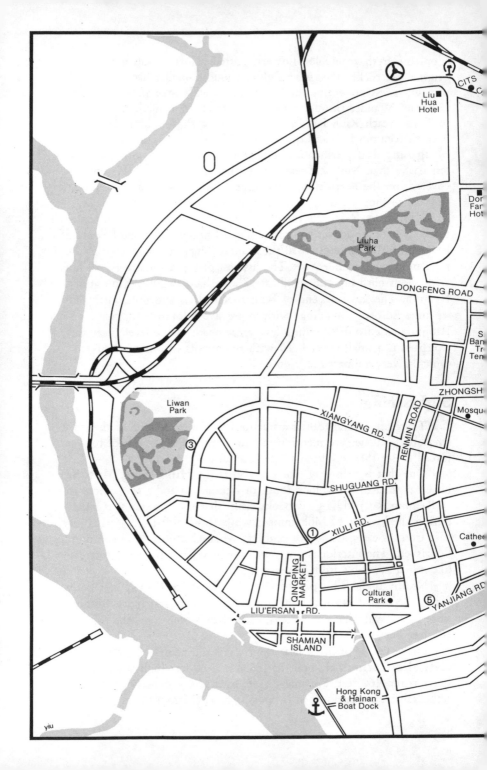

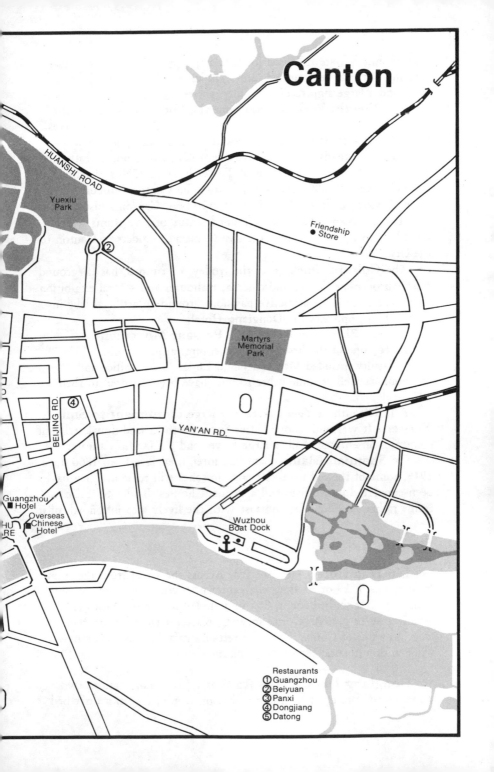

former churches are still used for secular purposes. One church near Renmin Rd. has been turned into a clinic; outside is painted a red cross and a large sign reading "Emergencies.")

The **Yuexiu Park,** covering one-third of a square mile east of the Dongfang Hotel, offers a landscaped garden, three boating lakes with islands accessible by hump-backed bridges, and quiet walks (although weekends are usually crowded). The outstanding feature of the park is the five-storey Zhenhai Tower built in 1380 and rebuilt as a watchtower in 1686. The tower houses the Canton Museum, each floor of which is devoted to different aspects of Canton's history. On a nearby hill is the much photographed Statue of Five Rams which, according to legend, brought the five demigod founders of Canton to the city.

The **Cultural Park,** near the trolley 3 terminus, has fairground rides, an open-air theater and cinema, teahouses and several exhibition halls. There are some attractive pavilions around an artificial lake in Liuhua Park, opposite the Dongfang Hotel.

On East Zhongshan Road is the **Peasant Movement Institute,** one of the first schools of communism in China (1925-7), whose faculty included Mao and Chou En-lai. Mao's office and bedroom, as well as some other rooms, have been restored to their 1925 style.

A little south of Yuexiu Park is a large **monument to Sun Yat-sen.** It was built shortly after Sun's death in traditional style and comprises an entrance hall, a large tower and a 5,000-seat theater.

On **Shamian Island,** Canton's foreign enclave from 1860 until 1949, some of the old mansions and churches still remain. They have been converted into offices and apartment houses. Today Shamian seems rather moribund by contrast with the lively area just north of it.

Hotels

Liu Hua Hotel, Huanshi Rd. Across the street from the train station, bus 5, 29 or 31 from the center of town. Dorms in the old wing 6 元 in a six-bed room, 8 元 in a three-bed room. Dorms are usually easy to get. A favorite meeting place for travellers on their way in or out of China. There's a restaurant and a cafe in the new wing with authentic Hong Kong plastic decor.

Dongfang Hotel, Xicun Rd. Bus 7 from train station, two stops. Dorms are open to students in China only; 8 元 in a three-bed room. This is Canton's best-known and most luxurious hotel. Its newly-opened International Club offers homesick expatriates a Western restaurant and cafe, as well as a poolroom and a flashy disco (10 元 disco admission; passport check at the door).

Overseas Chinese Hotel, Haizhu Square. Bus 29 from train station. Some travellers have managed to get into the 4 元 per person dorms, but this hotel is officially for Chinese only.

Guangzhou Hotel, Haizhu Square. Next to Overseas Chinese Hotel. 23 元 double room with bath. A well-maintained 23-storey building in the center of town. Good view of Canton from the higher floors.

Renmin Hotel, Yanjiang Rd. On the river — take bus 5, 29 or 31 and then walk. This hotel was rumored to have rooms for under 10 元 but was being renovated in recent months and refused to accept foreigners. When the work is completed, this policy may change. It's in a great location if you can get in.

Baiyun Hotel, Huanshi Rd. Bus 30 from train station. This luxury air-conditioned 33-storey hotel is the tallest building in China. Expensive, but a few single rooms are available for under 20 元.

Government Service Worker's Hostel. Superbly located on Shamian Island, this small, unpretentious hotel has recently been allowing foreigners to stay for 3 元.

During the twice-yearly trade fair the above hotels might be full, but other hotels near the train station, normally closed to foreigners, will take you.

Restaurants

The kitchens of Canton are world-famous, for most Chinese restaurants outside China are Cantonese. Like the French "nouvelle cuisine," Cantonese cooking strives to preserve and highlight the natural subtle taste of the ingredients. Fresh food is quickly cooked in a *wok* so that none of the flavor is lost.

Not surprisingly, some of the finest Cantonese restaurants in the world are to be found in Canton. It may be harder than in Peking to gain admission to the cheaper sections, but if you are politely adamant, you will almost certainly be served. For even cheaper food, try one of the hundreds of small sidewalk restaurants scattered throughout the city. Several are conveniently located just west of the Liuhua Hotel.

Guangzhou Restaurant, corner of Xiuli and Wenchang Rds. The least expensive dining room is on the ground floor in the back; this is a big restaurant and there may be other cheap dining halls. The food is excellent, and in terms of value-for-money perhaps the best in Canton. Many dishes are under 2元 each, and one per person is enough.

Beiyuan, 318 Dongfeng Rd., a few blocks north of Zhongshan Rd. Excellent food and old Chinese decor. The cheaper dining hall is the big room upstairs. This is more expensive than most, but worth it. It and the Panxi are often considered the two top restaurants in Canton.

Panxi, Liwan Park. An enormous place with some cheap rooms and even teahouse areas patronized by the workers who live in the area.

Dongjiang, 337 Zhongshan Rd. A smaller restaurant with very good food. Go upstairs. Most dishes are between 1元 and 3元. After dinner take a peek at the large temple that has been converted into a factory on a side street just opposite the restaurant.

Datong, 63 Yanjiang Rd. Occupies all of an eight-storey building overlooking the river. The sixth floor has the cheaper dining room. Very popular with Western businessmen, but decidedly overrated.

Sha He. A simple restaurant in a suburb of Canton (bus 11 from town). This restaurant invented the Cantonese flat rice noodle. Noodle experts claim the best in the world is served here (for under 1元), but you may be unable to detect the difference.

Sichuan Noodle Shop, across from Nanfang Department Store between Renmin Rd. and the Cultural Park. Good, cheap and very crowded — you can stuff yourself with dumplings or noodles for under 40 fen. The red sauce is *hot,* so beware.

Public Security

On Jiefang Rd. south of Dongfeng Rd. (bus 5 or 29 from

station). Open 8-12 in the morning and 2-5 in the afternoon. By presenting your passport and visa and filling in a form, you can get a travel permit listing 10 cities. If you ask for more than 10, they might omit some. They will give permission for most ordinary places and it doesn't matter if your original visa does not list Canton. As an added bonus, your travel permit will have your name written in Chinese — but check the translation before you have it engraved on a seal!

Transport

Express trains to Peking (via Changsha and Wuhan) and to Shanghai (via Hangzhou). The former is China's finest: 33 hours, 40 元 hard seat, 65 元 hard bed (60元/110 元 for tourists). The train ride to Guilin is very long (up to 36 hours) and indirect (change at Hengyang). The station's ticket office is usually very crowded and it is difficult to get the Chinese price; the CITS office just east of the station charges tourist price but is faster.

The bus station is a five-minute walk west of the train station. Buses to Zhanjiang (5 a.m.), to Guilin (6:30 a.m.), to Shantou, Jiangmen and Foshan. Buses to all open cities in Fujian Province (2-3 days). Foreigners have sometimes been refused tickets for the bus to Guilin, but the boat/bus combination via Wuzhou (q.v.) is an agreeable alternative. There are several departures for Macau daily, as well as a luxury minibus for 7元.

The wharf for riverboats to both Wuzhou and Jiangmen is near the bus 7 terminus (buy tickets in advance at the booking office). The 24-hour cruise to Haikou starts from the pier south of Renmin Bridge. This is also the departure point for the overnight ferries to Hong Kong and Macau.

Nearby

South of Canton stretch the rich ricefields of the Pearl River Delta. This area, one of the most prosperous and densely populated in China, is also noteworthy for its travel potential. In theory foreign tourists may go up to 100 km from Canton without a travel permit, and in practice one can probably wander a lot farther without raising any official eyebrows. Buses and riverboats connect even the smallest towns, and those wishing to explore in depth might be able to hitch or go by bicycle (by buying and reselling one in Canton). Since the area borders on Macau, transport costs are minimal. If you arrive in

Hong Kong with $100 and want to see China, this is the place to go. The following are the main tourist spots, to be visited or avoided as you see fit:

A few miles north of Macau is **Zhongshan County,** where Dr. Sun Yat-sen was born. His former home is in the village of Cuiheng. West of Zhongshan is **Taishan,** the ancestral town of many Chinese-Americans. The newly-built guest house is run entirely by solar power, and used to be a high point of environmental and soft technology tours run in conjunction with the *Whole Earth Catalogue.*

Northeast of Taishan is **Jiangmen,** an old town whose streets are lined with rows of multi-storied, colonnaded mansions built by rich merchants in the 19th century. Many of these houses front the bustling riverside boulevard. Jiangmen can also be conveniently visited from Canton: there are five buses a day from the main terminal (three hours, 2.50元), and two boats a day along the canals of Guangdong (2.50元 including a bunk). The Jiangmen Mansions, next to the bus station, has single rooms with bath for 9元; cheaper rooms are probably available. To get to the old part of town, cross the big street and continue down the small street with food stalls opposite the hotel; turn left at the end of this street, then right when that street ends. From Jiangmen you can catch a boat to Wuzhou and then a bus to Guilin. A few miles from Jiangmen is **Xinhui**, with a nearby lake suitable for swimming.

Ten miles southwest of Canton is **Foshan,** specializing in handicrafts. It was an important city during the Ming and Qing dynasties, and boasts a highly decorated Song Taoist ancestral temple. Foshan can be visited in a day's outing from Canton: buses leave every half hour from a small station on Dayun Rd., the east-west street one block north of the Guangzhou Hotel.

Shenzhen, at the Hong Kong border, is now being developed as a special economic zone. It's hardly a place to linger, but if you are coming from Hong Kong and can't get an immediate train out, a visit to the town center provides a good introduction to China. Walk down the broad avenue just outside the station to the T-intersection, then turn right and walk past the souvenir shops and fountain to Jiefang Rd. Although modernity has established a beachhead here in the form of several flashy new restaurants, most of Jiefang's buildings are old-fashioned. There are many small, poorly-stocked shops, mostly patronized by straw-hatted farmers from nearby villages.

Most Shenzhen restaurants cater to tourists and are overpriced, but there are some cheaper ones. One is down the small street to the left of the Friendship Restaurant. If you turn right instead of left, you will come to a small market.

Hainan Island

Hainan is a large tropical island just south of the Guangdong coast. When the mainland shivers in the grip of winter, you can sunbathe on the palm-fringed beaches of Hainan's southern end, which is sheltered from the icy northern winds by a central mountain range. In these higher regions live the Miao and Li people, the original inhabitants of the island. They helped the Communist forces in the years before 1949, and perhaps for this reason the center of the island has been made a Li and Miao Autonomous Region. Along the coast the people are Han Chinese, the descendants of those who migrated a thousand years ago from the mainland. Hainan is relatively undeveloped at the moment, but will not remain so for long, for the island has been made a Special Economic Zone.

You cannot, surprisingly, get your travel permit endorsed for Hainan in Canton, but you can in most other cities in China. Or you can get Hainan listed on your original visa in Hong Kong. Usually permission is given only for Haikou, but the whole of Hainan is open to tourists and may be visited with impunity.

Haikou is poorer than most Chinese cities. There is a large, very lively market with nighttime food stalls on a long street back from and parallel to the canal. Southeast of the center is an interesting suburb, reachable by city bus. Here are many small folk temples, doorways carved with religious motifs, and votive objects in homes — all of which have virtually disappeared on the mainland. If you spend the day in this part of town, sustenance is available at a restaurant on the second floor of a building on the main street 50 yards from the bus station, but beware of overcharging.

The eastern shore of Hainan has a number of large communes, including the cultured pearl industry of **Xincun,** populated by the Danjia minority, and **Xinlung,** a tropical fruit farm and hot springs complex administered by Overseas Chinese.

On the south coast of the island, nine hours by bus from Haikou, is **Sanya,** a large but attractive port. Four miles southeast of here is Luhuitou, the resort beach for which Hainan is famous (with bungalows). Dongfeng Beach, with an enclosed ocean swimming pool, is considerably closer to town. At dusk old men make the rounds of the guest houses rattling spoons to give massages, but beware: some are more rough than skilful.

North of Sanya is **Baoting,** a mountain town which is the capital of the Li and Miao Autonomous Region. It is a rather uninteresting place, with very few minority people in evidence (they're in the hills). The dirt road from here to **Dongfang,** a port on the west coast, runs through remote villages.

The Overseas Chinese Hotel in Haikou offers single with private bath for 8元 or dorm beds for 3.50元. Baoting and Sanya have inexpensive tourist guest houses, and there is no problem staying in any of the very cheap Chinese hotels all over the island.

There is a comprehensive network of buses on Hainan. The Haikou bus station is on the opposite side of town from the ferry. You can also buy bus tickets at the small port on the mainland before you get on the ferry to Haikou, and some travellers have found this easier. Hitchhiking is quite acceptable.

Hainan is accessible by daily boat, weather permitting, from Canton to Haikou. The trip takes 26 hours and starts from the quay south of Renmin Bridge in Canton. There are several classes, and prices begin at 13元.

Another way of getting there is via **Zhanjiang,** the nearest large city on the mainland. There is a daily bus (6元) from here to the tip of the Leizhou peninsula, and a connecting ferry makes the short hop to Haikou. Zhanjiang may be reached by daily direct bus from Canton, by train from Nanning, Guilin or Liuzhou, or by bus from Nanning (via Beihai).

Although Zhanjiang is not officially open, it is often visited en route to the island. The largest port west of Canton, it was leased to France from 1898 until 1949. Zhanjiang is divided into two parts separated by about five miles of countryside. One section comprises the harbor and the train station. There are many huge boulevards lined with run-down buildings and a large Friendship Store. The other part of town, near the bus station, is more interesting. The road from the port forks in two, and between these streets is a quiet neighborhood of narrow lanes and small houses. There is a hotel close to the bus station where a single with bath is 7元. There is a CITS hotel in the harbor section of town that has charged some travellers 1元 for a luxury double (but don't count on it).

Changsha

The plains of Hunan are among the most fertile in China, and it is therefore not surprising that Changsha — the provincial capital — has been a trading center for over two millenia. In 1904 it was opened to foreign commerce, and under the influence of its European and American residents, many small industries and schools were set up. Changsha's most famous student during this period was Mao Tse-tung, who attended the Hunan Normal School from 1912 to 1918. With a population of two million, the city is a food processing center.

Changsha has many quiet neighborhoods, some of which can be found by walking west along Zhongshan Rd. past the Youyicun Restaurant and turning left at Daqing Rd., the main shopping street. The big traffic circle south of Zhongshan, Wuyi Square, is the center of the old town, and the best areas for walking are to the southwest.

The **Hunan Provincial Museum** (bus 3 north) has a fine collection of treasures unearthed from the 2,000-year-old Mawangdui tomb. Early lacquerware items and fine silk paintings depicting cosmological scenes are displayed here, as well as the mummified corpse of the princess for whom the tomb was built. The **Hunan Normal School,** rebuilt in the 1950s, is open to visitors (bus 1 south). Just east of the hotel is the old District Headquarters of the Communist Party, founded by Mao; it, too, is now a museum.

The **Xiangjiang Hotel** is on Zhongshan Rd. (bus 1 from train station). Double rooms are 14元 per person and a bed in a triple is 8元, although you may have to fight for this price. There are also dorms, although the management is reluctant to let you use them. This seems to be the only hotel in town. The huge Hunan Guest House, recommended by many guidebooks, no longer takes foreigners.

The cuisine of Hunan is one of the most famous in China, and there are Hunanese restaurants in Europe and America. The best place to try it is the **Youyicun,** housed in a big building a few minutes' walk west of the hotel on Zhongshan Rd. The more expensive section has better food, and you can get some dishes there for under 3元. There are many other good, smaller restaurants throughout the city.

The Peking-Canton main line passes through Changsha's big new railway station. (Its clock tower plays "The East is Red" to mark the hour.) So do express trains to Kunming. Rather than merely using Changsha as a stopover en route to a major city, however, you might consider making a detour to **Shaoshan,** a place which offers the rare opportunity to observe village life. Of course, Shaoshan itself is hardly typical, because it is the birthplace of Mao Tse-tung and has been developed as a national shrine. During the Cultural Revolution it received three million pilgrims a year. But these visitors never left the main road, and the other villages in the area are, surprisingly, quite poor and neglected.

In the midst of a densely populated farming area, the Shaoshan Guest House is ideal as a base for a long walk in the country. Three paved roads intersect near the entrance. One goes to Mao's home and the train and bus station. Walk down either of the other two until you find a likely-looking dirt road, then follow it and see where it leads. The people in the area are very friendly. They may invite you to spend the night, but if you do you will probably receive a visit from the authorities.

The house where Mao was born is not unlike the houses in some of the neighboring villages, although it is somewhat larger than most. The interior furnishings have been restored. There is also a Mao museum in a modern building on the other side of the hotel, full of paintings, photographs and memorabilia. During the 1960s this museum had two identical sections, each displaying the same "original" exhibits.

The **Guest House** itself is about four miles from the train and bus station. There is an irregular bus service between the stations and the hotel. A country villa in a garden setting; the staff is exceptionally helpful and friendly. 5元 per person for a room with bath. Good, huge meals are 2元.

There is a slow train leaving Changsha for Shaoshan each morning and returning to Changsha each evening. Or you can take a local bus from Changsha to **Xiangtan** (a city of 300,000 open to foreigners), and then another bus to Shaoshan (many buses throughout the morning and early afternoon). Best, if you can, is to hitch a ride on a tour bus from the Xiangjiang Hotel. Ask the tour leader the day before; you should offer to pay about 5元. The tour bus takes two hours, while the local bus and train take from four to six. It is also possible to reach Shaoshan from Zhuzhou (see below).

Railway Cities

One of the major reasons to visit railway cities is, paradoxically, that they have few tourist attractions. This is especially true of the busy junctions in and around Hunan Province, and those either entering or leaving China might consider making a random stopover to get a feel for some of the more unbeautified aspects of the country's urban life.

Not all the cities on this portion of the line are modern. **Shaoguan,** the first stop north of Canton, was the second most important town in Guangdong in the time of Qianlong. Although this is not an open city, some travellers have stayed at the hotel just opposite the train station, where rooms are 6元. Cross the bridge outside the hotel and continue for a few hundred yards to a long street on the right lined with the overhanging upper storeys typical of the province. Most of the activity in Shaoguan takes place along this crowded road.

A few hours north of Shaoguan, at the junction of the train line to Kunming, is **Hengyang,** a poor industrial town. Travellers without permission for this open city may be forbidden to leave the station. The hotel, where a bed in a triple is 10元, is a 10-minute walk down the street opposite the station. There are two city centers, one fairly near the hotel and the other across the river.

The next major station is **Zhuzhou,** closed in theory but not in practice. From the station turn right, then right again: the hotel is just across the rail bridge, dorms 3元. A left turn from the ultramodern station entrance leads to a neighborhood of old wooden houses. Zhuzhou is linked by bus to nearby Shaoshan, and by rail to Nanchang and Kunming.

Thirty miles beyond Zhuzhou is Changsha. Farther north, at the Hunan-Hubei boundary, **Yueyang** has many streets of old houses and a famous but frail old pagoda mentioned in the poems of Li Bai (visible from the train). In **Xianning,** the next stop, there is an attractive guest house four miles out, at Wenquanzhen, located among farm villages with a hot springs nearby.

Two hours after leaving Xianning the train reaches the sprawling metropolis of Wuhan, followed some eight hours later by Zhengzhou (listed under separate headings). Other possible stopovers en route to Peking are discussed under *Peking-Canton Railroad.*

Wuhan

With a population of almost three million, Wuhan is one of the largest cities in China. Although few travellers go far out of their way to visit Wuhan, many pass through it, either on their way from Canton to Peking or at the end of the scenic Yangtse River cruise. Wuhan is a pleasant spot to break the journey, and while it is a far more typical Chinese city than either Canton or Peking, it is also livelier and less homogeneous than some of its smaller counterparts.

Wuhan is composed of three sections, once independent cities, straddling the confluence of the Yangtse and Han Rivers: Hankou, Hanyang and Wuchang. Of these, Hankou is now the most important, but Wuchang is the oldest. It was established during the Han Dynasty and became a regional capital under the Yuan. Hankou, by contrast, was little more than a village until the Treaty of Nanjing designated it a treaty port. Within a few years Hankou was divided into British, French, German, Russian and Japanese concessions, all grouped around the section of present-day Zhongshan Rd., north of the Xuangong Hotel.

The arrival of the railway in the first years of the 20th century spurred further growth and created one of China's first industrial proletariats. Wuhan also became one of China's main centers (along with Canton and Shanghai) for intellectual and revolutionary ferment. The 1911 revolution that toppled the empire began in Wuhan. In the next decade, a Communist School at which Mao briefly taught was established in Wuchang.

Today, Wuhan is a center of iron and steel production, of heavy and light industry, of transportation and, with 21 colleges and universities, of higher education.

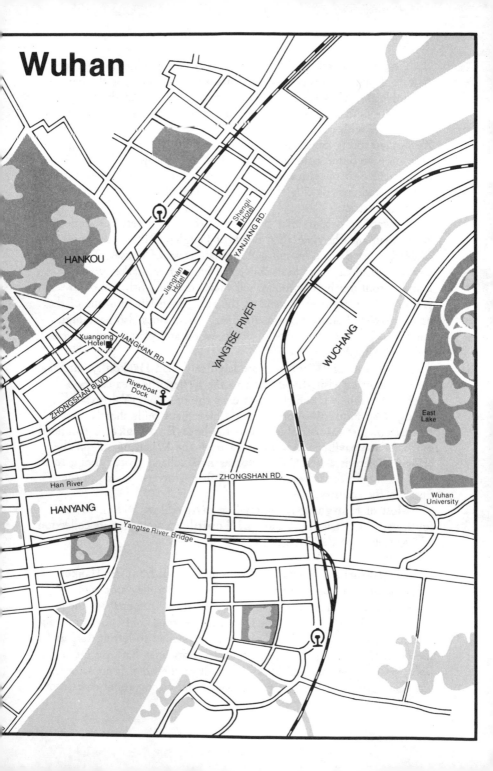

Despite its relative youth, **Hankou** is hardly a sterile metropolis. A walk down Zhongshan Rd., the main thoroughfare, is the best way to sample the city's variety. Toward the north, around the Jianghan Hotel, Zhongshan runs through a quiet neighborhood of mansions and row houses with carved facades in grey stone. Farther south, where Zhongshan meets Jianghan Rd., are grand old European buildings with massive fluted columns and Corinthian capitols. A few blocks beyond the old concession area ends, the architecture becomes more Chinese, and crowds clog the sidewalks. This is the city's main shopping district.

Rewarding detours may be made to the side streets between Zhongshan and the river. Just south of Jianghan Rd., for example, is a cobbled street flanked by unusually ornate rows of houses. This road, now closed to cars, has been converted into a free market where farmers from nearby communes sell their chickens, fish and other produce. Turn right at the end of the road, then left into one of the narrow streets leading toward the river. These lanes also have high buildings, but they are made of brick, wood and plaster and are less well maintained.

The streets of **Wuchang** are less lively than Hankou's, but they are also worth a visit. In addition to the ferries, the area can be reached by trolley 1, which passes over the mile-long **Yangtse Bridge,** an impressive engineering achievement built shortly after Liberation. Just east of Wuchang is the large **East Lake,** surrounded by parks and pavilions (bus 12 or 14 from the Wuchang side of the bridge). There is a steel mill in northern Wuchang worth trying to visit: to the south is the campus of Wuhan University, one of the finest in the country.

Most of **Hanyang** is a sprawling maze of low houses. In the southwest district is the **Yuangui Temple,** known for its collection of 500 statues of Buddha's disciples.

The **Jianghan Hotel** is a five-minute walk from the Hankou train station, on a side street next to the no. 2 trolley stop on Zhongshan Rd. (From the Yangtse boat walk to Zhongshan, then take the trolley.) The 5th floor is entirely devoted to 4-bed dorms, and the management has apparently become reconciled to letting foreigners use them (6 元 a bed). There are double rooms with bath on the fourth floor for 12 元 per person. Although most of the hotel is contained in a modern wing, the wood-panelled lobby and dining room date from the early 20th century.

Another possibility is the **Xuangong Hotel** on Jianghan Rd. (trolley 2 from the Hankou train station or a 10-minute walk from the Yangtse boat dock). Some travellers have stayed in cheap (6元 per person) rooms in the dingy annex across the street from the main building, but others have found that the receptionist might blandly deny their existence indefinitely. The luxury double rooms in the main building are 24元 and 34元, but students in China can stay in them for 6元. A good hotel in an old European building, tastefully modernized.

The **Shengli Hotel,** north of town near the river, has given some travellers dorm beds for 6元. Very near the train station on Chezhan road, the **Aiguo Hotel** has singles for the same price.

The **Sijimei Restaurant** occupies a three-storey building on Zhongshan Rd. near the Xuangong Hotel and next to the Foreign Languages Bookstore. The first two floors are nothing but dumplings, but more elaborate fare is available on the third. There are plenty of other good restaurants on and around Zhongshan Rd.

Wuhan has two **train** stations. Wuchang is larger and can reserve seats on some trains, but Hankou is more convenient. All trains stop at both stations. (When arriving at Wuhan by train, it's best to get off at Hankou.) Wuhan is on the main Peking-Canton train line. Express trains to Kunming and Xi'an also pass through. Tickets in Hankou are sold at the station (where student cards are carefully scrutinized) and at a smaller booking office on Zhongshan Rd. (where they aren't).

Boats leave every day for Chongqing, five days upstream, and Nanjing and Shanghai, three days downstream. The passage to Chongqing is spectacular, but most people prefer to take it downstream, which is two days shorter (see *Yangtse River Cruise*). The boat is also the most sensible way to go to Shanghai; it's far cheaper and not much slower than the train, which is indirect.

Jiangxi Province

Until the building of the Peking-Canton railway, the main land route between Guangdong and North China passed through Jiangxi, and Nanchang and Jiujiang became trading centers during the Han

Dynasty. Later the province, already a major rice-growing area, became noted as a producer of luxury goods: tea and oranges were grown throughout, and porcelain came from the kilns of Jingdezhen.

The main river port is **Jiujiang,** as it has been for over a thousand years. In 1862 the town became a treaty port, and although the main avenue, Poyang St., is now a strip of concrete apartment blocks, many European-style buildings lie between that road and the river, especially around the Dongfeng Hotel. The narrow, tree-lined streets in this area are alive with hawkers, vendors and other free-market activity, including a massage specialist (signboard in English). Also of interest is the seven-storey brick pagoda in the southeast part of town.

Foreign visitors to Jiujiang are expected to stay at the Nanhu Guest House, expensive (16元) and somewhat remote. The Dongfeng, which is also authorized to take in travellers, is neither. (From the boat dock walk straight out to Poyang St., turn left and walk three blocks. Bus 1 from train or bus station.) There is a good restaurant one block inland from the boat dock: look for the neon sign.

Jiujiang is linked to Nanchang by train and to Jingdezhen by bus. It is also the jumping-off point for nearby **Lushan,** a cluster of peaks rising almost 5,000 feet above sea level, overlooking the Yangtse and Lake Poyang. The hill station of **Guling,** nestled in the mountains, is an ideal refuge from the intense heat of the Yangtse Basin summer. In the 1930s European residents of Shanghai would sail to Jiujiang and be carried the six miles to Guling by sedan chair. Today, tour companies at the hotels and at the docks charge approximately 4元 for a bus roundtrip excursion, and there are also buses from Nanchang. Guling has three hotels open to tourists, two of which are old colonial-style affairs. There are many short scenic walks to such places as Long Shou Yan, a 1,000-foot hill with panoramic views, and the Cave of the Immortals, which was once home to several Taoist hermits.

East of Lake Poyang lies the ancient town of **Jingdezhen,** where for hundreds of years the world's finest porcelain was made. When, in the 12th century, the Song Emperors were forced to leave the north and flee to Hangzhou, many of the Imperial potters followed the court. They established kilns at Jingdezhen, which came under the Emperor's patronage during the Ming and Qing. The quality of the clay found in the nearby village of Gaoling was so high that the name of the hamlet entered the dictionary as "kaolin". This clay made possible the manufacture of brightly glazed polychrome ware that some historians consider the greatest art of the Ming Dynasty. During the first part of the Qing the Imperial kilns were enlarged, but by the 18th century artistic quality had begun to decline — as had the dynasty itself — though output increased. Grosier, a European who visited Jingdezhen in those years, found a sprawling city of a million inhabitants and 500 fiery kilns that lit up the sky. "When night falls it looks as though the whole town is on fire . . . foreigners are not allowed to spend the night."

Much of the town has changed little since Grosier's time, and though foreigners are now allowed to visit, few do. Jiushan Rd. has been widened and adorned with modern buildings, but Zhongshan Rd., the main commercial artery, has not. It pulses with activity for its entire length. Near the intersection with Jiushan are many old shops selling traditional handicrafts and medicines.

On either side of Zhongshan is a warren of narrow lanes overhung with poles of drying laundry; many are barely wide enough for two people to walk abreast. Between Zhongshan and the Chang River, the houses are fronted by enormous wooden panelled doors which are usually left open, and social life revolves around the streets outside, where people gather at all hours to visit, gossip, eat, and play Chinese chess.

East of Zhongshan the texture changes. The wide doors are replaced by high whitewashed walls, some of which enclose courtyards where porcelain is made (to spot a kiln, look for the smokestacks). Porcelain here is a cottage industry: clay is prepared in one yard and moulded in another before reaching the kilns, situated in a third. In other courtyards, the china is glazed, packed and put on hand carts. Those who want to observe the process in a more modern setting should visit the showpiece Renmin Porcelain factory (bus 1).

Finally, the riverbank is worth investigating. Apart from the hawkers, the washerwomen and the bridge traffic, every evening at dusk five blind storytellers draw audiences of 50-200 (two give matinee performances). They intersperse their prose monologues with chanting punctuated by castanets and drums.

Those spending several days in Jingdezhen might visit the **Fuliangcheng Pagoda,** in the village of the same name. This slender Song Dynasty tower is situated on the west bank of the river 10 miles north of town. Buses go straight from the village at 7 and return at 5, and there are more frequent bus-and-ferry services via the east bank. The ride along the west bank goes through many small settlements with earth-walled houses.

As for lodging, there are two options: the Jingdezhen Guest House in the north of town (expensive), and the shabby Jingdezhen Hotel at the head of Jiushan, where rooms are 5-8元 (negotiable). Take bus 2 from the train or bus station. There is a mediocre restaurant around the corner on Jiushan, and a slightly better one at the Zhongshan intersection. From Jingdezhen there are buses to Jiujiang and Huang Shan (via Tunxi), trains, buses and planes to Nanchang, and rail service to almost anywhere via Yingtan (see below).

Nanchang is the provincial capital. Despite its long history, the city is best known as the site of a 1927 uprising in which Chou En-lai and Chu Teh led an armed force of 30,000 men to victory against the KMT. Although these early Communist leaders probably didn't cruise through town in long limousines, their present-day successors do, and this provides a striking contrast with the poorer neighborhoods by the river. Recommended areas for walking include the streets east and west of Shengli Rd. a few blocks south of Bayi Rd., the long stretch between Bayi and Zhongshan just east of Ruijin Rd., and the street running south from the corner of Zhongshan and Bayi, where stands the building in which the 1927 uprising was planned. On Bayi, the main drag, the architecture is what Italians call ''Mussolini modern,'' and its two plazas are graced with many inspirational sculptures and monuments.

On the whole Nanchang is a less pleasant stopover than the more relaxed cities around Lake Poyang, and accommodation is more expensive. The Hongdu Hotel, cattycorner from the Public Security office (bus 2, seven stops from the train station) has inexpensive rooms, but are sometimes full. Due north of the Hongdu is the Bingjiang, where a surly staff charges 11元 per person for doubles with ample meals for 2元. At the posh Jiangxi Guest House, the cheapest accommodation is 34元.

Nanchang is 10 miles north of the main Shanghai-Canton line, but many trains from those cities make the short detour. There is also rail service to Jiujiang, Jingdezhen and Peking, and buses to Lushan and Jingdezhen. To get to other destinations you must change trains at **Yingtan,** a small town well-known to rail travellers. Expresses to Fuzhou, Xiamen, Shanghai, Canton and Kunming pass through, and those changing trains may have to spend the night. Thus, Yingtan, officially a closed town, has learned to tolerate *short* visits. There are three hotels, all on the left-hand side of the main road leaving the train station, two of which take foreigners. The first charges a hefty 24元, while the last has been known to rent singles for 5元 with dinner included (very hospitable). If you continue down Hotel St., turn right at the traffic circle and then left, you will reach the older part of town, built along the bank of a large river.

The only open area in Jiangxi that cannot be conveniently reached from Yingtan — or anywhere else — is **Jinggang Shan,** a remote and beautiful region of hills and villages 200 miles southwest of Nanchang. Jinggang Shan was used by Mao and Chu Teh as a base area until they were driven out in 1934 and forced to retreat to Yan'an. Some of the farmers in Ciping, the main town, can still remember the battles against the KMT, and farmhouse walls are daubed with outdated political slogans.

Xiamen

The seaport of Xiamen (Amoy) was founded at the end of the 14th century, at a time when the rest of China was walling itself off from the outside world. Many of its traders went to live abroad, and by the end of the 16th century tens of thousands resided in Sumatra, Japan and the Philippines. In 1653 the son of one of these Overseas Chinese, the famous buccaneer Koxinga, established his headquarters at Xiamen. The last of the Ming loyalists, Koxinga attacked Manchu garrisons as far north as Nanjing before turning his attention to Formosa, then a colony of the Netherlands, and driving the Dutch out. 200 years later Xiamen became a treaty port and the Europeans came back, carving out an enclave on the island of Gulangyu. During this period the exodus of Chinese continued unabated, and the remittances they sent their relations helped boost the region's economy — and still do today. During the late 1950s Xiamen's economy stagnated as PLA troops exchanged artillery barrages with the Nationalist garrison on the nearby island of Quemoy. In recent years, Xiamen has begun to regain its commercial pre-eminence. The city was opened to tourism in 1980 and, a year later, became a special economic zone, with foreign investment encouraged by surprisingly favorable terms.

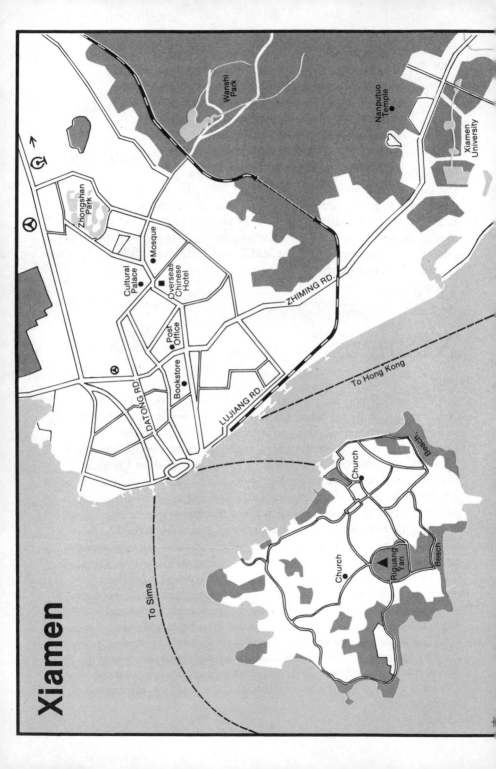

Xiamen

Wanshi Park

Nanputuo Temple

Xiamen University

Zhongshan Park

Mosque

Cultural Palace

Overseas Chinese Hotel

Post Office

ZHIMING RD.

Bookstore

DATONG RD.

LUJIANG RD.

To Hong Kong

To Sima

Church

Church

Riguang Yan

Beach

Beach

Despite its key role in China's modernization program, Xiamen remains a charming city. The pace of life is as Mediterranean as the aging stucco buildings that grace much of the town. Its winding streets seem designed for meandering, their tall row houses decorated with bright blue wooden shutters, in happy contrast to the peeling facades. Cobbled, crooked side streets abound, particularly in the area west of Zhiming St. and north of Zhongshan Rd., the main arteries. Be sure to visit the western end of Datong St., lined with streetside clothing and knicknack vendors and closed to traffic for much of its length.

A short ferry ride from the end of Zhongshan Rd. lies the island of **Gulangyu.** Here, the Mediterranean flavor is more pronounced. Narrow lanes wind past small whitewashed houses and ornate salmon-pink stucco mansions. Old men gather in the main piazza when the sun goes down. Cars are banned. There are two sand beaches, of which the east is cleaner, quieter and better for swimming. The island is hilly inland, and there is a good view from the highest peak, **Riguang Yan.**

Though there's really no need to leave Xiamen port and Gulangyu, there are several secondary attractions in other parts of town. The **Nanputuo Temple** (bus 1 or 2 from Zhongshan) is a large, functioning Buddhist complex with a good vegetarian restaurant. Nearby is **Xiamen University,** established with Overseas Chinese funding, one of the most famous in the country. Another touted educational attraction is on the mainland at **Jimei** (bus 20 from the suburban terminal on Zhiming), where several middle schools and colleges share one enormous campus. Though the Chinese-style architecture is not without appeal, it is far from town and not worth the trip.

The **Overseas Chinese Hotel** is on Zhongshan Rd. (bus 1 from train station; from the bus station or ferry, it's best to walk). 3 元 per person in a comfortable three-bed room. The CITS office on the ground floor is very helpful, and acts as intermediary for travellers dealing with Public Security (as they do everywhere in Fujian Province).

There is no lack of things to do in the immediate vicinity of the hotel. Just opposite the square is the huge Worker's Cultural Palace, which offers everything from calligraphy and chess classes to rather sterile storytelling and a teahouse. The opera house adjacent to it is worth investigating. A few yards east on Zhongshan, to the left, is the inevitable bomb shelter restaurant (there is another one on Gulangyu). Further down, in a side street to the right, is a tiny, dilapidated but functioning mosque.

A posh (but not exclusive) guest house is within walking distance of the Overseas Chinese building, and an enormous high-rise tourist class hotel in the area will soon be completed. There is rumored to be another hotel for foreigners on Gulangyu.

There are daily trains to Shanghai, Yingtan, Fuzhou and Zhangzhou. Despite their "express" billing, these move at a leisurely pace. Buses to Fuzhou, Quanzhou and Zhangzhou (via ferry), plus CTS specials to Shenzhen every Tuesday and Friday. The boat service to Hong Kong is expensive (90 元).

Quanzhou

Quanzhou was founded in the 8th century A.D. and within 300 years had become one of the world's greatest entrepôts. Fleets of trading ships crammed its busy harbor, and its shops overflowed with goods from all over the world. Quanzhou was known to the merchants of the Middle East and Europe as the fabulous city of Zaitun, and thousands of them came to settle by the banks of the Jinjiang River. In the 14th century Italian missionaries built a Catholic cathedral and Franciscan monastery. After the fall of the Yuan Dynasty the town declined rapidly in importance, and the harbor became silted up

Quanzhou today is still rich in color. Its sunny streets and bustling markets are noticeably gayer than those of other Chinese towns. The carnival air is especially pronounced on Zhongshan Rd., the main street, jammed with brightly-dressed strollers and bicyclists for its entire length. (There are few cars and no city buses in Quanzhou.) Away from the main street are mazes of flagged alleys whose one-storey houses are interspersed with the remains of Song and Yuan walls. The large market area just south of the hotel is full of peasant women wearing flowers in their hair.

The main attraction in Quanzhou is the **Kaiyuansi Temple,** 200 yards down West St. from the head of Zhongshan Rd. Founded under the Tang, it reached its apogee under the Song, when a thousand monks lived there. The present buildings mostly date from the 14th century, including the palatial Great Hall. This and the rear temple to Guanyin both contain unusually fine (though neglected) statuary. In front of the temple is a large flagstone-paved terrace lined with stone tortoises and enormous shade trees. On either side of this square are "twin" 13th-century stone **pagodas** whose multiple roofs are hung with wind chimes and, on holidays, paper lanterns. In the evening the plaza stays open, and is a favorite gathering spot.

Dozens of other temples, both small and great, are scattered about the city as if strewn by a prodigal hand. One, on a side street west of the square at the northern end of Zhongshan Rd., has recently been restored and is now a middle school library: some of the original beam paintings are still intact. Another, huge but in wretched condition, lies between Zhongshan and the main market. Below the market, to the right of the T-intersection south of the hotel, a door in the wall opens onto a tiny complex used for ceremonies (weddings, funerals). 100 yards south of here (from the hotel, take a left-right zigzag) is a Tang Dynasty temple with some beautiful interior woodwork. It is now the setting for occasional free concerts of traditional music and other public entertainment. The shell of a mosque built under the Song is 50 yards left of the T, southeast of the hotel.

Many fine temples once stood on the outskirts of town, but most were ransacked during the Cultural Revolution. Recently some were restored, but in unbelievably hideous fashion. For those spending several days in the area, however, there are some sites that are worth visiting. Three miles to the west, **Mount Juri** is covered with prayers for favorable winds inscribed by officials about to set sail. An ancient statue of Lao-tzu, covered with moss, stands on a hill northwest of town. The **cemetery** of a few Arab tradesmen, dating from the town's heyday, is to the east. Farther east, on the road to Fuzhou, is an 11th century **stone bridge.** Quanzhou's suburban bus terminal sits on the square at the northern edge of Zhongshan, though the statue and cemetery are more easily reached if you can borrow a bicycle. The surrounding countryside is dotted with villages, many of whose brand new houses were financed by gifts from relatives abroad.

The **Overseas Chinese Hotel** is wonderfully situated, just off the main intersection of Zhongshan Rd. Walk from the bus station, or take a rickshaw. Bed in a triple 3 元; fan 50 fen. Most of the front courtyard has been converted into a popular cafe, and there are many restaurants nearby. There are buses to Xiamen, Fuzhou and Shenzhen (twice-weekly, CTS). No boats, no trains.

The Coast Road

Highways skirt the South China coast from Hong Kong to
Shanghai. The circuitous rail link between Canton, Xiamen, Fuzhou
and Hangzhou is thousands of miles longer than the road. Along the
coast, the route passes through many small villages, where architecture
varies from region to region. Open cities are conveniently strung out
along the way, and the entire trip may be made with only one stop in
a theoretically closed town. At least along the first stretch, the buses
are efficient, going from Hong Kong to Fujian in a day and a half,
although it is fair to add that the journey becomes more arduous
beyond this point.

This remarkable speed is made possible by the CTS luxury buses
that leave from Shenzhen, across the border from Hong Kong. There
are daily departures at noon for Zhangzhou, near Xiamen, branching
off into twice-weekly service to Fuzhou, Quanzhou and Xiamen. Most
passengers book their seats in advance from Hong Kong, but it is
usually not difficult to procure one on the spot. The terminal is in the
Overseas Chinese Building across the tracks from the train station.
The only drawback is the expense: 55 元 to Zhangzhou, including food
and a night's accommodation. The public buses from Canton are
approximately half the price and also run as far as Fuzhou, though
they take considerably longer. Note that Canton is sometimes
reluctant to sell foreigners bus tickets.

The way to **Shantou,** the first open city, is dotted with small
villages of earth-walled houses, many of which have "bandit"
watchtowers. Shantou was once one of China's largest ports, and its
stately architecture seems quite out of place amidst the cheerful squalor
that now permeates it. Broad avenues lined with tall colonnaded
buildings radiate from a central circle. Coming from Fujian, walk from
the first stop or take a trishaw from the bus station (1 元) to the
Overseas Chinese Hotel, where beds in a triple are 3 元. To reach the
downtown section take bus 2 from the hotel or walk (turn left, then
right down the long avenue lined with streetlamps).

A two-hour ride inland from Shantou is another old trading

center, **Chaozhou,** also called Chao'an. From the rear of the
Overseas Chinese Hotel (4 元) it's a pleasant walk to the city center
through a residential neighborhood of narrow lanes and family
courtyards. The downtown area has typical colonnaded architecture
painted an atypical lemon yellow. Some of the old city walls remain,
as well as an impressive gate by the Han River.

Daily buses leave both Shantou and Chaozhou for **Zhangzhou,**
along the banks of the Jiulong River, 30 miles inland from Xiamen.
In the older part of town, by the river, low buildings perch on rickety
piles and straw-hatted farmers patronize its shops and foodstalls. Just
across the westernmost bridge is a busy market; on Sundays a cattle
fair is held nearby. South of the market is the Nanshansi, a Buddhist
temple full of worshippers burning incense and throwing divining
sticks. There is an unusual pure-white figure of the Buddha visible
through the pane-glass doorway of the right rear prayer hall.
Zhongshan Park, at the northern edge of the old town, has a large
outdoor teahouse near which hawkers and storytellers compete for
attention. Unfortunately, the hotel is located in the ugly modern
district, a short distance west of the bus station. (If you've come by
train, take a rickshaw half a mile or walk south; there are no city
buses.) A bed in a triple is 4 元.

From Zhangzhou many trains and buses make the short hop to
Xiamen. But, if you have any time to spare, take a bus to **Longhai**
(also called Sima) and the afternoon boat from there to Xiamen
(departure time depends on the tide). This coast town is a smaller and
more rural version of Zhangzhou. Watch for the tiny, desecrated
temple northeast of the long kiosk. A travel permit valid for
Zhangzhou and Xiamen will allow a few hours' stopover in Longhai,
and possibly even an overnight stay at the CITS hotel in town.

After a visit to Xiamen and nearby Quanzhou (q.v.), it is possible
to leave the coast, either by train for Jiangxi Province or by boat to
Hong Kong. For those wishing to continue north, there are frequent
buses to Fuzhou. Many of the villages along this stretch are building
new houses at a frantic rate. Most are multi-storied brick affairs with
brightly colored curved roofs, elaborate enough to indicate that the
construction is being fueled by rich relations overseas.

Fuzhou, the present-day provincial capital, was founded during
the 6th century A.D. and within a few hundred years had become a
thriving commercial entrepôt, second only to Quanzhou. Under the

Ming, walls were built around a roughly triangular area whose corners were three wooded hills. The town was made a treaty port in 1842, and many Europeans settled on Nantai Island south of the walled city.

Today, the ramparts are gone, and the district they once enclosed now laid out with broad boulevards and brick residential side streets. The once-renowned Hualinsi temple has apparently been reduced to rubble and its site is closed to visitors, though two ancient **pagodas** still stand in the center of town west of the Mao statue overlooking an enormous plaza. Farther south, the old port and cantonment area is now a squalid shantytown, and the famous pair of arched bridges passing over the Min River have lost much of their former charm.

The **Overseas Chinese Hotel** (bus 2 from bus or train station) is more expensive than others in Fujian Province, with a minimum rent (for a double) of 8 元. The panoramic view from the hills just south of the river is the site of a number of better restaurants. In addition to the buses, express trains run from Fuzhou to Beijing and Shanghai, and there is also an irregular boat service to Shanghai from the nearby port of **Mawei.**

The first open town north of Fuzhou is Wenzhou, in Zhejiang Province. There is no direct bus service linking the two cities. Instead, you must take a boat from Fuzhou to an intermediate destination, and then another bus the next day to Wenzhou. One possibility is **Fuan,** where an overnight poses no problem. Rates at the principal hotel (turn right from the bus station, a short distance) range from 1 元 to 14 元: the latter rooms receive zero maintenance. Fuan itself is a poor town with a very popular storyteller. The approach is especially attractive. Shortly after leaving Fuzhou the bus climbs into the hills, and the ornate brick houses of the plains yield to smaller, earth-walled structures. This scenery holds until the border of Zhejiang Province (q.v.).

5. The Southwest

Guilin

Guilin, situated on the bank of the Li River 225 miles northwest of Canton, is one of China's most famous beauty spots. The river and karst limestone peaks of the surrounding area bring to life the classic scenery celebrated on Chinese scrolls and, although most visitors overlook the fact, a visit to some of the smaller towns and villages around Guilin provides insight into life in rural China even more rewarding than the landscape.

Guilin itself is an ancient city, founded in the 3rd century B.C. when the first Qin emperor built the nearby Ling canal to link the Yangtze and Pearl River systems. Capital of Guangxi Province from the Ming Dynasty to 1914, Guilin today is a regional center of manufacturing with a population of 300,000.

To See

With block after block of stolid modern buildings, most of central Guilin will seem drab and monotonous to those coming from Canton or Kunming. Worse, it is rapidly becoming a tourist trap. Nevertheless, a walk along Zhongshan Road north of the Guilin Hotel leads to a more interesting neighborhood. About a mile north, a few blocks beyond Jiefang Rd., the street is lined with smaller, older houses and flanked by rocky precipices.

There are several steep but climbable crags jutting right out of the center of town. **Solitary Beauty Peak** offers a sheer climb up 306 stone steps, past innumerable stone inscriptions, to a good view of the city and its surroundings. **Fubo Hill,** beside the river, offers a similar panorama, as well as Tang and Song Buddhist carvings in the caverns that riddle its base. **Elephant Trunk Hill,** so named because it resembles an elephant drinking from the river, is on an island just south of town and can be seen from the roof of the Li River Hotel.

Some of the most extraordinary limestone scenery is underground. **Reed Flute Cave** (take bus 3 to last stop) is the best, with chamber after chamber of stalactite and stalagmite clusters, luridly (some would say magically) lit. **Seven Star Cave** has more of the same.

A local train leaves Guilin each morning at 10:30, heading northeast; another returns the same afternoon. You can go to the small market town of **Xingan** for the day or, better yet, buy a ticket to Xingan but get off at a small station at random and investigate.

Another way of exploring the countryside is to rent a bicycle (in a shop on Zongshan north of the road leading to the Li River Hotel; look for a small cardboard placard). Some people have spent days roaming around and camping out at night with sleeping bags, although this may not be strictly legal.

Li River Boat Trip

The trip by tourist boat 50 miles down the Li River to Yangshuo provides an opportunity to see a beautiful montage of karst scenery as the boat moves through a landscape of cliffs, villages and bamboo groves. The six-hour cruise is, however, exorbitantly priced at 40 元 (25 元 for students in China). One way of doing it for less is to go to Yangshuo by bus and be at the dock at noon when the boats arrive. The ferries go back to Guilin empty, and sometimes the crew will let you come along at a reduced rate (between 5 and 15 元). Some travellers have tried to do this and were refused passage, but the beautiful scenery to be seen on foot around Yangshuo proved adequate compensation.

In winter, when the water in the river is low, the cruise goes from **Yangti** to Yangshuo. The 40 元 standard tour provides a bus from Guilin to Yangti. If you take the boat from Yangshuo upstream you must spend the night at Yangti (hotel 2 元) and take the morning bus, hitch, or walk to the main road, where there are frequent buses to Guilin. The approach to Yangti passes through many small villages, and you might want to overnight there even if you don't take the boat.

Yangshuo itself is a small town set in the midst of brooding crags. It is a good place to spend several days. There is a serviceable hotel in town (room with bath 9 元 per person, 5 for students; good meals 3 元, fix the price before eating). The scenery is better than that of Guilin, and there are many old villages nestled among the karst outcrops. Go down the main road over the big bridge and keep walking. Many dirt roads and paths lead off to small settlements with earth or stone houses, some of which appear to be hundreds of years old. A few roads on the right go to the Li River, which can be crossed on wooden barges rowed by old ferrymen straight out of

Siddhartha. This area has been settled for a very long time, and you may stumble upon such surprises as carved stone lions by the river or ancient stone tablets with inscriptions in a field.

Hotels

Guilin Hotel, Zhongshan Road. Bus 1 or 11 from train or bus station, or ten-minute walk. Double room with bath 14元 without bath 9.60, single room (only a few available) 6元. Dorm 6元 (4 for students). These prices may vary depending on the whim of the receptionist. Drab, unheated (but hot showers).

Osthmanthus Hotel, Zhongshan Road. Just south of Guilin Hotel. Dorm, unheated, 5元. Bed in a heated corridor 7元. A newly built, apparently prefabricated hotel.

Li River Hotel. Bus 1 or 11 over Banyan Lake Bridge — one stop after Guilin Hotel — then walk down the lakeside street on the right. Rooms for students in China 6元 per person (15元 regular price). A luxury tourist hotel with heat, private bath, disco, panoramic view from roof.

Overseas Chinese Hotel. On the same street as Li River but the other side of Zhongshan Road; from Zhongshan turn left, it is close by on the right. Four bed room for 12元.

There are many small private **restaurants,** some rather good, on the main street between the Guilin Hotel and the train station. Some of these have "zoos" of exotic fauna ready for the pot.

The bank at the Li River Hotel will change money and also cash checks with American Express and other credit cards. In the past few months, several black market money changers have set up "shop" in the street outside the Osthmanthus Hotel. They have approached every passing foreigner, and unscrupulous travellers have received a premium for changing their FEC into People's Money. *Caveat emptor.*

Transport

There is good direct rail service to Peking, Shanghai and Kunming. To go to Chongqing one must change trains at Guiyang;

service to Canton is also indirect (change at Hengyang). Because the railway line makes a large detour to the north, it takes at least 24 hours to go from Guilin to Canton, 225 miles as the crow flies.

The one-hour plane flight from Guilin to Canton costs 60 元 and avoids the long train journey.

The bus to Canton, which leaves every morning at 6:30 (buy ticket in advance, 20 元) is another alternative to the arduous train trip. It takes two days, but the night is spent in **Wuzhou**, now a small town but in the early years of the century so important a center of foreign trade as to have a British Consulate. Wuzhou is normally closed to tourism, but they have let bus travellers stay the night in the hotel (2.50 元); walk over the bridge to explore the town. The bus ride passes through remote, beautiful areas with many small villages. Some people take a bus from Guilin to Wuzhou, and then a boat the next day downriver to Canton. This is cheaper, but has the disadvantage of reaching Canton at 4 a.m.

Stopovers

The train from Guilin to Kunming takes 36 hours, and travel time to Chongqing is even longer given the unavoidable layover in **Guiyang,** the capital of Guizhou Province. For the tourist, the most salient fact about Guiyang is that it is "closed." Thus, although many travellers pass through there, they are not in theory permitted to leave its cavernous train station. Nevertheless, it is sometimes necessary to spend up to half a day in Guiyang waiting for a connection, and the police will often let you out if you are persistent (or say you want to buy food, medicine, etc.).

Some people have actually been given permission to visit Guiyang by a quirk of fate that may soon become permanent, since the provincial government is thought to be on the verge of opening its doors to tourism. One possible harbinger of such a shift in policy is the CITS office, with English and French interpreters, now operating about two miles from the station. Very recently they have begun offering stranded travellers tours to a set of nearby caves (guide 2 元, taxi 8 元), worth it for groups of two or more who can't get out of the station otherwise. (Note that even if you have permission for Guiyang the police are not required to honor it, and they have sometimes exercised this prerogative.)

The station itself is a long way from the center of town (there is a nearby checkroom for luggage). Take bus 2 past the huge Mao statue to the end of the wide boulevard. The main shopping street runs north (left) from here. Walk along this lively avenue and, if you have time, explore the side streets running west. They lead to an area of small houses perched over canals, with many outdoor markets and food vendors.

The only hotel officially open to non-Chinese is a small building, formerly a private home, 10 miles outside the city. Public transport goes there in the daytime; at night, a taxi there and back (arranged by CITS) is 17元. There is also a hotel opposite the train station that might let you stay.

Those heading south from Guilin to Hainan Island will have to change trains for Zhanjiang in **Nanning,** the capital of the Guangxi Zhuang Autonomous Region. A trading center since the time of Khublai Khan, Nanning has mushroomed in recent years, and much of the town is architecturally uninspiring. A few older streets remain around the large, interesting market near the train and bus stations. To get there, cross the street from the bus station and keep going in that direction. Another older area, where you can find pre-1949 Guangdong-style houses with overhanging upper storeys, is west from the Yongjiang Hotel, more or less following the bend of the river.

Every year on the fifth day of the fifth lunar month (early summer) dragon boat races are held on the Yong River, and this lively festival adds color to a city in need of it. Nanning's only other tourist attraction is the Yiling Cave, a garishly lit series of limestone caverns 12 miles northwest of the city. If the plethora of caves around Guilin whetted your appetite, then go. If not, pass it by.

Most travellers stay at the Yongjiang Hotel (bus 5 from train station), where a bed in a comfortable three-bed room costs 7 元. There is also a nearby Friendship Hotel where students in China pay 6 元 each for a double room with bath.

Near the Yongjiang, just past the bridge, is a floating restaurant where you can get a good Mongolian Hot-pot. Another restaurant, specializing in seafood, is by the water in People' Park.

The Nanning Public Security office is not far from the train station. Just go down the main street to the first traffic circle, and turn left.

In Nanning you can get permission to visit **Beihai** (eight hours by bus, enroute to Zhanjiang), an old fishing port with a long canal and dark, quiet streets. The most interesting part of town is along the canal inland from the sea. To find it, turn left at the bus station exit, walk along this street until it forks, and take the right-hand road. The canal and older neighborhood will be on your right. To the left of the fork is the entrance to the hotel, where a single with bath is 6 元. There is a Vietnamese refugee camp near town.

At the fork of the railways to Guiyang and Nanning is seldom-visited **Liuzhou,** a small, boring industrial city with a long tradition of coffin-making.

Kunming

Yunnan Province, of which Kunming is the capital, was one of the last regions of China to come under the central government's control. Until a few hundred years ago the area was inhabited mainly by non-Chinese, and even today Yunnan contains about half of China's 55 listed national minorities, including the Yi, the Dai, the Naxi and the Bai. Most of these peoples formed their own independent states administered by hereditary chieftains. During the 8th century one of these principalities, the Bai kingdom of Nanchao, became the most powerful state in the region and routed several Chinese armies sent to subdue it.

Although the Bais rejected Chinese superiority, they were eager to learn from its civilization, and Dali, their capital, soon became a cultural center. Indeed, it is probable that Thailand derived several of its mores from Buddhist Nanchao, since most of its people are descendants of emigrants from the Nanchao area. In the 13th century, however, the Bai state lost its independence to the Mongol invaders who eventually brought all China under their dominion. From that time on, Yunnan slowly lost its autonomy. Many Chinese moved into the area, and today they make up well over half the province's population.

The minorities remained ever-ready to revolt against their Chinese overlords. The most serious rebellion was a 19th-century Muslim uprising that lasted 15 years and was put down in 1872 with French aid. Minority resentment of Chinese dominion did not vanish with the Communist takeover. It was fueled during the Cultural Revolution by the government's suppression of folk festivals and demolition of temples. In recent years, however, the minorities' cultures have been allowed to bloom once more.

Despite its location in a frontier area, Kunming is historically a Chinese city. It was founded over two thousand years ago and has been a Chinese outpost ever since, except for a 500-year period when it was annexed by Nanchao. Marco Polo visited the town, which he thought a "very great and noble city." Later Chinese governments, however, considered it a remote backwater of the empire, since it took three months to reach from Peking. But development was spurred in 1910 by the building of a railroad to Hanoi and, three decades later, by the flight of many rich Chinese to Kunming from the Japanese-occupied eastern seaboard. Expansion has continued after Liberation and Kunming has become an important manufacturing center with a population (including suburban areas) fast approaching two million.

The Town

Despite its recent growth, Kunming is one of the best places in China to see what life was like before 1949. Of course, Kunming has its share of modern housing projects, but there are still many old streets of picturesque two-storey houses with red and green carved wood facades. Some of these can be found by walking either north or south along one of the many small lanes that intersect **Dongfeng Rd.,** the main street, between the department store and the Panlong River. There is an outdoor food market on the street behind the small park facing the department store, and on sunny days the park itself is filled with old men playing cards. **Changchun Rd.,** the first big east-west avenue north of Dongfeng, is a bustling shopping district lined with older shops and houses, as is **Wucheng Street,** just north of Changchun's western end (bus 1 goes along both of them). **Daguang St.,** the western continuation of Wucheng, features many streetside medical practitioners including wart removers and dentists. Walking north from the department store to Changchun you will see a large, pagoda-like mosque, still functioning, just behind the store. Farther north, down a side street on the right, is a sidewalk market crowded with villagers come to sell their Yunnan ham, vegetables and cheese. **Jin Bi Rd.,** the main street parallel to and south of Dongfeng, is also good for a walk. From the alleys south of Jin Bi you will see two ruined **pagodas** towering over the houses. They were built in the Tang Dynasty but are now inaccessible. At the northern end of town is a beautiful old prayer hall, the **Yuantong**

Temple, set in a large park.

Three **minority stores** are devoted to handicrafts produced by Yunnan's peoples. One is located on the corner of Dongfeng and Daguang, and another, catering primarily to group tours, on Changchun. The emporium on the south side of Dongfeng just east of the department store is mainly intended for the minorities themselves, and the gold and silver jewelry is not sold to foreigners. It is nevertheless worth a visit to see the crowds of shoppers, some wearing huge headdresses, who come here from the remoter parts of the province.

Kunming also has several **universities,** including the illustrious Yunnan University and a minorities institute. Of the nine Mao statues that once graced the city, two remain, one just north of the Green Lake Hotel, the other on the campus of the Engineering College.

Teahouses

In the cities of pre-1949 China, teahouses were a focal point of life. Each had its own unique ambience and regular clientele, and most specialized in a specific variety of evening entertainment — storytellers, opera singing, or whatever. Today, in most cities, the teahouses have disappeared. A few can be found in Guiyang, Chengdu and Shaoxing, but the best place to see them is Kunming. They are easy to spot along most side streets, always crowded with older men playing cards, smoking huge bongs full of tobacco, talking, snoozing, and sometimes even drinking tea. For the price of a cup (5 or 10 fen) you can sit as long as you like.

Best of all are those teahouses that still offer afternoon or evening entertainment. One is found by walking along the main street north from the department store and then taking the first turn left; it is on your left, a few hundred feet down, with many outside tables. Here storytellers perform every day at 1:30 and 7:30 p.m. The stories, based on Chinese history and legends, are told in soap opera form; one tale might take three months to complete. There are musical performances nightly at a slightly larger place just west of the Green Lake Hotel.

About a mile north of Dongfeng near the canal are two more possibilities. At the first, just west of the river, there is very informal opera singing each evening. The second, on the other side of the river, is set in an abandoned temple where storytellers, musicians, etc., give shows at 2:30 and 8 p.m.

Finally, some teahouses deserve mention even though they do not

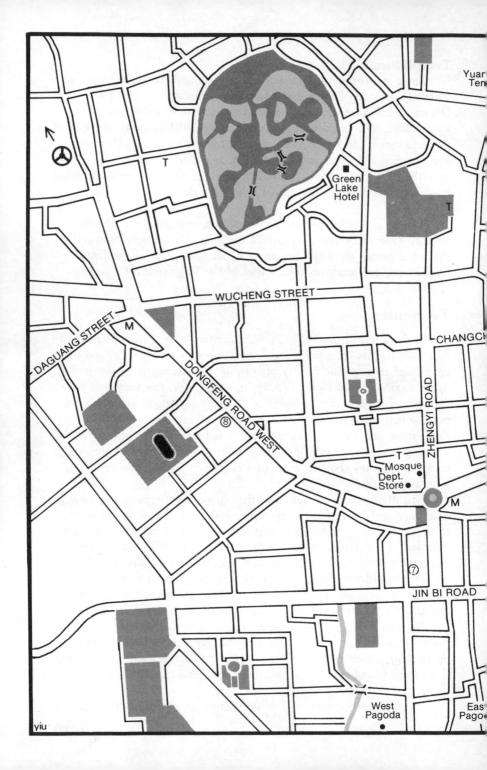

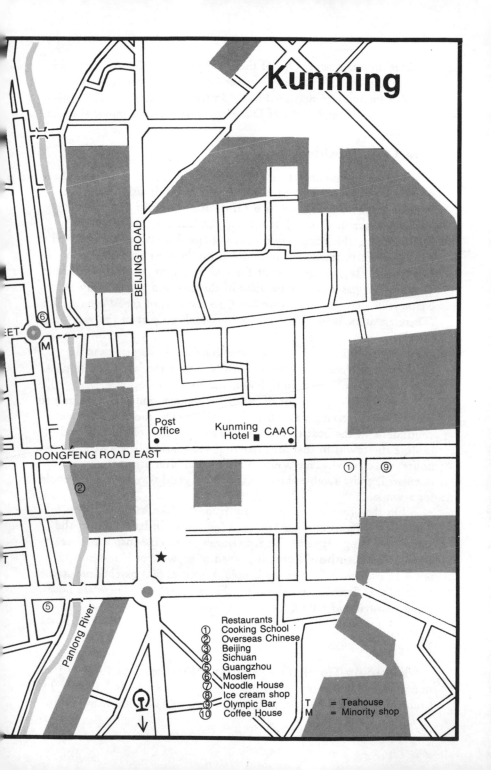

Kunming

BEIJING ROAD

EET

M

⑥

DONGFENG ROAD EAST

②

T

⑤

Panlong River

Post
Office
●

Kunming
Hotel
■

CAAC
●

①

⑨

★

Restaurants
① Cooking School
② Overseas Chinese
③ Beijing
④ Sichuan
⑤ Guangzhou
⑥ Moslem
⑦ Noodle House
⑧ Ice cream shop
⑨ Olympic Bar
⑩ Coffee House

T   = Teahouse
M   = Minority shop

organize entertainment. One of these, filled during the day with old men playing chess, is on Five Flowers Hill, a large mound north of the department store that used to be dotted with temples. The others are on Daguang, and south of Dongfeng near the two movie theaters.

The Countryside

There are some attractive lakes, hills and temples in the area that provide a good change of pace from the hubbub of city life. A short distance from Kunming is **Lake Dianchi,** the sixth largest freshwater lake in China. Just west of the lake are the **Western Hills.** There, the Yuan-period Huating and Taihua temples, as well as a group of three smaller Qing temples, can be seen on the way to the **Dragon Gate,** a stone arch at the end of a path cut into a cliff face. Dragon Gate has a panoramic view of the lake and surrounding countryside. To get there, take bus 6 to the foot of the Western Hills. (There are sometimes public minibuses which go part of the way up the cliff.)

Every morning at 8 a.m. a public boat leaves its pier near the canal running from Kunming and cruises across the lake. The ship passes by fleets of tiny fishing boats, and makes a stop near the Western Hills. You can get off, visit the temples and perhaps climb to the gate before taking a bus 6 back to town. The more energetic can continue with the boat to the southwestern section of the lake and explore the towns in that area (Anning Hot Springs is about four hours' walk away). The Western Hills themselves are sparsely populated, and a ramble through them is a good way to escape people for a while.

On the other side of Kunming from the lake is the **Golden Temple** on Phoenix Song Hill (bus 10). Its main hall, built at the end of the Ming Dynasty, is made largely of bronze that was once gilded. The **Bamboo Temple,** seven miles west of Kunming (take bus 5 to end, then 7, then walk uphill) features 500 psychedelic statues of Buddha's disciples carved during the 19th century. These are now being restored and only a few can be seen.

Hotels

Kunming Hotel, Dongfeng Dong Rd. (Bus 2 or 23 from train station to the big square, then bus 5 or five-minute walk.) Dorms 9元 (students 6元), double rooms 15元 per person. There are many dorm rooms but the reception often claims that they are fully booked to encourage you to take a double room. The dorms rank among the nicest in China; they are beautiful two-room suites with private bath. A new luxury high-rise wing has just opened, but there is no cheap accommodation therein.

Green Lake Hotel (bus 2 from station). Dorms 8 元, may be limited to students in China. This is a newer, Japanese-built hotel.

Kun Hu Hotel, Beijing Rd. (fairly near the station) has 3 元 beds but is in a very dull part of town.

Restaurants

The Kunming Hotel offers bland, à la carte dishes for between 1 元 and 3 元 each. Better (and cheaper) food can be found at the **Cooking School Restaurant** just east of the hotel, on the opposite side of Dongfeng (1). Another eatery close to the hotel is the **Overseas Chinese Restaurant** just off the big square near the river (2). Its friendly owner speaks English. In the center of town is the **Beijing Restaurant** (3), which most Chinese consider the best in town. Specialties of the region are available here. There is a wider selection on the second floor, where dishes range between 2 元 and 5 元. Nearby, the **Sichuan Restaurant** (4) serves dishes from that province, and Cantonese food is available at the **Guangzhou Restaurant** (5). There is a **Hui (Muslim) Restaurant** on Changchun St. (6), less expensive than those already mentioned. It has good food and serves beer in barrels. Even cheaper is the **Yunnan Chau Gwo Mi Sien Noodle House** near Jin Bi Rd. (7), which features across-the-bridge noodles cooked in chicken broth, the best-known specialty of the province. This dish, which costs 20 元 at the Kunming Hotel, may be ordered for 1.25 元 here. (If you develop a taste for this and other Yunnanese dishes and later visit Peking, be sure to visit the Kang Le, which is the most famous Yunnanese restaurant in China.)

Two other eating places should be mentioned where, although the food is quite good, the main attraction is the bistro-like ambience. One is the many **sidewalk restaurants** near the two movie theaters east of the Beijing Restaurant. The other is a **riverside cafe** with outdoor tables and a wide selection of dishes located just off Changchun by the river.

Also worth a visit are the **ice cream shop** on Dongfeng Rd.

West (8), which is open late and a young people's hangout, and the **Olympic Bar** on Dongfeng Rd. East (9), whose slick plastic decor makes it the "in" place in town. The **Vietnamese Coffee House** on Jin Bi Rd. (10) serves coffee made from the excellent, but hard to find, beans grown in Yunnan.

Transport

Direct rail service to Guilin (36 hours), Shanghai (70 hours), Chengdu (24 hours) and Peking. The ride to Chengdu is one of the most beautiful in China — it passes through rugged mountains and river valleys inhabited by the Yi people. Much of the ride is through tunnels laboriously carved and blasted through the mountains (the highest pass is at 10,000 feet). Indirect to Chongqing (change at Guiyang) and Canton (change at Hengyang); both of these journeys take a long time.

Planes to Simao (for Jinghong) 42 元. To Chongqing 85 元. Also to Peking and Canton. International flights to Hong Kong and Rangoon (a Burmese visa is required).

Nearby

24 miles from Kunming is the town of **Anning Hot Springs,** a good place to spend a few days. It's best not to loiter in the town, but to hike around the surrounding hills, which are dotted with small villages. The hotel in Anning has dorm beds for 1.20 元 and rooms for 8 元 and you can bathe in water from the spring. To get there from Kunming, take bus 18, and book your return ticket in advance at the hotel.

The strange rock formations of **Shilin,** the **Stone Forest,** are 75 miles from Kunming. The stone "trees" are quite different from anything to be seen in Guilin. Jagged stone columns stand up to 100 feet tall surrounded by trees, pagodas and small lakes. Although hordes of tourists (mostly Chinese) descend on Shilin daily, the forest is large enough for you to escape the crowds. The nearby village, with many traditional mud-brick houses, is quite attractive, although its people (from the Sani branch of the Yi minority) are used to having foreign visitors.

Shilin is very quiet at night after the tourists have gone. There are two hotels, the cheaper of which (turn right when you get off the bus) has beds for 2元. The other, more luxurious hotel offers rooms for 9元. You might also be able to spend the night at nearby **Lunan,** an interesting town, especially on market days.

There are daily buses to Shilin leaving at 7 a.m. from a bus stop opposite the Kunming Hotel. You can buy a ticket at the hotel for 4元 the morning of the day before departure, or on the bus (3.50元, but you might not get a seat).

Two days from Kunming by bus is the beautiful lakeside town of **Dali,** once capital of Nanchao. Dali is now closed to foreigners, but a big hotel has just been built there and tourists may soon be allowed to visit. Go if you can. Dali is a fascinating city whose cobbled streets are lined with old stone houses. The nearby Erhai Lake is very deep, and is fringed by snow-capped mountains. One of these, called Chicken Foot, is a Buddhist holy mountain, but almost all of its 200 temples were razed during the Cultural Revolution. In early April Dali holds a big week-long market fair which draws villagers from all over Yunnan.

Xishuangbanna

For the people of Imperial China, Xishuangbanna was a semi-mythical paradise. One of the farthest outposts of the Empire, it was 120 days' arduous travel from the capital. Today, Xishuangbanna can be reached from Kunming in two days (if the plane is on schedule), but much of the region remains a remote, peaceful and forgotten corner of Southeast Asia. Bordering on Burma and Laos, its main ethnic group (there are over ten) are the Dais, who are racially and culturally similar to the people of Thailand.

As early as the 13th century Xishuangbanna was a Dai state loosely controlled by a Chinese governor from a capital at Jinglan. Now named Jinghong, the former imperial stronghold on the Mekong River is still an administrative headquarters. Before 1949 the region was more or less autonomous, and according to official Chinese publications it was under the sway of rapacious and bloodthirsty feudal lords whose favorite recreation was oppressing the masses. While this must be taken with a grain of salt, it appears that the local chieftains exercised far more power over the populace than did their Thai or Burmese counterparts.

To diminish Xishuangbanna's traditional autonomy, the Chinese government has populated it with thousands of Han settlers from Shanghai and other urban areas. Relations between Han and minorities were unusually good, and many hospitals and schools were built. During the 1960s, few publications on the regions of China failed to include an article about Xishuangbanna's devoted doctors, selfless cadres, etc. Nevertheless, as the traveller will observe, nearly every Buddhist temple in the region was gutted during the Cultural Revolution, and although some of these have been restored and a few are currently in use, the saffron-robed monks who are a common sight throughout the rest of Southeast Asia have virtually disappeared.

Jinghong

Jinghong, the capital of Xishuangbanna, is built in typical Chinese monolithic architecture. Nevertheless, the palm trees and the crowds of colorfully-dressed and graceful Dai women shopping on the central market street give the town a unique tropical flavor. But do not linger there, for the villages outside the capital are far more interesting.

The town is in a river valley surrounded by hills. In the valley are numerous Dai villages with ramshackle wooden houses on stilts, muddy main streets shaded by huge trees, and farm animals peacefully resting in the yards or under the houses. Each hamlet has its own temple, most of which have been converted into storehouses. In addition to the Dai communities, there are many Han settlements formed by people sent to Xishuangbanna during the 1960s. High in the hills around the valley are the villages of the Hani tribesmen, whose women dress in black culottes and blouses decorated with old coins. These people do not welcome visitors, and one was recently detained at gunpoint.

One particularly recommended route goes south along the street outside the hotel (turn left at the hotel gate). This paved road leads to a large but attractive Dai village whose big temple is now under restoration. From here the street, now a dirt path, goes past a tiny village on the left, a small park on the right, then through a long, narrow third village ("Man Loh Hohn") beyond which is a tributary of the Mekong fordable by log canoe (5 fen). On the other side are many more Dai settlements hidden in groves among the rice paddies.

There is another cluster of stilt houses west of Jinghong. To reach it, take the main road (towards Menghai, see below) four miles out of town. You will see a large bridge on your left. Just before the bridge, a dirt road intersects the main road on the right. This track leads through ricefields to many villages, some of which have temples that appear to be functioning. You can hitch back to town from the bridge.

The hotel is by the Mekong about a mile from the bus station. The cheapest rooms, which are good, are 3元 per person; others are 6元 8元 and 12元 Set in an exuberant garden with quiet paths shaded by palm trees, it's almost worth the trip from Kunming just to stay there.

In the hotel, they give you a choice of the 2元 and the 3元 meal. They're exactly the same! The food is quite adequate; if they let you order à la carte, your meal will be even cheaper. There are other small restaurants in town, including one just outside the hotel (turn left) where you can eat for about 50 fen.

Finally, don't overlook the local theater, on the same side of the same road as the police station in the direction of the hotel. Usually this presents "Peking" opera of painfully poor quality (overpriced at 30 fen), but with luck you may be in town for the famous Dance of the Peacock, Dai ethnic and beautifully choreographed. The prince's arrival in the land of the peacocks is based on the legend of the discovery of Xishuangbanna.

Travel Permit

You must apply at Public Security in Kunming (or Peking) for permission to visit Xishuangbanna. The Kunming authorities usually give permission routinely, but have sometimes been known to be capricious (especially with those who speak fluent Chinese). It is also difficult to get permission during Spring Festival, because hundreds of Westerns working in China spend their vacations in sunny Jinghong.

If you succeed, your travel permit will be stamped "travel by air only"; it is impossible to buy tickets for surface transport, and at least one would-be hitchhiker was deported. You must fly to Simao, and spend the night.

Simao itself has an interesting old section, with many cottage industries: from the bus station, go right, then straight into the narrow lane on the other side of the main street. If you follow the main street right, there is a hotel with comfortable beds for 2元 on the right. (To find the CAAC office go one block farther and turn right again.) Farther down, on the left, there is a better hotel with double rooms for 6元per person, complete with private bath and hot water; a third, next to the bus station, offers beds for 60 fen.

Buses leave Simao every morning for Jinghong. There is a roadblock at the Xishuangbanna border where your permit is checked. When you arrive in Jinghong the hotel will forward your permit to the police, who will establish the maximum duration of your visit. Recent travellers have been limited to three days unless they obtained specific authorization in Kunming to stay longer. Moreover, travel is officially limited to the Jinghong valley.

Outside the Valley

Menghai is a rather boring town 30 miles west of Jinghong whose main attraction is a large temple. Twenty miles beyond it is **Mengtze,** also with a temple, reputedly nicer than the one at Menghai, that has recently recruited several new monks. Although you are not supposed to go to these places, some buses will take you (they stop on the main road just beyond the post office). You can easily make the roundtrip journey in a day.

Some travellers used to take the morning boat leaving Jinghong at 8:30 for the beautiful village of **Gan En Bang,** 20 miles downriver. They would spend the night there (hotel 50 fen) and return by boat the next day. Recently, however, a policeman has been stationed at the landing to prevent foreigners from taking this scenic cruise. If the situation changes and you do succeed in going, do not check out of the hotel in Jinghong and do not spend more than one night away.

The large **Tropical Plant Research Institute** is in the jungle, half a day away by bus. There is both a hotel and a bus heading back to Simao, but considering the roadblock it would be best to try and do this one officially. It is reputed to be very worthwhile. (There is a similar institute in Jinghong which is quite easy to get to, but a waste of time.)

Emei Shan

Emei Shan, perhaps the most beautiful of China's four sacred Buddhist mountains, rises 6,500 feet above the Sichuan plain and over

10,000 feet above sea level. Several pleasant days can be spent hiking along the verdant trails to the summit, with overnight stops at monasteries along the way. In addition to the beauty of the countryside and of the many temples that dot the mountain, the walk offers a chance to meet the occasional Tibetan and other Buddhist who come to Emei on pilgrimages.

Visitors to the mountain must first pass through its namesake, **Emei Town,** whose train station (five miles out) is on the Kunming-Chengdu line. There is also a regular bus service connecting Emei with Chengdu and with nearby Leshan.

Emei itself is worth an overnight stop. There is a hotel five minutes' walk from the bus station (turn left, then take first right). Rooms are 3-5元. Emei's streets are always filled with farmers from nearby villages come to shop, and the liveliest market area is near the hotel. The Emei Restaurant (big billboard in English) is surprisingly good.

Located at the base of the mountain a few miles from town is **Baguo,** the largest monastery in the area. Although not as quiet or scenic as those farther up the mountain, it is a good place to spend the night before the trek. Like all the monasteries on the mountain, Baguo offers spartan accommodations for 1.50-3元 a night, and has a mess-hall. Even if you decide to spend the first night at Wanniansi, you must stop here to get your hiking permit. You might also want to visit the nearby 6th-century Fuhusi (Tiger Taming Temple), where monks are resculpting the statuary that has recently been destroyed.

The northern route up, a two-day climb, is the one favored by most hikers. From Baguo you can catch a bus (about 3元) to the roadhead about two miles from **Wanniansi,** the 10,000-year Temple, which features a huge statue, cast in 980, of the Buddha riding an elephant. If you spend the night here you will be awakened by the crashing of cymbals and gongs announcing the morning prayers.

From Wanniansi to the next monastery, **Xixiangsi** (Elephant's Bathing Pool) is a five-hour walk. Most of the trail after Xixiangsi consists of stone steps, encrusted with ice during the winter months. If you go then, be sure to rent crampons, tie-on spikes for your shoes, at the monastery for 1元 (plus 2元 deposit). Monkeys are often a nuisance on this part of the trail. To disperse them, clap your hands and thrust your palms forward to show them you have no food.

Jinding, the Golden Summit, is another five hours of spectacular mountain scenery ahead. At the top, on a sunny day, circular rainbows and one's own shadow can be seen in the cloudbanks below. Sunrise and sunset are especially memorable. It is said that many an inspired pilgrim has leaped from the mountain in exhilaration. (Not recommended.)

The once-magnificent **Golden Summit Temple** was gutted by fire several years ago. China's economic progress is neatly symbolized by the nearby television tower visible through the temple's charred arches. The monastery guest house, however, is intact (sometimes it doubles as a military installation), and provides heavy coats and quilts to ward off the nighttime chill.

Although you can retrace the above route back to Baguo in a day, there is an interesting two-day alternative descent, with waterfalls, dragon bridges and innumerable stone inscriptions along the way. Just below Xixiangsi there is a fork: going right, you proceed to (and possibly overnight at) **Jiulaodong** (Nine-Olds Cave), followed by **Qingyinge** (Clear Sound Pavilion). This monastery is in a beautiful area of streams and forests, and offers peaceful walks in the surrounding area; many Chinese who do not want to climb to the summit hike from Baguo to Qingyinge and back. This 10-mile walk passes through many small villages clinging to the base of the mountain; if you do this, it's worth continuing on the trail half a mile past Qingyinge to where it threads a river pass with steep cliffs and rushing torrents.

The temptation after climbing Emei is to go directly to Chengdu or Kunming. If you are not in a hurry, however, consider a visit to nearby **Leshan.** It is an old town, founded over 1300 years ago, and although many modern apartment buildings have been constructed, its bustling streets, markets and teahouses still retain much of their cachet.

Most of the activity in Leshan takes place along the main street running from the bus station in the direction of the guest house. Close to the station is an area of hawkers and streetside stalls, with the larger stores a few blocks beyond. Both are usually quite crowded, for Leshan is the market town for the many villages in the area. Between the main street and the hotel is a neighborhood of older houses with several teahouses, a food market and a small park. Parts of the old city walls remain by the nearby riverbank.

On the far side of the river, reachable by boat from the town center or a three-mile walk across the bridge near the bus station, is the 230-foot **Dafu,** or **Big Buddha.** An entire cliff was carved in the 8th century to create this colossal statue, easily the largest stone sculpture in China and one of the world's biggest Buddha images. The area around Leshan is dotted with tiny villages, some of which are only a few miles out of town. Many buses ply the roads, especially the main route going past the Dafu, and you can catch a ride for a few miles and then get off and explore.

Leshan's most well-appointed guest house is about a mile west of the bus station, at the terminus of Leshan's one local bus route (service is casual and irregular). A room with bath is 9元 per person. Gargantuan seven-course dinners for 3元 (order at least a few hours in advance). Another very pretty guest house has just been opened near the Big Buddha (dorm bed 2.75元). Less comfortable but cheaper and more interesting is the hotel just next to the bus station (turn left). This is one of the few ordinary hotels in China to admit tourists. Itinerant cobblers and street vendors sometimes sleep in beds in the corridors, with their wares stacked next to the bed. A double room is 3.30元

There are frequent buses to Emei, several a day to Chengdu, and one morning bus a day (7 a.m.) to **Neijiang,** from where trains leave (at 3:30 and 11 p.m.) for Chongqing. This is a beautiful ride along dirt roads through a remote but densely populated region of verdant, rolling hills, with a lunchtime stop in a tiny town with a huge old pagoda.

Chengdu

Set in the fertile plains of one of the most densely populated areas of China, Chengdu is an ancient city, founded over 2,500 years ago, that rose to prominence during the time of the Three Kingdoms as the capital of the state of Shu. It has long been an intellectual and artistic center. During the 2nd century B.C. the governor of Sichuan, Wen Ong, established a school system in Chengdu that the Emperor later held up as a model for the rest of the country to follow. Almost a thousand years later the great Tang poet Du Fu wrote many of his best poems in Chengdu, where he lived for three years. Still the cultural hub of the region, the city before Liberation was also one of the most beautiful in China, rivalling Peking, with its own viceregal palace. During the Cultural Revolution the palace was destroyed, and Chengdu is now an industrial center with a population of 1.5 million.

Despite modernization, there are still an unusually large number of streets lined with the traditional Sichuanese half-timbered houses that look remarkably like Tudor cottages. One attractive part of the city may be reached by taking bus 16 two stops north of the Jin Jiang Hotel. Turn right (east) along the busy shopping street, and then left at the first intersection and walk north. In the area north and east of **West Jade Dragon St.** are several busy produce markets and teahouses with bamboo chairs on the sidewalk where you can comfortably sit and watch the throng of passersby. A bit farther north, on Renmin Bei Rd. (bus 16 four stops from the hotel) is the **Wen Shu** Monastery, a beautiful, functioning Buddhist temple complex.

If you don't feel like walking, there's a bicycle rental shop near the hotel; turn left, left, and left again. Or try the **Chengdu Municipality Blind People's Massage Parlour** (opposite the Mapu Dofu Restaurant) where you can get a vigorous 20-minute massage for 40 fen.

To the south of the city (bus 1) is the **Wu Hou Si,** a temple complex replete with statuary commemorating Zhuge Liang, the great military strategist of the state of Shu. Farther out (bus 5 or 25 to the end, then walk) is the **Du Fu Cottage,** a replica of the thatched hut of the great Tang Dynasty poet Du Fu.

A more interesting excursion is to the **Divine Light Monastery,** a well-maintained and functioning complex founded about 1,900 years ago. The present buildings were erected in the 17th century. It is located in **Xindu,** a lively town with many fine teahouses and street stalls. To get there, take a bus (several every morning) either from the traffic circle just south of the train station or from the main bus station.

Thirty miles north of Chengdu is the **Dujiangyan Irrigation System,** a vast dam and water conservancy project built in 250 B.C.

The **Jin Jiang Hotel** is on Renmin Nan Rd., bus 16 from the train station, seven stops. A triple is 9元 per person (5元 for students) plus 1元 in winter for heat. A bed in a crowded dorm is 6元. A large hotel with a bank and many shops, as well as a bar with stereo tape player open to midnight on the second floor.

Sichuan food is world-famous, and deservedly so. Some famous Chengdu specialties are: *mapo doufu,* spicy bean curd; *gong bao rou ding,* meat cubes in a peppery sauce; *yu xiang rou ding,* meat cubes in a sweeter sauce.

The **Furong,** Renmin Nan Rd. (five-minute walk north of the hotel) is Chengdu's best-known restaurant. Most dishes are under 2 元; menu in English has prices slightly higher than the Chinese menu. The food at the Chengdu Restaurant on Shengli Rd. is as good or better than the Furong and the service much friendlier; best to eat on the ground floor. Also be sure to try the **Ma Pu Dofu**.
Restaurant, West Jade Dragon St. (bus 16 three stops north of the hotel). Very cheap, very crowded, specializing in the spicy dofu they invented 100 years ago, dofu is 40 fen, and most other dishes are in the same price range.

Public Security is on Xin Hua Rd. (bus 16 four stops north of the hotel, turn right at the movie theater). This is where most people get permission for Emei Shan and Leshan.

There is direct rail service from Chengdu to Kunming (24 hours, a beautiful ride), to Xi'an (24 hours), to Lanzhou, to Chongqing (12 hours, four times daily), to Hefei and to Peking. Guilin is accessible via Guiyang (q.v.). The Kunming train stops at Emei, and there are several buses daily to Emei and Leshan.

Chongqing

The site of Chongqing has been settled for three thousand years; it received its present name during the Song dynasty. Until the 20th century it remained a small town, still surrounded by its ancient walls. Modernization began in 1928 and accelerated during the war. Chongqing today is one of the largest urban areas in China; about a million people live in the old city, and another five million in the surrounding suburbs. It is a major center for heavy and light industry.

Chongqing is perched on a rocky promontory at the confluence of the Yangtse and Jialing rivers. Those who explore this hilly city will have to climb many stairs. Central Chongqing is unusually poor and has fewer new buildings than most Chinese cities, as well as a far greater number of outdoor food stalls and private markets. Most visitors find the combination attractive.

The **Liberation Monument,** a large clock tower, stands at the center of town, and a walk along any of the streets radiating from its base is recommended. In the direction of either river are districts of muddy lanes and small houses — even some jerry-built shanties — clinging to the steep hills above the water. Some of these buildings house small factories that produce plastic teddy bears, artificial limbs and other equally exotic products. The narrow streets in these districts often surprise the stroller with panoramic views of the river 1,000 feet below. For an even more spectacular sight, take the cable car (10 fen) which rides on a seemingly-fragile wire high above the Jialing River.

At the confluence of the two rivers is a ferry dock where you can take a boat across either of them. On the southern bank is a busy market area where freelance "barefoot doctors" subject their patients to unusual remedies. You can return to Chongqing proper by city bus. In the western suburbs is the **U.S.-Chiang Kai-shek Criminal Acts Exhibition Hall,** with interesting photographs. In theory it's not open to Americans; in practice, no-one cares. Pleasanter entertainment can be found at the Chongqing Theater near the clock tower. Most evenings you can see colorful and beautifully choreographed Sichuan opera for 40 fen.

City maps are sometimes harder to find than in other towns. They are usually sold at three locations: the main Xinhua bookstore, the Friendship Store, and a smaller bookstore next to a tiny post office. All of these are near the clock tower, which is also the best neighborhood for restaurants. There is a bank in the Friendship Store.

The **Chongqing Guest House** is centrally located. Take the funicular from the train station (or walk up 320 muddy steps) to bus 1, which goes straight to the hotel. Dorms 4元 per bed. This cavernous Russian-built hotel has apparently not been repainted since it was first opened. Freezing in winter but otherwise comfortable. The small building across the street housed Chou En-lai's office during World War II, and was also used by Mao in 1945.

Another possibility is the **Renmin Hotel,** which has dorms for 6元; from the station take bus 1, then 13. It's worth a visit just to see its monumental architecture, part of which is modelled after the Temple of Heaven in Peking.

There are express trains to Chengdu four times daily, to Guiyang (change for Guilin), and to Peking. Boats leave every day for Wuhan, a very beautiful three-day cruise (see separate section).

Eight hours by bus from Chongqing is **Dazu,** a very small town near which are found Northern Mountain and Precious Summit Mountain, both adorned with huge bas-reliefs sculpted about a thousand years ago. Get permission from Public Security before you go. Precious Summit is ten miles outside town; take a bus (40 fen), the countryside is fabulous. The guest house in Dazu charges 6 元. There is probably a bus from here to Wanxian, the last port before the gorges on the Yangtse River cruise.

Yangtse River Cruise

The wild beauty of the rugged Yangtse Gorges has impressed travellers for thousands of years. It is an area haunted by many ghosts, for until recently the passage was fraught with danger. The river rushed through treacherous reefs and shoals at speeds of up to 20 miles an hour. Hauling on hawsers, hundreds of underpaid coolies towed boats against the current. If the pilot was unskilled or unlucky, his craft would be dashed against the rocks and the coolies thrown to their death in the water. Nevertheless, since 1,000 B.C. countless boats have made the journey, as the river was virtually the only link between Sichuan and the rest of China. After Liberation the channel was enlarged and the deadly rocks blasted away. Today, although the danger is gone, the romance and beauty of the trip remain.

(It is fair to point out, however, that the gorges themselves are not one of the natural wonders of the world, such as, say, the American Grand Canyon. Many travellers expecting to be dwarfed by mile-high cliffs have been bitterly disappointed. The scenery is highly enjoyable, provided it's not spoilt by overanticipation.)

There is a ship every day from Chongqing to Wuhan and vice-versa. Beginning in Chongqing (downstream and therefore two days shorter) tickets may be bought near the landing (bus 1 east to last stop) or at the CITS office in the Renmin Hotel. The former often has tickets when CITS doesn't (some travellers have reserved their third class berth the afternoon before departure), but has been known to claim that third class was fully booked when in fact it was half empty. If this happens, try again the next day.

There are four classes — second, third, fourth and fifth. Most travellers take either third (about 40元)or fourth (25元).Fourth class is adequate if spartan, with bunks in cabins of 24; bedding is provided. Third class is more comfortable, with better-furnished eight-berth cabins. Second class has a lounge with a bay window, while fifth-class travellers sleep huddled on the floor in the hallways.

Meals are not included in the ticket price, but a restaurant on the lower deck serves fairly good meat or vegetable dishes for about 60 fen each. Soup and rice go for 25 fen. You must pay with meal tickets, bought from a counter amidships.

Departure is at 7 a.m. but you can sleep on the boat the night before by purchasing a 1元ticket at the booking office. Passengers may board at 8 p.m.; go early to get a good place in line.

The first day a hilly and verdant landscape is visible on either side of the river; many small, remote villages perch on the summits of the hills or cling to their sides. That night the boat stops for about six hours at **Wanxian,** allowing it to traverse the river rapids by daylight. Passengers can go ashore and wander through the town.

Early the next morning the steamer, having left Wanxian a few hours earlier, enters **Qutang Gorge.** Farther on is **Wushan Gorge** ("Sorceress Mountain"), an eerie place whose name was derived from the belief that an enchantress haunted its slopes. In winter, when the skies are bleak and the mountains hemming in the river are covered with snow, the name still seems appropriate. Some consider the sheer cliffs of the **Xiling Gorge** even more impressive.

Early that afternoon, the boat reaches the town of **Yichang.** Here, the majesty of the gorges gives way to the monotony of the plains. Everyone on board crowds the deck to see the boat pass through the newly opened locks of the huge dam. It is possible to go by train from Yichang to Luoyang, changing trains at Xiangfan. A few hours later, the boat reaches **Shashi,** a city of 200,000, open to tourists, with a smaller walled town a few miles away (bus 1). Some may wish to disembark and spend a night or two before taking a bus onwards. Or you can leave the boat at a landing near Yueyang and take a bus into town from the pier. If the boat is on schedule (which it usually isn't) it reaches Wuhan early that afternoon.

Service along the Yangtse continues to Jiujiang, Wuhu, Nanjing and Shanghai. Sometimes this involves a boat change at Wuhan.

6. Beyond The Wall

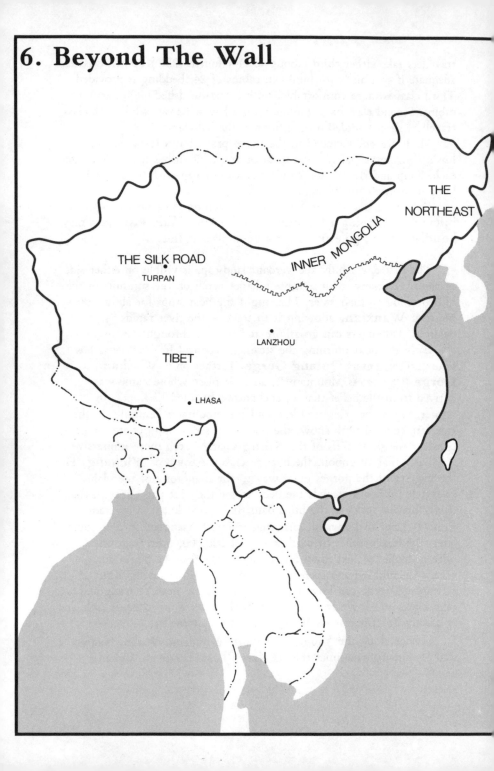

The Silk Road

Xinjiang, today one of the remotest parts of China, was once the crossroads of Asia. For over a thousand years it was a strategic stop on the overland route linking China with India, Persia and Rome, and countless traders and wanderers passed through its barren desert. Most of the merchants carried bales of silk, China's best-known export, which were so highly prized by fashionable ladies of the Roman and later empires that the entire route became known to Europe as the Silk Road.

For China, the cultural interchange with the rest of Asia proved more important than the commerce that inspired it. Buddhist missionaries from northern India travelled along the Silk Road to introduce their faith to the Middle Kingdom. Later, Chinese pilgrims journeyed to India, the most famous being Xuanzang, who passed through Xinjiang in 629 on his famous Journey to the West. He returned to China fifteen years later having spent the intervening period immersing himself in Hindu and Buddhist metaphysics. His writing expounding Indian philosophy opened new realms of thought to the Chinese, and catalyzed the intellectual ferment that culminated in neo-Confucianism. Nor were the notions that traversed the Silk Road limited to such heady doctrines: the Chinese also learned the use of sugar and wine.

It is hardly surprising, in light of the volume and variety of commerce that passed through them, that the lush oases of Xinjiang were extremely cosmopolitan. Their inhabitants were Caucasians who spoke Indo-European languages, their religion was Buddhist, and their art and culture was a synthesis of Indian, Persian and Hellenic elements. Each oasis was an independent city-state, but the strategic location of these tiny kingdoms made it inevitable that they would become prizes sought after by all the major powers of the region. Mongols, Arabs and even Tibetans vied for their possession, but the main contender was, of course, China. The Chinese were in almost continuous control of all the territory east of Dunhuang, a frontier post and garrison town. Their dominion over the kingdoms beyond waxed and waned, depending on the strength of the ruler in

Chang'an. Thus, during the Han and Tang dynasties, the kings of Xinjiang became vassals of the emperor, but reasserted their independence during the period of Chinese weakness in between.

The 9th and 10th centuries mark a watershed during which the composition of the region was radically altered. The Uygurs, a warlike Turkic people who were allies of the Chinese, migrated in force from their homeland in Mongolia to Xinjiang, where they established a kingdom with Turpan as capital and intermarried with the Indo-European inhabitants. Arab expansion closed the Silk Road to travel, and the Uygurs were soon converted to Islam. When, in the 13th century, the Mongols conquered the greater part of Asia, trade flowed once more, only to diminish to a trickle during the isolationist Ming and Qing dynasties. The Uygur territories continued to be ruled by descendants of Genghis Khan, and were not decisively annexed by China until the 18th century. The Sungars, the last of the Mongols, were ousted by the Qianlong Emperor, and the new province received its present name of Xinjiang, or "new land."

Xinjiang today is very much a border area, worlds removed from the plains of China. The region's Han Chinese are outnumbered by the five million Uygurs. Like the people of neighboring Afghanistan, the Uygurs are proud, volatile and devoutly Muslim. They are also as restive as the Afghans under what they consider foreign domination, and Uygur-Han relations are often uneasy. The Chinese, who view themselves as having brought industry, hospitals and female emancipation to a backward area, are surprised by the sporadic riots that jolt the autonomous region. Two in 1980 were especially severe, and Peking responded by appointing as governor a man known for his good relations with the Uygurs.

One of the People's Republic's undisputed accomplishments is the building of the rail line that links Xinjiang with the rest of the nation. Five expresses a day ply the route between Urumqi and the East, one each from Peking, Shanghai, Zhengzhou, Xi'an and Lanzhou. They cover the 1600 miles between Xi'an and Urumqi in slightly over two days; the cost, including sleeper, is about 60元. The Marco Polos of the rail age are permitted to break their journey in only five places: Lanzhou, Jiuquan, Jiayuguan, Dunhuang and Turpan.

The Gansu Corridor

The first of these, **Lanzhou,** is an industrial center of over two million, the largest city west of Xi'an. Sandwiched between a range of high bluffs and the Yellow River, Lanzhou is narrow, very long and somewhat bland — like a hot dog. There is a good view of the town from the top of **Baita Shan,** a hill in a park across the river from the city center. The main part of town is to the east, and the busiest streets are those east and south of the Xiguan traffic circle, directly opposite Baita Shan. The low brick buildings in this area, though old and brightly painted, are curiously devoid of character. One exception is the former **Temple of the Town Gods,** just north of Nanchang Rd., the street that runs east from Xiguan. The complex has been repainted and is now a public park.

Across the street from the hotel is the **Provincial Museum,** whose star exhibit is the sculpted bronze "Flying Horse of Gansu." Farther afield are the **Binglingsi Caves** at Yongjing, with Buddhist sculpture and paintings from the Tang, Song and Ming dynasties. In summer the grottoes can be reached by boat, a 35-mile ride along the Yellow River.

Also accessible from Lanzhou is **Xining,** the capital of Qinghai Province. This large and interesting city is closed to tourists. Those lucky enough to get permission for it should also try to visit the Qutansi, a large Buddhist monastery near Ledo, the railway station one stop before Xining.

The main hotel in Lanzhou is the large, seemingly-deserted **Youyi Guest House** (bus 1 or trolley 31 from the Xiguan or the train station), where a bed in a triple is 6元. There are two good restaurants in the center of town, both on Jiuquan St. One is the huge Lanzhou Canting, where the best food, reasonably priced, is on the third floor; a two-storey building a block north houses the other.

After leaving Lanzhou, the train follows the old caravan route through the Gansu Corridor, a narrow strip of fertile land dividing the Gobi Desert from the Qinghai Plateau. Beyond the green fields and earthen houses of the corridor, the snow-capped peaks of the Qilian range are clearly visible. An occasional camel plods the roads that skirt the tracks. 500 miles west of Lanzhou is **Jiuquan,** a Chinese administrative headquarters for two thousand years. A large red brick pagoda stands in the center of this old town; nine miles away are the cave temples of Wenshushan, the earliest of which date from the 5th century.

The next major station is **Jiayuguan,** whose large gate tower marks the end of the Great Wall. Built in 1372, it has recently been restored. The gate is just north of the tracks and can be clearly seen from the train. There is a hotel in town, single rooms 5元, if you want to stay the night. There are buses each morning from the hotel to the fort.

Dunhuang

South of the small town of Dunhuang lies the treasure trove of Buddhist art that has come to be known as the **Mogao Caves.** A monastery was founded at Mogao during Dunhuang's heyday as a stop on the Silk Road, and between the 5th and 14th centuries countless shrines were chiselled into the surrounding cliffs. In later years the monastery was abandoned and the caves came to be forgotten. Around 1900, a man named Wang chanced to enter a cave containing a vast hoard of Buddhist scrolls and other Tang Dynasty documents and paintings. To the historian these artifacts were priceless, and since the Manchu government expressed no interest, the Sinologists of Europe descended upon Dunhuang and carried off documents by the crateload. But Dunhuang's greatest treasures, the art that adorns its grottoes, was not so easily transported and remain for the traveller to rediscover.

The focal point of each of these rectangular chapels is a group of brightly painted statues depicting the Buddha, his acolytes and guardians, placed either at the center of the cave or in a niche in front. Most of these sculptures are terracotta since the soft sandstone of the caves is difficult to carve. Even finer than the statuary are the murals that cover every square inch of the walls. They were painted in tempera — in effect, watercolors — applied over several layers of clay and cement. Most depict either parables or episodes from the life of the Buddha, although interspersed between these realistic scenes are abstract designs. Commonly, hundreds of tiny Buddhas are arranged in a decorative pattern. The paintings are crammed with a surfeit of detail, and repay intensive examination. Often, tiny figures of surpassing grace float in the background, and exquisite landscapes are tucked away at the border of a larger work. Although much of the Mogao art has been well preserved, some was restored in later years, and many of these renovations, especially those done under the Qing, are noticeably inferior.

Virtually all the Dunhuang art dates from the Wei, Sui and Tang periods. The Wei artists, like their contemporaries at Datong and Luoyang, tried to depict people who, through asceticism and self-sacrifice, had succeeded in transcending the material world. As a result, their portraits often appear inhuman or primitive, a quality that oxidation has enhanced over the years by blackening the once-red pigment. The Sui sculptures, with their curiously oversized heads and elongated torsoes, represent a period of transition. Both the Wei and Sui grottoes are easily overshadowed by the dazzling variety of works produced under the Tang.

Far from appearing distant and abstracted, the figures in the Tang grottoes are full of emotion. Several sculpted disciples have cunning smirks (cave 79), while others laugh outright (85). Bellicose, fiercely mustachioed warriors guard the Buddha in cave 173. The accompanying paintings are equally lively: many depict scenes of contemporary Chinese life. Some are peopled by Tang aristocrats (237), and portly gentlemen in wide hats and flowered robes bear offerings to the Buddha. A few murals feature large Chinese houses and pagodas (197), while others portray battles from Tang military expeditions (156).

Some of the largest murals are the best. Here, the figures that swirl with sinuous grace are all subordinate to the larger design. Cave 158, dominated by a huge statue of the dead Buddha, has two paintings on the end walls that deserve special attention. They depict Buddha's mourners, including Turks, Arabs and other "barbarians," and their powerful figures, distorted in grief, are unlike anything else in the caves. Also worth notice, for size rather than artistic merit, are the huge sculpted Buddhas in caves 96 and 130. 96 is the taller (100 feet), though the other is far better carved.

The magnificence of the Mogao Caves is marred by their presentation. Only 40 grottoes are open to the public. Some of the 460 closed caves are in poor condition, while others contain Tantric art whose explicit sexual portrayals are apparently viewed as corrupting influences. Even the 40 caves cleared for exhibition are barred by locked doors which must be opened by a guide. Many of these custodians are shockingly apathetic, and the "tours" consist of brief visits to five or six caves. Since there are usually several groups at the caves at any one time, you can extend your time in each cave by moving from one to the other. (It's best to bring a flashlight, for the caves are unlit and viewing is at times unsatisfactory without one.) Foreign tour groups of the $100-a-day variety are given a more comprehensive excursion, and you might be able to tag along, especially if you spend several days in Dunhuang. If not, you are liable to be very disappointed by your visit to Mogao. Those who come a long way just to see the grottoes are taking a great risk.

Getting to Mogao presents another problem; the caves are 15 miles from town. Every second day at 7:30 a.m. a bus leaves from the large traffic circle in the center of town, one block from the guest house (turn right at the gate). The 70 fen one-way fare includes a cursory tour of the caves. The bus leaves Mogao at 11:30, although those wishing to stay longer can probably hitch back on one of the many tour buses. Or you can cover the distance by bicycle, which can be rented at the hotel. If none of these possibilities appeal to you, try the rest house at the caves. It is not normally open to foreigners, but will probably put up those who are stranded. Another option is the hotel jeep, which holds four: 20元 buys a morning or afternoon tour. Be sure to specify jeep rather than car (which costs 35元), since the hotel staff makes a practice of overcharging the unwary. Note that the caves are closed between 11:30 and 2:30, when lunch is served at the rest house for 1元.

Dunhuang itself is a dull town dominated by grey concrete structures, set in the middle of a fertile oasis. Fairly close to town is an area of huge sand dunes, one with a road leading to the top, surrounding a beautiful crescent-shaped lake. 40 miles south, reachable by rented jeep, is the **Yangquan Pass,** known for its Han Dynasty walls and beacon towers.

Most foreigners stay at the Dunhuang Hotel. From the bus station turn left, then right at the T: the hotel is one block beyond the traffic circle. Dorms are 6元. There is a big new hostel on the same street as the bus station where a place in a spartan but clean four-bed room is 3元, and a bed in a double is 6元. Between the hostel and the station is one of Dunhuang's better restaurants. There are also two ice-cream shops, one adjacent to the hotel, the other, run by unemployed youths, between the hotel and the traffic circle: both stay open until 10:30 p.m.

The nearest train station to Dunhuang is at **Liuyuan,** 100 miles across the desert. Walk straight out of the terminal and down the main street: the bus station is a few minutes' walk away, cunningly concealed behind a building on the left. Buses to Dunhuang leave at 7:30 a.m. and noon. If you come later, you must spend the night at this dismal town (hotel 3元) unless you can hitch a ride. A recommended alternative is the daily bus from Jiuquan direct to Dunhuang. From Dunhuang, there are two daily departures for Liuyuan and one for Jiuquan. The hotel will book Liuyuan tickets, though you can usually get a seat when you board.

Turpan

West of Liuyuan lie the deserts of Xinjiang. After a 12-hour journey across a wasteland of dun-colored rock and howling winds, the train arrives at the Turpan oasis.

It is easy to fall under the spell of this charming town. Turpan has been spared the uglification inflicted upon most Chinese cities. Its aging whitewashed buildings, some of which have pretentious stucco porticoes and pediments, belong to an earlier era. As in Kabul, water used for washing and waste disposal flows in a canal by the side of the main street. Old men with long beards and embroidered prayer caps lend to the prevailing Central Asian ambience.

Down a small alley opposite the bus station is a large market surrounded by over a dozen tiny restaurants. Farther west along the main street, a garishly painted mosque stands at the edge of town. There is another mosque, now being restored, half a mile farther on, with the ruins of an ancient minaret nearby. A short distance beyond this district, the main street reaches a large crossroads with brightly painted buildings and a bazaar much more lively and colorful than the one in town.

Another pleasant walk is towards the well-known **Sugongta Mosque.** Turn left at the hotel entrance and, after a few yards, left again along a dusty, lively road crowded with donkey carts and bands of naked children shouting a welcoming "bye bye!" After about 20 minutes the starkly beautiful silhouette of the mosque will be visible in the distance. Built in 1779, its tall minaret, with a geometric mosaic of brick, may be climbed. (If the doors are locked, ask at the small white gatekeeper's lodge next door.) Next to the minaret is a huge smokestack ornamented with an inspirational Mao quotation.

The Turpan oasis is densely populated, and for those willing to go farther afield there are many villages of earth-brick houses, some of which are surrounded by fortress-like ramparts. These houses' stark walls conceal richly carpeted interiors. Each community has its mosque, and most villages have cemeteries, some of which contain huge tombs with vaulted roofs.

A spiderweb of small dirt roads radiate from Turpan. Since the town is set in the north-center of the oasis, the likeliest directions for exploration are towards the south. (A very detailed map of the oasis is hidden in one of the back offices of the guest house.) The road running due south from the guest house (turn left at the gate) soon becomes a cart track that ultimately leads to several villages. Or, south from the main intersection one block west of the guesthouse, turn right at the T, then left onto the first paved road and keep going. A third option is the road that runs south from the crossroads bazaar one mile west of Turpan. After several miles (and one right-left zigzag) there is a large village with well laid-out streets.

A word of warning to walkers: in summer, Turpan is the hottest place in China and the sun is dangerously strong. Count on walking both ways when you visit a village. You may be able to hitch a ride on a cart, but traffic is often sparse, especially at midday.

About 20 miles east of Turpan is **Gaochang,** the old Uygur capital. A flourishing city between the 7th and 14th centuries, its earth-brick remains, which sprawl over a square mile, are slowly reverting to desert. It can be difficult to distinguish between wall and bluff. West of Turpan is another old city, **Jiaohe,** set on a high cliff above a dried up riverbed. Its buildings are in slightly better condition that those of Gaocheng, and a few narrow street are visible.

North of Gaochang are the **Bezeklik 1,000-Buddha Caves.** Most of the Tang frescoes that ornament the seven caves are in bad condition, many having been destroyed by Moslem zealots. The artwork is overshadowed by their awe-inspiring setting in the midst of the Flaming Mountains.

Gaochang and Jiaohe are not served by public transport. Taxis can be hired at 50 fen a kilometer, or one of the many tour groups that visit the area might accept an extra passenger, for which privilege CITS charges about 10元.

The **Turpan Guest House** is the only hotel in town. From the bus station turn left down the main street, then right at the second intersection. The hotel is in the first whitewashed compound on the left. 5元 for the dorm, 9.50元 per person for a double in the old wing. 15元 for a double with shower in the new wing. Hotel dinners are exorbitantly priced at 6.50元 (negotiable), though the portions are Brobdingnagian. The food is especially good when a tour group is in town. Cheaper options include the eateries in the bazaar, the evening food stalls by the cinema, and the small restaurant next to the bus station. (Be careful what you eat, because Xinjiang has a reputation for causing diarrhoea.)

In summer, the sky stays light until after 10 and people stay up late to enjoy the cool of the evening. When tour groups are in residence there is a performance of Uygur music and dances in the hotel garden starting at 9:30 (admission free).

Although the railway station is signposted as "Turpan," it is in reality **Daheyon,** an unbelievably ugly place 30 miles from where you want to go. There are two buses a day to Turpan, at 8 a.m. and 5 p.m. Walk straight out of the train station and take the first right; the bus park is on the left side of the road, about 200 yards down. To avoid the Daheyon detour, take a bus from Turpan to Urumqi. They leave at 8 a.m. and 4 p.m., a six-hour ride. In Turpan itself, transport is by communal donkey cart (10 fen for a short ride, 1元 for a return charter to the Sugongta).

End of the Line

Nobody likes **Urumqi.** A modern industrial city, it was apparently designed by Han settlers pining for the uninspired architecture of their hometowns. You can climb Hongshan (four stops south of the hotel by bus 1 or 2), a crag topped by an old pagoda, for a panoramic view of factories, smokestacks and desert. A few Uygur houses stand forlornly among the industrial plants. One small Uygur neighborhood, nicer than most, with a long covered market that houses many small restaurants, is across the street from the Hongshan Department Store, next to the hill.

The **Kunlun Hotel,** Urumqi's cheapest, offers beds in four-bed rooms for 3元. Bus 2 from train station. From the bus depot turn right, walk to the main street and cross it, then take bus 2. Public Security is near the former town center; take bus 1 six stops from the hotel, then walk about 200 yards farther down the street. Nearby is a long block of older houses.

Most of Xinjiang is closed to foreigners. The exceptions are the **Southern Pastures,** a grasslands on the fringe of Urumqi, reachable by taxi; **Shihezi,** a modern Han outpost about 100 miles west of Urumqi, famous for its cotton mill; and **Tianchi,** on the Tianshan range. 30 miles from Urumqi, Tianchi is a small lake fringed by fir-clad hills and snow-capped mountains. You can visit for the day, or overnight in a bungalow. Buses make the round trip from Urumqi twice weekly in spring and daily in summer. Tickets are available next to the bus depot, which is at a small kiosk near Hongshan (take bus 1 from the hotel four stops south, then walk 100 yards beyond the stop).

Off-limits is the string of Uygur oases that skirts the southern desert. The largest and reportedly least Sinicized of these is **Kashgar,** or Kashi, a fabled city near the Pakistani border. There are buses from Urumqi for those willing to try. The four-day ride costs about 30元. Close to Kashgar are two of the world's highest mountain ranges, the Karakorams and the Pamirs: the Silk Road passes over these peaks on its way to the West.

Inner Mongolia

The nomads who inhabit the windswept steppes of Mongolia were once the most feared people on earth. In the 4th century A.D., hordes of Xiongnu warriors from Western Mongolia rampaged through much of Europe, where they became known to the terrified inhabitants as The Huns. Nine centuries later Mongolian armies once again swept across Asia, forging the largest empire the world had yet seen. Throughout the ages, the various Mongolian tribes posed a more or less constant threat to China — the Great Wall was built to keep them out, and numerous military expeditions were sent to Mongolia under the Han, the Tang and the Ming. Finally, under Kangxi, the Mongol princes swore fealty to the Emperor. When the Qing Dynasty fell, however, the Mongols considered themselves released from their oath, and Outer Mongolia became independent, falling later under Soviet domination.

In 1947 the Communists designated what remained of the original territories the Autonomous Region of Inner Mongolia, although only one-fifth of the area's nine million people are Mongols. (The remaining inhabitants are mostly Han, who are concentrated in the two largest cities, Hohhot and Baotou.) Nonetheless there are some two million Mongols in China as against only one million in the Mongolian People's Republic.

Hohhot, the capital, is a 12-hour train ride from Peking. It was founded in the 16th century, and despite recent industrial development many interesting neighborhoods remain. Several fine temples are still standing in what appears to be the old city (bus 1 or 2). The Dazhao, a Ming monastery built in modified Tibetan style, is now a factory; the Wutazhao is an 18th-century terrace on which five small pagodas stand. There is also a Qing Dynasty mosque and minaret. In the eastern suburbs, a half-hour by train from town, is the Wanbuhuayanjing, a large octagonal brick pagoda built in the 11th century. At Hohhot's guest house, near the train station, beds in a triple are 6 元.

Baotou, Inner Mongolia's largest city, lies west of Hohhot. Get off the train at the East station and take bus 5 to the Donghe Hotel, dorms 5 元. The large Tibetan-style monastery of Wudangzhao is a few hours away. Founded during the 18th century, the lamasery at one time owned 16,500 acres of land, 500 slaves and a coal mine. Its many white flat-roofed halls are in excellent condition. Although CITS will urge you to join a tour, long-distance public buses to Guyang County stop at the Wudangzhao.

North of Hohhot and Baotou stretches the **Inner Mongolia Plateau,** many of whose inhabitants still move their livestock across the vast grasslands, living in felt yurts. CITS offers two- and three-day tours to the grasslands from Hohhot. Nights are spent in carefully selected communes, where guaranteed genuine Mongols take off their Mao suits, don native garb and perform traditional dances. These tours are expensive (50-100 元), but they do include a three-hour drive over the Daqing Mountains and across the grasslands, where herds of horses, sheep and cattle are visible. This is the only officially approved way of seeing the grasslands, and the Hohhot bus station will not sell tickets to foreigners.

There are other possibilities. **Xilinhot,** a small city on the plateau, accessible only by plane, is open to tourists, and you may be able to get to the grasslands outside town. Xilinhot itself has a large Qing monastery, the Beizimiao, and a mostly Mongol population. Or, with luck, you might get permission to visit some of the other towns of Inner Mongolia. **Hailar,** northwest of Harbin, is close to the Siberian forests, which are still inhabited by nomadic hunters.

The Northeast

The Northeast is China's last frontier. Its fertile plains, mostly virgin until the beginning of this century, are still relatively underpopulated today. The explanation for this anomaly must be sought in the region's history. In the 17th century, the Manchus, who then lived in present-day Heilongjiang, conquered the southern half of the region and went on to wrest control of the whole Empire from Chinese hands. During the entire Qing Dynasty the Manchu emperors closed their homeland to Chinese settlers. Japan and Russia were not oblivious to this vacuum on their borders, and both vied for control of the resource-rich territory. The Japanese occupied the area from 1931 until 1945, establishing a heavy industrial base in the puppet state of Manchukuo. Russian troops invaded Manchuria in 1945 and sacked the factories.

After 1949 the Chinese rebuilt and expanded the assembly lines, and today nearly a third of China's industrial production is concentrated in the Northeast. A quarter of the nation's steel comes from the huge mills of Anshan, a like proportion of all domestically made machines are manufactured in Shenyang, and until recently four-fifths of China's oil came from the fields of Daqing. Nor has Manchuria's potential as a breadbasket been overlooked. Immigration has been encouraged and large state farms, where workers are paid set wages, have been established in sparsely-populated Heilongjiang.

The huge cities of the Northeast offer the traveller the chance to observe China's industry and mix with her proletariat. But, though attractively laid out, they are largely devoid of color. The only city with any historical remains is the largest, **Shenyang,** about 12 hours by rail from Peking. In 1625 the Manchu leaders, having evicted the Chinese from the area, established their capital at what was then called Mukden. Hoping even then to rule China, the Manchu kings built an **Imperial Palace** which still stands today (trolley 10 or 13 from the center of town). Though it pales by comparison with its Peking namesake, it is an attractive complex in its own right. The main halls are in the series of courtyards to the left of the entrance. In the pavilions surrounding the far courtyard are displayed a wealth of jade and ivory, as well as fine examples of Qing porcelain.

Around the Imperial Palace is the **old city.** Its heart is bustling Zhongyang Rd., crowded with multi-storied architectural fantasies, some with Moghul-style towers on top. Numerous alleys wind through the area south and west of Zhongyang, but the traditional houses in this workers' neighborhood are outnumbered by larger brick buildings. The western part of the city, just outside the train station, is more modern. The main streets are Zhonghua and Zhongshan; the latter avenue runs into a big plaza at the center of which stands one of China's finest Mao monuments.

Behind the statue is the former Liaoning Guest House, one of China's more exuberant architectural curiosities. This grand old hotel has recently closed its doors; the only guest house still open to foreigners is the huge **Liaoning Mansions** north of the city (trolley 6 from station, 3 from Mao square). A bed in a double costs about 10 元 (negotiable). In a large park near the hotel is the tomb of Abahai, the Manchu ruler who declared himself emperor of China in 1636 but died in 1643, one year prior to the fall of the Ming Dynasty.

South of Shenyang is **Dalian,** located at the tip of the Liaodong Peninsula. Dalian is a spacious, well-organized city, much influenced by the Japanese and Russians who occupied it during the early part of the century. It is also a seaside resort — mainly patronized by Shanghainese — with four landscaped beach parks. From Dalian, daily boats make the short hop across the Bohai Gulf to Yantai in Shandong Province, but departures for Shanghai are less frequent.

North of Shenyang is **Changchun,** once capital of Manchukuo, whose administrative buildings were erected by the Japanese.

Four hours from Changchun by train, **Harbin** is the northernmost city in China open to tourists. A small fishing village at the turn of the century, Harbin's growth was spurred when the Tsarist government built a railway from Siberia to Vladivostok across Manchuria. The city's Russian community, swelled by refugees fleeing the Bolsheviks, remained in Harbin until the end of the last war. The flamboyant buildings they erected set the city's tone today. Most are fronted with yellow stucco, though some feature elaborately carved stone facades.

These architectural transplants from pre-war Europe are nowhere more in evidence than along Zhongyang Blvd., a cobbled street just west of Shangzhi Blvd. reachable by trolley 1 or 3 from the hotel. On Toulong St., near the large plaza on Shangzhi, is a former **Russian Orthodox church** with a large onion dome. Much of Toulong is a produce market, closed to traffic. Another market area sprawls behind Dongdazhi St., across the traffic circle from the hotel.

A different sort of Russian influence can be felt in **Stalin Park,** a landscaped garden by the Sungari River. (The entrance is at the end of Zhongyang.) The park is dominated by blaring loudspeakers and "Socialist Realist" statuary, both of which would doubtless make the old dictator feel at home.

In winter the river freezes over and is used for skating and sledding (you can rent the equipment). Just after Chinese New Year the city adds its own twist to the traditional Lantern Festival, lighting their candles in ice sculptures.

Harbin's main hotel is the Guoji (trolley 1 or 3 from train station, or five-minute walk), where single rooms are 17元 and doubles are 24元 There are dorms, but it will take a struggle to get in; budget travellers are rare in these parts. There is a good restaurant on Fendou St., the Jiang Nan Chun. The ice cream sold by street vendors is the best in China.

Several non-Han peoples live in Heilongjiang, and some are still hunters in the northern forests. These areas are, needless to say, closed to tourism. With luck, you might be allowed to go to **Dailing,** a small logging town northeast of Harbin, or to **Hailar** in Inner Mongolia. Easier but perhaps less exciting to visit are the oilfields of **Daqing,** held up as a model for industry during the Cultural Revolution.

Tibet

Until this century, so little was known about Tibet that most world maps left it blank. A steady stream of adventurers, including burly Swedes disguised as Indian pilgrims and female missionaries in Tibetan costume, risked their lives for a glimpse of the forbidden city of Lhasa, but only a handful succeeded. Some were deterred by the inhospitable terrain, but most were frustrated by local officials fearful of outsiders and their influence.

In the 7th century, when recorded Tibetan history begins, it was their neighbors, not they, who lived in fear. Tibetan armies were considered as great a scourge as the Huns, and under the famous King Songsten Gampo, they occupied Nepal and collected tribute from Nanchao, in Yunnan. Shortly after Songsten's death his warriors moved north, briefly controlling the Silk Road oases of Kashgar, Khotan and Kucha. Chinese troops vigorously contested these appropriations, and in 763 the Tibetans responded by sacking the capital city of Chang'an.

Tibetan expansion came to a sudden end when, in 842, the King was assassinated. In the ensuing struggle for power Tibet was fragmented into feuding principalities. Never again were Tibetan armies to leave their high plateau.

As the secular rulers' authority waned, that of the Buddhist clergy increased. Ever since reaching Tibet in the 3rd century, Buddhism had had to compete with bon, the traditional Tibetan form of animism. In time Tibetan Buddhism incorporated many bon beliefs and rituals — such as the ever-present prayer flags — and this may explain its deep-rooted place in the life of the Tibetan people. The monasteries became increasingly politicized, and in 1641 the Yellow Hat sect, a reformist movement advocating stringent monastic discipline, used the support of the Mongols (who were Buddhist) to crush the Red Hats, their rivals.

The Yellow Hat leaders adopted the title of Dalai Lama, or Ocean of Wisdom, and became both the spiritual and temporal rulers of Tibet. Each Dalai Lama was considered the reincarnation of his predecessor; upon the death of the God-King, monks searched the land for a baby who showed a sign (usually recognition of the holy possessions) of embodying his eternal spirit. Sometimes test results would be swayed by political considerations. The Yellow Hats converted the Mongols to their cause by finding the Dalai Lama's fourth incarnation in the family of the Mongol ruler.

But the Mongols came to regard Tibet as their domain. In 1705 the Qosot Mongols succeeded in ousting the Dalai Lama, and a decade later the Sungar Mongols drove the Qosot from the holy city and occupied Lhasa themselves. At that time the Sungars were the most powerful of China's enemies, and the Emperor Kang-xi sent an army to Tibet to expel them from their new stronghold. The Chinese left behind two commissioners to direct Tibetan foreign relations. Riots incited by Tibetan nationalists in 1750 led to the return of Chinese troops the next year. Though the Emperor recognized the Dalai Lama as King of Tibet, the Chinese commissioners wielded full political power.

After the Qing Dynasty was overthrown Tibet proclaimed itself independent, but in 1950 the PLA entered the region and re-established the protectorate. The Chinese planned to leave the Dalai Lama in power while they slowly converted the Tibetans to communism. Land ownership at that time was more concentrated in Tibet than it had been in China, and the Chinese expected the Tibetan peasantry to welcome them as liberators. Instead, an armed uprising broke out in 1959. The PLA suppressed the revolt, the Dalai Lama fled to India, and Tibet became an "autonomous region" of China.

The new Chinese rulers introduced a program of social reform, both secular and monastic. Large estates were distributed among the landless. Roads, schools and hospitals were built. Nevertheless, the economy stagnated, and what improvements were made failed to benefit the Tibetans: the roads were used by the military, and the schools taught in Chinese. Worse, farmers were required to plant hopelessly alien lowland crops. During the Cultural Revolution the government's primary aim was to "civilize" the Tibetans and turn them into Chinese. Buddhism received special attention. Over 2,000 lamaseries were disbanded, and their monks put to work in the fields. Temples were closed, and many were reduced to rubble.

Several of China's current leaders, notably Party Chairman Hu Yaobang, opposed the Maoist policy of assimilation. In 1980 the regional party boss was sacked and replaced by a more liberal administrator. The following years brought other changes. State subsidies to the region were increased, taxes were waived, and farmers were allowed to grow what they liked and sell their produce. Several monasteries and temples were restored and re-opened. In 1982 members of the Dalai Lama's cabinet-in-exile visited Peking to discuss his possible return. The Chinese, of course, would be happy to co-opt him as a religious figurehead, but it appears that the days of the all-powerful God-King are at an end.

Getting There

Though roads and airfields now link Lhasa with the rest of the nation, Tibet remains the remotest part of China, and for many travellers it has become a sort of grail. The primary obstacle today, as it was a century ago, is not logistical but bureaucratic. Tibet is officially closed except to those willing to join exorbitantly priced group tours. But not all Public Security offices seem to be aware of this fact, and in the spring of 1982 a few dozen travellers managed to have Lhasa added to their travel permits in Datong, Hohhot and other places. The word of each discovery spread along the tourist grapevine, and within a few weeks puzzled policemen found themselves playing host to hordes of Lhasa-seekers. Irate telephone calls from Peking brought each bonanza to an end, and those who came too late moved off in search of other police stations. But most of those who got permission succeeded in reaching Tibet.

The best way of finding out the current situation is to ask every traveller you meet. Or you can pioneer new areas, such as smaller towns or seldom-visited provincial capitals. Ask for a lot of other cities as camouflage, be persistent, and be prepared for failure. That Lhasa chop grows more elusive every day.

If you are lucky, keep away from other Public Security offices. Many have developed the irksome habit of confiscating travel permits endorsed for Lhasa. Get on a plane right away. There are flights most days from Chengdu (322 元), with slightly less frequent departures from Xi'an. When you arrive in Lhasa, don't miss the CAAC bus; it's an 80-mile ride to town. Some travellers have gone to Lhasa overland, hitching from Liuyuan or Dunhuang on the Silk Road. Trucks go fairly regularly from Liuyuan to Golmud, and from Golmud to Lhasa. Don't advertise your presence in Golmud, which is a very closed town. The drive from there to Lhasa is arduous, but the scenery on the last day provides at least partial compensation. There are also roads from Sichuan and Yunnan, but the police in those provinces quickly detect and deflect any foreigners who use them.

In Lhasa itself the police are far less peevish. As of mid-1982 a friendly officer would inspect travel permits, and those whose papers were in order were permitted to stay as long as they liked.

The Town

Lhasa is really two cities. The modern Han section has broad boulevards and modern buildings. But the paved roads end at the Tibetan part of town, and the dusty gravel streets are lined with old, two-storey whitewashed houses whose flat roofs are used to store barley and animal feed. At the center of the old city is the **Jokhang Temple.** Founded by King Songsten Gampo and expanded in later years, its buildings are a potpourri of Indian, Chinese and Tibetan architecture. During the Cultural Revolution this holiest of shrines was reportedly converted into a pig slaughterhouse. It has now been restored and is open for worship six days a week. The street that encircles the temple contains Lhasa's liveliest market, the **Bargor bazaar.** There are many Tibetan artifacts on sale, but prospective buyers should remember that jewelry not bought in state shops is liable to be confiscated.

Lhasa's most famous landmark is the 17th-century **Potala,** the winter residence of the Dalai Lama, which took 50 years to build. The Dalai Lama lived in the upper storeys of the Red Palace, which also contains temples, shrines and tombs (chorten). The White Palace once housed monks and administrators.

About two miles west of the Potala is the Dalai Lama's summer palace, the **Norbu Lingka,** where the pavilions are more Chinese in character. The surrounding gardens are a favorite picnic spot.

Slightly farther from town are two of Tibet's most renowned monasteries, the **Sera** and the **Drepung.** The Sera is the closer, four miles north of the Potala. The Drepung, about six miles northwest of town (you can hitch), was founded in 1416. At bne time it housed over 10,000 monks and was the largest monastery in Tibet and possibly the world. About 300 monks live there today. The main halls are richly decorated, dimly lit with devotional lamps, and permeated with the smell of yak butter.

Several other temples in the Lhasa area were demolished during the Cutural Revolution, though one or two may have been rebuilt since. These include the Xiaozhao Temple, half a mile north of the Jokhang, and the Medicine King Temple, built atop a hill southwest of the Potala. But don't try to see too much in one day. The air is thin in this 12,000-foot-high city, and visitors may suffer from exhaustion, mild dehydration and insomnia.

Despite CITS-inspired rumours that the only hotel in town is the 200元-a-day No. 3 Guest House, most travellers stay at the No. 1 Guest House (Diyi Binguan), just west of the Jokhang, where the cheapest bed is 1.50元. Rooms whose windows face the sun cost 50 fen more per bed, but those 1.50 rooms, though not so well lit, face the Potala. Hot showers are 70 fen. There are several cheap restaurants near the hotel on the street leading to the market.

Beyond

Though the Lhasa police rarely give permission to visit other towns, some travellers have gone to Gyantse and Xigaze 'unofficially'. There are buses to both towns, but tickets cannot be bought without a valid travel permit, so it's best to hitch. The road to Gyantse climbs to 15,730 feet to cross the Kamba La mountain pass and skirts the brilliant blue waters of the Yamdrok Tso, a 14,400-foot-high lake fringed with tiny villages. **Gyantse** is dominated by an old citadel perched on a rocky crag overlooking the town. Its most famous landmark is the 15th-century Golden Temple, whose four storeys of chapel are surmounted by a huge white stupa like those in Nepal.

There is a cheap hotel in Gyantse, and some travellers have spent a week there.

From Gyantse a road runs to **Xigaze,** Tibet's second largest city. (If this track is flooded out, as sometimes happens, use the road that goes directly from Lhasa.) Xigaze is the seat of the Panchen Lama, second only to the Dalai Lama, and his monastery, the **Tashilumpo,** ranks among Tibet's most prominent. With its red and brown halls topped with sculpted bronze, it is one of the most beautiful as well. There are several hundred monks in residence, but the Panchen Lama himself was taken to Peking in 1965 and has lived there ever since. West of Xigaze are two old towns, **Lhaze** and **Tingri,** which are worth the effort required to reach them.

Leaving Tibet overland is far easier than getting there; after all, the police in the neighboring provinces are unlikely to send you back. A road runs east from Lhasa to Chengdu. There are reportedly buses between the two cities, and hitching is also possible. Walk out of Lhasa before daybreak and avoid army trucks. Nights are spent at small roadside rest houses, with Tibetan villages often close by. South of Qamdo the road forks, with one branch leading to Lijiang, Dali and Kunming. Those who strike out in this direction, however, face deportation if caught in Yunnan. (There are twice-weekly buses from Zhongdian, the first large town in Yunnan, to Kunming, and this might be a safer alternative.)

Another possibility is the road north; hop one of the trucks heading for Golmud. From there, either hitch to Dunhuang or try to get permission from the Golmud police to head for Xining. (This has worked in the past even though Xining is theoretically closed.)

The only officially sanctioned way of exiting Lhasa overland is also the most exciting: the road to Kathmandu. There is a Nepalese consulate in Lhasa that issues visas, or you can (in theory) get the stamp when you cross the border. The Chinese travel and exit permit must be obtained from Public Security in Lhasa, and may take a week to arrange. From time to time the police also grant re-entry permits; the recipient can visit Nepal and return to Tibet. There is one bus a month to Kathmandu, but many trucks make the journey, so it's always easy to get a ride.

Nepal is linked by road to just about every corner of the globe. You can hitch to Kampala, to Rome, or to Timbuktu.

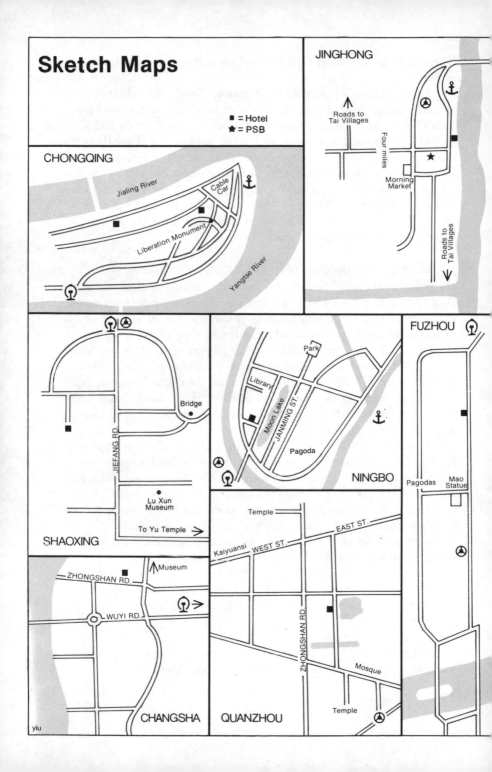

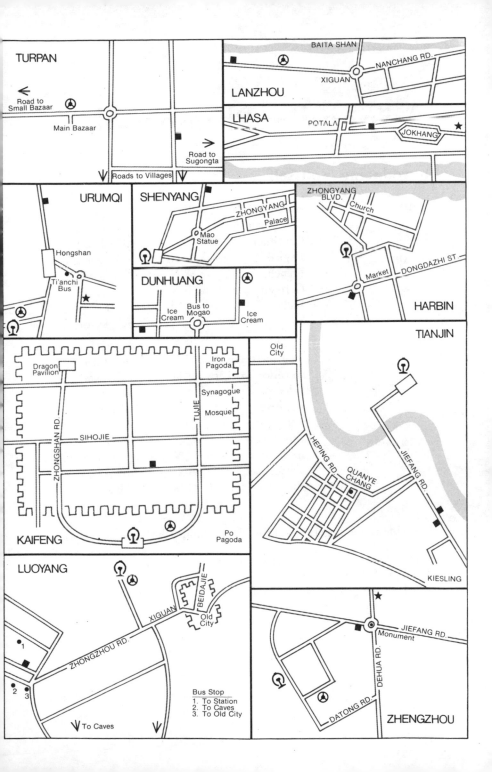

Appendix-Phrasebook

Introducing Yourself

I am

我是

wǒ shì

American	美國人	*měi guó rén*
Australian	澳大利亞人	*ào dà lì yà rén*
Canadian	加拿大人	*jiā ná dà rén*
English	英國人	*yīng guó rén*
French	法國人	*fà guó rén*
German	德國人	*dé guó rén*
Italian	義大利人	*yǐ dà lǐ rén*
Swiss	瑞士人	*ruì shì rén*
an artist	畫家	*huà jiā*
a businessman	商人	*shāng rén*
an office worker	文員	*wén yúan*
a doctor	醫生	*yī shēng*
a lawyer	律師	*lù shī*
a student	學生	*xúe shēng*
a journalist	記者	*jì zhě*
an engineer	工程師	*gōng chéng shī*
a diplomat	外交家	*wài jiāo jiā*
a teacher	教師	*jiào shī*

In Chinese, the negation is formed by adding "bù". For example,

I am not American, I am Australian.
我不是美國人，我是澳大利亞人。
wǒ bú shì měi guó rén, wǒ shì ào dà lì yà rén.

Requests

Do you have any/Is there any.....?

這裏有.....嗎？

yǒu méi yǒu.....?

tickets	票	*piào*
single rooms	單床間	*dān chuáng jiān*
double rooms	雙床間	*shūang chuáng jiān*
hardseat (on a train)	硬席	*yìng xí*
hard sleeper	硬臥	*yìng wò*

fish	魚	*yú*	beef	牛肉	*niú roù*			
soup	湯	*tāng*	rice	飯	*fàn*			
tea	茶	*chá*	beer	啤酒	*pí jiǔ*			
water	水	*shuǐ*	cold	冷	*lěng*	hot	熱	*rè*

English newspapers	英文報紙	*yīng wén baò zhǐ*
noodles	麵條	*miàn tiáo*
vegetables	蔬菜	*shū cài*
chicken	雞	*jī*
chopsticks	筷子	*kuài zǐ*
knives	刀	*daò*
forks	叉	*chà*
menu	菜譜	*cài dān*

soap	肥皂	*féi zào*
shampoo	洗髮劑	*xǐ fà zhì*
toilet paper	手紙	*shǒu zhǐ*
sanitary napkins	衛生巾	*wèi shēng jīn*

I want	to visit	a	commune	公社	*gōng shè*
我想	參觀	一間	school	學校	*xúe xiào*
wǒ xiǎng	*cān gūan*	*yì jiān*	university	大學	*dà xúe*
			hospital	醫院	*yī yuàn*
			factory	工廠	*gōng chǎng*
	to see		a play	話劇	*huà jù*
	看		an opera	戲劇	*xì jù*
	kàn		a film	電影	*diàn yǐng*
			a martial arts demonstration	雜技	*zá jì*
	to go to		the bus station	汽車站	*qì chē zhàn*
	去		the train station	火車站	*huǒ chē zhàn*
	qù		the airport	飛機場	*fēi jī chāng*
			the dock	碼頭	*mǎ tóu*
			the Friendship Store	友誼商店	*yǒu yì shāng diàn*

Direction

A simple way to ask direction is to put the object in front of the interrogative. For example:

Where is

the washroom?	洗手間	*xǐ shǒu jiān*	在那裏？
the telephone?	電話	*diàn huà*	*zài nǎ lǐ*
the post office?	郵政局	*yóu zhèng jú*	
the bank?	銀行	*yín háng*	
the public security bureau?	公安局	*gōng ān jú*	
foreign affairs bureau?	外事科	*wài shì kē*	

Numbers

One	two	three	four	five
一	二	三	四	五
yī	*èr*	*sān*	*sì*	*wǔ*

six	seven	eight	nine	ten
六	七	八	九	十
liù	*qī*	*bā*	*jiǔ*	*shí*

Twenty (= Two ten)	Twenty-five (= Two ten five)
二十	二十五
èr shí	*èr shí wǔ*

Hundred	百	*bǎi*
Thousand	千	*qiān*
Ten thousand	萬	*wàn*

Time

One O'clock	Half-past One (= One O'clock half)
一點鐘	一點半
yī diǎn (zhōng)	*yī diǎn bàn*

Money

Dollar(s)	元		*yúan*
Cent(s)	毛		*máo*
$3.40	三元四十毛	*sān yúan sì shí máo*

Fourth Floor   四樓   *sì lóu*

Number Nine Bus (= Nine number bus)
九號車
jiǔ haò chē

Useful Words

Passport	護照	*hù zhào*				
Travel Permit	旅行許可	*lǔ xíng xǔ kě*				

Letter	信	*xìn*	Telegram	電報	*diàn bào*
Stamps	郵票	*yóu piào*	Postcard	明信片	*ming xìn pīan*

Surface mail	平郵	*píng yóu*	Air Mail	航空	*háng kōng*
Mail Box	信箱	*xìn xiāng*			

North	北	*běi*	South	南	*nán*
East	東	*dōng*	West	西	*xī*

Male	男	*nán*	Female	女	*nǔ*

Today	今天	*jīn tiān*	Yesterday	昨天	*zuó tiān*
Tomorrow	明天	*míng tiān*	Tonight	今晚	*jīn wǎn*

Useful Phrases

Hello!	你好	*nǐ hǎo*
Goodbye	再見	*zài jìan*
Excuse Me	對不起	*duì bù qǐ*
Help!	救命	*jiù mìng* (only when your life is in danger)

I don't speak Chinese	我不說中文	*wǒ bù shuō zhōng wén*
I don't understand	我不明白	*wǒ bù míng bái*
I don't feel well	我不舒適	*wǒ bù shū fú*
How much?	多少錢？	*duō shǎo qián*

I am not rich.　　　　　　　　　　我沒有很多錢。

I want a bed in the dormitory.　　我想住在宿舍裏。

I will wait here; maybe a bed will become available soon.
我在這裏等，或者很快有牀空出來。

I always pay student price.　　　　我平常都付學生價。

Main Trains

47	37	15	5	1 ↓		↑ 2	6	16	38	48
1920	1815	2243	2359	657	**Peking**	2122	910	601	1254	1032
2245	2140	155	324	1023	**Shijiazhuang**	1744	526	236	916	654
432	315	718	849	1610	**Zhengzhou**	1149	2352	2106	330	100
1203	1108	1432	1610	001	**Wuhan (Hankou)**	410	1624	1349	1933	1720
1746	—	1957	2200	600	**Changsha**	2235	1040	822	—	1132
2049	—	2250	100	—	**Hengyang**	—	732	521	—	817
—	—	—	641	—	**Guilin**	—	112	—	—	—
—	—	—	1448	—	**Nanning**	—	1716	—	—	—
600	—	754	—	—	**Canton**	—	—	2054	—	2240

243	143	171	53/52	69 ↓		↑ 70	54/51	172	144	244
—	—	—	—	1214	**Peking**	2209	—	—	—	—
—	—	—	1249	—	**Shanghai**	—	2254	—	—	—
—	—	2240	405	2140	**Zhengzhou**	1243	734	632	—	—
—	2231	827	1326	713	**Xi'an**	316	2213	2001	1213	—
1125	1434	002	401	2218	**Lanzhou**	1230	709	354	1918	1404
605	913	1836	2148	1532	**Jiuquan**	1938	1329	951	2357	1721
1421	1720	148	438	2232	**Liuyuan**	1244	650	241	1616	948
435	753	1601	1806	1154	**Turpan**	2325	1724	1210	139	1915
755	1130	1904	2111	1453	**Urumqi**	2035	1420	914	2233	1616

183/ 182	163	131/ 130	9	7 ↓		↑ 8	10	132/ 139	164	184/ 181
—	1938	—	858	550	**Peking**	2243	2022	—	1121	—
1123	558	1928	1754	1450	**Zhengzhou**	1322	1101	956	005	1922
2124	1620	527	324	009	**Xi'an**	406	136	2320	1405	930
1335	935	2230	1839	1540	**Chengdu**	1310	1011	700	2120	1740

9 to Chongqing; **131** from Hefei; **182** from Shanghai.

125	119	45	21	13 ↓		↑ 14	22	46	120	126
1150	1910	1712	2108	1250	Peking	1004	1424	535	1103	850
2000	252	2345	319	1901	Jinan	342	804	2256	253	041
2112	405	—	—	—	Tai'an	—	—	—	139	2333
2240	601	—	—	—	Yanzhou	—	—	—	005	2203
631	1335	906	1219	356	Nanjing	1843	2304	1338	1619	1400
—	1650	1231	—	—	Suzhou	1603	—	1024	1307	—
—	1804	1348	1619	750	Shanghai	1455	1909	844	1131	—
—	2140	1659	—	—	Hangzhou	—	—	532	800	—
—	—	1239	—	—	Fuzhou	—	—	944	—	—

275	109	49 ↓		↑ 50	110	276
1016	—	918	Shanghai	2310	—	1940
1321	2125	1206	Hangzhou	1942	1546	1613
2328	748	2133	Yingtan	1051	554	639
1708	—	—	Xiamen	—	—	1255
—	1032	—	Nanchang	—	306	—
—	1909	613	Zhuzhou	207	1959	—
—	926	1805	Canton	1425	720	—

17	39	11 ↓		↑ 12	40	18
1550	2007	800	Peking	1848	631	1135
—	2148	941	Tianjin	1656	441	—
—	—	1252	Beidahe	1347	—	—
129	642	1849	Shenyang	800	1939	144
829	1405	—	Harbin	—	1227	1832

79	61 ↓		↑ 62	80		289 ↓		↑ 290
—	037	Peking	1733	—		740	Chengdu	1850
—	1719	Wuhan	004	—		827	Kunming	1955
—	2303	Changsha	1821	—				
1617	—	Shanghai	—	543				
1429	—	Hengyang	—	642				
2049	—	Guilin	—	010				
1436	1123	Guiyang	2148	615				
550	1123	Kunming	810	1640				

Above schedules can change at any time.

Hong Kong

For most travellers, the British colony of Hong Kong is the gateway to China. Those coming direct from the West will get their first taste of Chinese civilization in Hong Kong. For those leaving China, there will also be culture shock. All the bright lights, tall buildings, nightclubs and other symptoms of "bourgeois decadence" that China lacks are concentrated here.

It sometimes seems as if Hong Kong's sole purpose is business. This is not an inaccurate view of its history. The island of Hong Kong was ceded to the British by China in 1841 in consequence of the First Opium War, the Kowloon Peninsula was added after the Second Opium War in 1860, and the islands and hinterlands of the New Territories were leased for 99 years from the Chinese in 1898. From the very beginning Hong Kong was a convenient entrepôt between China and the West, and its wealth was founded on this trade. Even today, almost half of China's foreign exchange is derived from Hong Kong. Manufacturing has become the major source of income for the colony, which also serves as the banking and financial hub of the region.

To See

Hong Kong's major urban area consists of the north coast of Hong Kong island and the southern tip of the Kowloon Peninsula, linked to the island by subway, tunnel and ferry. The rest of the colony, about 280 square miles of mainland north of Kowloon and 100 square miles of islands, consists of the New Territories. Leased rent-free to Britain in 1898 for 99 years, they are now the main industrial area, though many parts are still rural.

With its modern skyscrapers and well-stocked shopping emporia, the **Central District** on Hong Kong island may well be the most modern city center in Asia. Seemingly out of place in this high-rise jungle are the antiquated trams that sedately cruise along Des Voeux Rd., the major avenue. If you board the tram in either direction, it will take you to areas where the flavor is noticeably Chinese. Going west it traverses the Western District and eventually ends up in Kennedy Town. The eastward route leads to Wanchai, Causeway Bay and North Point. All of these areas are also worth exploring on foot.

South from Central is **the Peak,** the poshest neighborhood in town, at the verdant summit of which there is a spectacular view of the harbor. You can reach it by the peak tram, which starts near the Hilton Hotel, or by bus 15 from Central. Walking trails lead through the woods around the Peak; one path, all downhill, leads to **Aberdeen** on the other side of the island. More easily reached by bus 70 from Central, Aberdeen is known for its many fishing boats and sampans, but extensive high-rise development has changed its character considerably in recent years. The town of **Stanley,** also on Hong Kong's south coast, is smaller, and the approach offers superb views of hills and ocean (bus 6).

Tsimshatsui, the part of Kowloon opposite Hong Kong, is one vast shopping center and is reputed to have more stores per square mile than any other place in the world, although the chic-est boutiques are located in Central. This is the place to find the ''bargains'' for which Hong Kong used to be famous. (You may find things cost more than you expected). Prices are often negotiable, but beware the sleazier shops. Stores that are members of the Hong Kong Tourist Association are usually reliable. Tsimshatsui is depressingly commercial, but about a mile north of the harbor the mood changes. The districts of Yaumatei and Mongkok, the Chinese sections of Kowloon, are fascinating places to wander. To get there, just go up Nathan Rd. to Jordan, turn left, then go north along one of the smaller streets such as Temple, Shanghai or Reclamation until you run out of steam. Temple St. is best visited after sunset, when it is transformed into a lively night market.

Perhaps the most interesting area of Hong Kong is the New Territories, which consists of both islands and mainland. The largest island, **Lantau,** is twice the size of Hong Kong but supports a population of under 30,000. It boasts a staggeringly beautiful mixture of mountains, beaches and monasteries. There are hourly ferries linking Silvermine Bay, the port on Lantau's east coast, to Central. Buses go from Silvermine along the south coast to Tai O, a 200-year old fishing town, and to the Po Lin Buddhist Monastery, which offers dormitory accommodation. The wilderness in the island's interior is good for hiking. There are many marked trails, and it's easy to get lost if you stray from them. Also worth a visit are Hong Kong's two other main islands, **Cheung Chau** and **Lamma,** on both of which you will find small Chinese towns with narrow streets as well as wilderness and beaches. (Try not to visit the islands on weekends, when they are swamped by hordes of Hong Kong residents.)

The **mainland New Territories** are a mixture of industrial boom-towns and small villages set amidst vegetable gardens and rice paddies. Most of these areas can be reached by buses from the Jordan Rd. bus terminal in Kowloon. Execeptions are the fishing villages of **Tolo Harbor** which are not accessible by road. They are served by the twice-daily ferry from Tai Po Kau. The four-hour round trip, with stops at several villages, affords an excellent glimpse of rural life.

For further information on things to see, the Hong Kong Tourist Association's offices at the Star Ferry (Kowloon side) and in the huge Connaught Center Building in Central will supply you with a stack of informative maps and brochures. One of these leaflets is a complete list of Hong Kong's many beaches, with directions on how to get there. Another lists major festivals in Hong Kong. If you are in town during one of them, don't miss it. Most of these colorful affairs commemorate local folk deities and for this reason have been banned in the People's Republic, which considers them to be remnants of feudal superstition, though they are still observed in some places even there.

Hotels

Hong Kong is one of the world's most expensive cities. There are, however, several hostelries catering to the impecunious that offer beds in very crowded dorms for HK$20. They are all centrally located in Tsimshatsui:

Travellers' Hostel, 16th floor, "A" Block, Chungking Mansions, 40 Nathan Rd. (opposite the Hyatt Hotel).

International Youth Accommodation Center, 6th floor, 21A Lock Rd. (behind the Hyatt).

Hong Kong Hostel, 11th floor, 230 Nathan Rd.

If you want to meet your fellow travellers, these are the best places to go. The Chungking Mansions on Kowloon's Nathan Road is a huge complex of five buildings each of which has many apartments that have been converted into cheap guest houses offering rooms for HK$30-$100. Shop around until you find a deal that satisfies you.

The grande dame of the budget hostelries is without doubt the **YMCA,** ideally located on the Tsimshatsui waterfront next to the Peninsula Hotel, with singles for HK$50 and cheaper dorm beds. All the cheaper rooms are reserved long in advance, though with luck you can get a room for which the reservation was cancelled. Even if you don't get in, visit the rooftop cafe, which has a spectacular view of the harbor and the skyscapers of Central. Finally, members can get a bed for only HK$8 at the **Mount Davis Youth Hostel,** a brand new complex of large, modern dormitories located at the top of the hill about half a mile beyond Kennedy Town, far from Central and a long walk from the nearest bus stop (take 5B to terminus). A new membership card is HK$72, worth it if you're planning to stay a while.

Restaurants

Hong Kong claims to have the world's best Chinese food and, for Cantonese cuisine, this boast has some substance. Unfortunately, Hong Kong's better restaurants are far more expensive than their Canton counterparts. There are, however, a plethora of street stalls, particularly in the area north of Jordan Rd., where you can eat well for under HK$10. Those coming from China might well head for the ubiquitous MacDonalds, Burger Kings or Creamery soda fountains. Many of the hostels have kitchens, and Hong Kong's supermarkets feature an amazingly wide range of European and American food including sirloin steak flown in from New Zealand (under HK$25 a pound).

Nightlife

Unlike China, Hong Kong doesn't close after dark. Nathan Rd., whose bright neon-lit signs are an obligatory feature of every Chinese film about decadent Hong Kong, buzzes with life until the wee hours of the morning. The areas with the highest concentration of clubs and topless bars are Tsimshatsui and Wanchai. For the price of a beer (HK$7) you can listen to good, live Dixieland jazz at **Ned Kelly's Last Stand** in Tsimshatsui. The **Front Page** on Lockhart Road, Wanchai, has rock and disco dancing and is especially lively after midnight on weekends. (Don't order a drink; the cheapest is HK$15). If you want to meet the expatriate men and women who work in Hong Kong, their favorite after-hours haunts include the **Bull and**

Bear in Central and the **Blacksmith's Arms** in Tsimshatsui. Both of these are "traditional" British pubs, complete with ersatz Tudor decor.

Macau

The tiny Portuguese colony of Macau is a sleepy backwater compared with Hong Kong, and therein lies its charm. Founded in the 1550s, it still retains much of its cachet, complete with Baroque churches and stucco-fronted houses nestling among much taller buildings. There are no fast food shops, no supermarkets and no discos. Macau, which has only five square miles of land to Hong Kong's 400, consists of a town on the mainland and two islands joined to it by causeway. Its major attractions are the Senate building and the 17th-century St. Paul's Church, of which all that remains is the facade.

During daylight hours there are frequent hydrofoils connecting the two colonies. (The Hong Kong pier is in Central, west of the Star Ferry.) These cost HK$40 plus an $8 tax and take only 75 minutes. There is also a slow boat with may be purchased upon several classes, beginning at $18. Visas may be purchased upon arrival. Avoid weekends. Macau's main industry is weekend tourism from Hong Kong.

From the Macau ferry pier, take bus 3 to the main street, Avenida de Almeida Ribeiro. Both food and lodging are noticeably cheaper than Hong Kong, and there are many hotels near the floating casino at the far end of the Avenida where rooms go for about HK$25. Or you can splurge at the **Bela Vista Hotel,** a 19th-century rococo extravaganza on a hill overlooking the bay. Its rates are HK$80 for a single, HK$115 for a double with bath.

Bibliography

There are several books which provide a good introduction to Chinese history and culture:

C.P.Fitzgerald, *China: A Short Cultural History* (Holt, Rinehart 1961)
C.P.Fitzgerald et al.,*China's 3000 Years* (Times Newspapers 1973)
R.Grousset,*The Rise and Splendour of the Chinese Empire* (University of
      California Press 1952)
D.J.Li, *The Ageless Chinese* (Scribner's 1971)

Other books provide traditional China with a more human dimension, examining the lives either of those who helped direct the flow of history, or of ordinary people swept up in the current:

J. Gernet, *Daily Life in China on the Eve of the Mongol Invasion*
      (George, Allen & Unwin 1962)
R.Huang, *1587, A Year of No Significance* (Yale 1981)
J. Spence *The Death of Woman Wang*
      Emperor of China:Self-portrait of K'ang Hsi (Peregrine Books)

Two books use this approach to illuminate China's turbulent passage from Empire to People's Republic:

E. Snow, *Red Star Over China* (Pelican 1938, 1968) (Life in
      Communist-held Yan'an, by a journalist who went there)
J. Spence, *The Gate of Heavenly Peace* (Viking 1981) (20th-century
      Chinese intellectuals, authors and insurrectionists)

Books dealing with modern China can be divided into two categories: those written before 1978 and those after. The former were usually written by academics who had never set foot inside the Peoples' Republic and often portray the Maoist vision of the New China rather than the real thing. One example, more profound than most, is R. Solomon, *Mao's Revolution and the Chinese Political Culture* (University of California 1971). In recent years, works by journalists and others who have spent years in China have appeared. These give a sober, penetrating (though at times unduly pessimistic) view of life in China today. One of the first to be published was J. Fraser, *The Chinese, Portrait of a People* (Fontana 1981). It is in large part devoted to the 1978 Democracy Wall movement and its suppression, and its view of China is a bleak one. D. Bonavia, *The Chinese, A Portrait* (Penguin 1980), is a more balanced account, and deals with such aspects of today's China as law, education, industry and family life. Chinese behavior and customs are the primary concern of D. Bloodworth, *The Chinese Looking Glass* (Farrar, Strauss 1980). Two other major books were published very recently:

F. Butterworth, *China, Alive in the Bitter Sea* (Times 1982)
R. Garside, *Coming Alive! China after Mao* (McGraw Hill 1981)

Two more books, though written earlier, were ahead of their time in perceiving Chinese political trends:

S. Leys, *Chinese Shadows* (Penguin 1977)
G. Orwell, *Nineteen Eighty-Four* (Penguin 1948)

Many of the books listed above, especially those by Bonavia and Butterworth, also contain information on the Chinese economy. Other works dealing with the subject include various monographs issued by the Food and Agriculture Organisation (FAO), the *Background Notes on China* published by the U.S. State Department, and R. Hofheinz and K. Calder, *The Eastasia Edge* (Basic Books 1982), a comparative economic survey of East Asia.

Another surprisingly informative source is *China Daily*, an English-language newspaper published in Peking and available in large Chinese cities and in Hong Kong.

Finally, there are the novels and short stories written by the Chinese themselves. Finding a good translation is a problem; here are a few:

Cao Xueqin, *The Story of the Stone*. (D. Hawkes, tr., Penguin Books 1973, 1977, 1980) (better known as *The Dream of the Red Chamber*)
Lao She, *Rickshaw* (J. James,tr., University of Hawaii 1979)
Monkey (A. Waley, tr., Allen and Unwin)(better known as *Journey to*

the West)
Straw Sandals: Chinese Short Stories 1918-1933 (H. Isaacs, ed., MIT Press
      1974)
Yu Luojin, *Le Nouveau Conte d'Hiver* (M. Mandares, tr., Christian
      Bourgois 1982)(in French)

Somewhat inferior translations of works by Lu Xun and Mao Dun
are widely available in China.

Among other guidebooks to China, the most noteworthy is the
Nagel's *China,* (1979). This is more an encyclopedia than a guide.
Unfortunately it is largely based on outdated information. Also
deserving of mention are:

Arlington and Lewisohn, *In Search of Old Peking* (1935, Paragon
      reprint 1967)
China Bound: A Handbook for American Students, Researchers and Teachers
      (U.S. China Education Clearing House 1981)
Delta Voyages, *Chine* (1980) (in French)
E. Garside, *China Companion* (Deutsch 1981)
B. Till, *In Search of Old Nanking* (Joint 1982)

— and, of course, the other books in the China Guides Series: *All
China, Peking* (3rd edition), *Shanghai, Canton and Guilin, Hangzhou and
the West Lake, Nanjing Suzhou and Wuxi, and Hong Kong.*

Index

1985 Supplement

by Steven Edelman and Robert Strauss

China is now in the midst of a massive drive to open up new areas to tourism. Pending completion of a new edition this brief supplement aims to pinpoint some of the major changes for travellers.

For those travelling in China the general mood now is undoubtedly buoyant. Recent changes in government policy have produced a more liberal and relaxed attitude. Massive economic reform is underway. Politics and ideology have taken second place to the economic necessities of productivity. As a result, a far greater choice and variety of goods is available and these are now also within the reach of peasants whose incomes have greatly increased through government approved, responsibility schemes. At present the leadership is concentrating on weeding out those elements in the party still refusing to accept the change. Provinces have recently been provided with wider powers to make independent contact with foreign countries and to promote tourism.

It is hard to keep track of the many new projects to restore sights, construct hotels, and improve transport facilities. New hotels catering to domestic tourists as well as to foreign travellers are opening. A number of joint-venture hotels, run by foreign management teams, are already operating in major cities, and many more are planned. These offer international-standard facilities and service, with prices to match. In general, prices for transport, food and hotels have escalated considerably since the publication of this book in 1983.

Offically, there has been a dramatic rise in crime and the campaign to stamp out criminal elements continues — outside each courthouse hang lists of names complete with their crimes and a red tick for execution.

For foreigners, however, China is still one of the safest places in the world. Nonetheless, as in any other country, do not tempt through carelessness. A tiny number of travellers in China have experienced pockets picked, bags professionally slit or cameras stolen on buses and trains in places such as Urumqi, Tianchi and Dali.

Exchange of FEC for Renminbi at a premium continues to be illegal and is now punishable by heavy fines (see page 52). Tourists have been caught by plainclothes police in Beijing and, as has been the case in other large cities, hefty fines imposed.

Visas and travel permits: Visas are still available in Hong Kong from various agencies (see page 36) at reasonable prices normally for an initial period of four weeks, but sometimes for five weeks. Extensions in China are usually granted for at least another four weeks but second extensions are now sometimes hard to acquire. Even though 257 places are officially open in China your visa still does not grant automatic entry to all of them and a separate travel permit (Lu Xing Zheng), available at public security bureaux, is necessary for 159 of these places. The 98 category 'A' cities listed on page IV at the beginning of this book do not require travel permits. The remaining category 'B' cities are steadily, one by one, joining the ranks of those that require no special permit.

Travel agents such as Phoenix Services, Traveller's Hostel, and Wah Nam can provide a visa for HK$80 in two or three days. A 24-hour express visa costs around HK$120, and a four hour superfast visa around HK$200.

Phoenix Services has a new address: Room 603, Hanford Road, 221D Nathan Road, Tsimshatsui, Kowloon, 3-7227378, 3-7233006

Travel: Increased mobility within China is clearly demonstrated at massive free-for-alls around train-ticket windows. During July, August

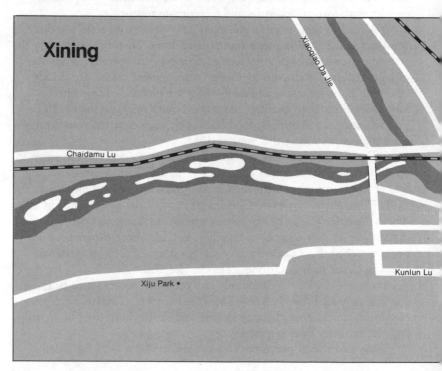

and September and at Chinese New Year, it is worth booking in advance. You can opt for the less troublesome method by booking through CITS but they will almost always require the 70% tourist surcharge in FEC (see page 45).

On main rail routes from Peking to Shanghai and Canton tickets are checked meticulously and a surcharge demanded on local price tickets if you are not entitled to them.

A tip for desperate souls unable to convert a hard seat ticket without even a seat number into a hard sleeper ticket: for a few extra yuan the restaurant car sometimes provides late night seats after the last sitting.

Airfare increases in the order of 30% were implemented in September 1984 (see page 47). The formation of new regional airlines companies proposed for 1985 may alleviate extreme pressure on ticket availability during the peak season. Alternatively, the shake-up within CAAC may lead initially to further chaos in reservation and ticketing systems. Although timetables are in short supply make sure you beg, borrow or whatever one in Hong Kong or major cities in China. Frequent changes make them an indispensable aid.

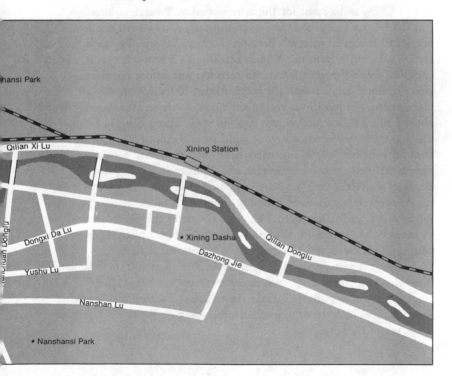

New open areas

Three important new open areas of major interest to travellers are Xining (see page 225), Kashgar (see page 215) and Tibet (see page 220).

Xining

The capital of Qinghai province is now open (see page 225). A spartan but friendly Chinese hotel accepting foreigners (3¥ per bed) is the **Xining Dasha** (two stops from the train station on bus 1). Xining is an interesting town in its own right as it attracts members of minorities (Tu, Tibetan, Mongol, etc.) to its shops and markets. But it is chiefly used as a stopover before travellers head to the town of Huanzhong and Taersi monastery. Public Security in Xining grants permits for Taersi but is unwilling to do so for Ledo (Qutansi monastery).

Taersi is one of the six most famous monasteries of the Yellow Cap sect in China and a must for those interested in Tibetan culture.

The bus to Taersi takes just over an hour, costs 70 fen and leaves when full at regular intervals between 7 am and 6 pm. To reach the bus station take bus 1 from the Xining Dasha, ride 5 stops due west then continue down the main street and turn left just before the river into a street running parallel with the river. About 150 yards on the left is the bus station. The bus drops you in the main square in Huanzhong. Walk about half a mile up the hill past rows of stalls selling Tibetan knick-knacks, then turn left at a row of eight stupas. About 30 yards up the road on your left, monk's quarters have been converted into a hotel with superb architecture combining Han and Tibetan styles. The rooms (7¥ per bed) above the courtyard are less damp than those at ground level.

At weekends crowds of gawping, giggling Chinese tourists jam the temples and meditation halls. This does not deter the sizeable population of monks and throngs of colourfully dressed Tibetan pilgrims from celebrating festivals and worshipping in traditional fashion.

Six temples are open. Tickets must be purchased at a small window beneath a large map of the monastery area opposite the stupas. Photography is not allowed inside the temples. Taersi is also an excellent base for hikes into the rolling hills surrounding it. Remember to take some warm clothing.

Kashgar

Recently opened, Kashgar, also known as Kashi, is now accesible from Urumqi by bus or plane (see page 215). Plane tickets from Urumqi to Kashgar are virtually unobtainable during August unless booked well in advance. However, for some reason, tickets in the opposite direction are usually available at short notice. The flight lasts around 3½ hours with a stopover in Aksu. No food is provided but at Aksu airfield beaming ladies sell dumplings in the transit lounge. A ticket one way is 215¥.

The usual bus route starts from Urumqi but buses also depart from Dunhuang and Daheyon (Turpan). From Urumqi to Kashgar buses take an average of three or four days to cover 940 miles passing through Turpan, Korla, Kuche, Aksu and Artux. The time taken depends on the driver's state of health, breakdowns, duststorms and other factors. Buses can be moderately comfortable or vintage boneshakers with a few parts left intact to keep up appearances. (Bus 79 belongs to the former type whilst bus 76 easily joins the latter class). A ticket costs 38.9¥ and buses leave from Nianzigou bus station at 9 am (in theory).

To reach the bus station from the Kunlun Hotel take bus 2 southwards for six stops, get off and walk due north to a large crossroads then continue a short distance due west to the bus station.

During the trip you will not be able to get at your luggage. It is stowed on the roof so strap it up securely to keep out the dust. Keep a small bag with essentials (overnight gear and wash things, valuables, food and clothing) with you.

The overnight stops are basic. Women and men are usually kept separate unless you also pay for the unoccupied beds in the room. Beds cost between 2¥ – 3¥ per person. Water for washing is unavailable or in short supply. Sanitation can involve long treks to walled holes in the ground.

The food stalls and roadside restaurants serve basic meals. Inevitably, you will be struck by the notorious Xinjiang belly. Try using Chinese medicine which usually proves effective. Western antibiotics can sometimes cause complications if they destroy the stomach's immunity.

Kashgar has that wild, anarchic air and fierce, Moslem pride that may remind some of Afghanistan.

Two hotels, the Xin Binguan and the Lao Binguan, are open to foreigners. Foreign tour groups usually land up in the **Lao Binguan**, a cosy complex of leafy courtyards close to the town centre, whilst individuals and Chinese conference groups reside in the **Xin Binguan**, a large, Soviet-style, concrete complex a long way out of town. This is

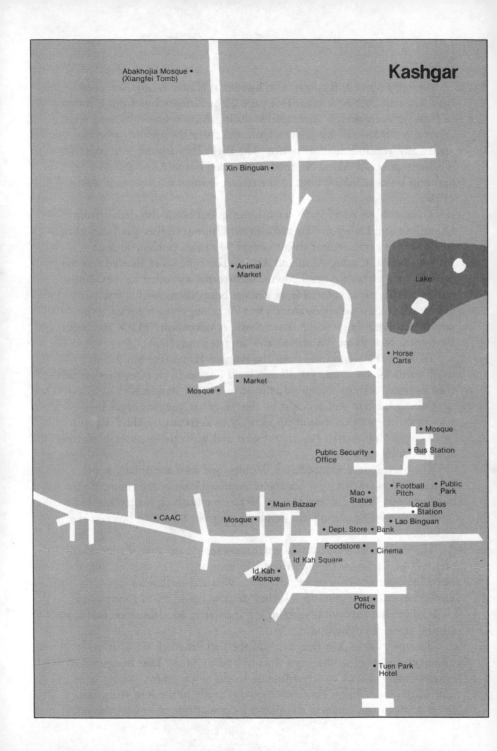

good news for the horse and donkey cart drivers who charge between 20 and 50 fen for a ride back to town.

The Xin Binguan provides budget accomodation at 6¥ per bed in a four-bed room. For this class of accomodation hot showers are provided on Saturday, Monday and Thursday from 9.30   10.30 pm. So, if you arrive on a Tuesday after a three-day bus journey, warm water can only be obtained with much cajoling of the manager. On Tuesday afternoon and Wednesday morning the hotel shop is closed for political study. The hotel restaurant provides mediocre fare to its trapped clientele except when high-ranking delegations cause an astonishing improvement. During the high season large groups of Hong Kong Chinese provide excitement noisily echoing up and down the corridor until the early hours. More expensive rooms, with hot showers available daily, are located in a block on the other side of the compound.

The **Tomb of Xiangfei**, a concubine of the Qianlong Emperor, is a half hour walk from the hotel. The mosque, located in peaceful, shady surroundings, contains not only Xianfei's tomb but also those of her relatives. A disinterested guide checks your ticket (50 fen) and then gives a rapid mono-syllabic tour. Behind the mosque is an extraordinary cemetery with large holes in the ground revealing the occasional bone. Whether or not Xiangfei is buried in the mosque is debatable but the area is worth a visit for its drowsy eccentricity.

Sunday is market day in Kashgar. Literally hundreds of horse carts, donkey carts, men on horseback and people on foot, stream into town raising clouds of dust, to sell everything from carpets, doorframes and knives to melons, camels and goats.

The **Id Kah Mosque** in the centre of town is surrounded by the main bazaar: row upon row of merchants and dealers, beckoning, haggling and dozing. Here you can find carpets; pewter, brass and copper articles; the famous daggers from Yengisar; fruit; nuts; local tobacco in three different grades, sold with papers (back copies of the local newspaper torn into strips) to roll your own; imported and smuggled goods. The food stalls offer kebabs, *lamian* (noodle dish) and *samsa* (type of pasty with mutton).

As a result of foreigners hopping onto buses at will and disappearing over the horizon, the Public Security bureau is no longer generous with permits. Unauthorised travellers have been heavily fined at the Pakistan border and in Khotan. Day trips are possible to places such as Artux and Yengisar. Most buses leave between 7 am and 8 am.

Tibet

The Forbidden Land has finally opened a crack. As of 1 September, 1984, Lhasa, capital of Tibet, is an open city. This means you can routinely have Lhasa added to your travel permit. The overland route from Lhasa to Nepal is now open, which allows for stopovers in the fascinating towns of Gyangze and Shigatse. Permits are routinely given by Lhasa Public Security.

The border between Nepal and Tibet officially opened in Spring, 1985 and an airlink between Nepal and Lhasa has been agreed by both sides, probably to commence in 1986.

The only permissible way to travel to Lhasa is by air. Daily flights on a CAAC Boeing 707 from Chengdu are 288¥. Though it is possible to catch a bus or truck into Tibet from Chengdu or Golmud, you may be turned back. Travellers have had far better luck leaving Tibet via Golmud than entering.

The view from the plane is spectacular. Flying at 35,000 feet above sea level, it is sometimes only 10,000 feet above the peaks. When checking in for the flight make it clear you want a window seat.

Tibet's only commercial airport is not much more than a runway and a concrete building, nestled between the peaks at close to 12,000 feet above sea level, more than 80 miles from Lhasa.

The journey to town takes approximately two hours. A new tarmac road is scheduled for completion by 1986, but until then the route follows the half-finished road and the riverbed. Old hands know to rush from the plane and claim a less bottom-jarring front seat while a companion collects the baggage.

The bus drops you at the CAAC office next to the Potala in the Chinese part of town. Of the several hotels open to foreigners, two are within walking distance. The **Number Three Guesthouse,** is only used by prepaid packaged tours. A major new hotel near Norbulinka Park is due to open in September 1985.

Closest to CAAC, and also in the Chinese section is the **Number One Guesthouse** (see page 224). Dormitories in the front building (facing the sun) now are 4¥. Tickets for hot showers (the doors should be opened 4 pm daily) are available at the front desk. A second building in the rear of the compound is nicer. The rooms have carpets and private baths, but the staff seem reluctant to place guests there, preferring to use them themselves.

For a shower you might also try the public solar heated showers directly across the street, which open at 9.30 am. At either place, make sure there really is hot water before getting too excited.

On the other side of town, in the old city, is the **Hotel Banak Shöl**. A new building, constructed in Tibetan style, this hotel is much favoured by budget travellers for its homliness and adherence to traditional construction techniques. A major disadvantages as of August 1985 is the lack of hot water. Dormitories are actually small rooms for four to eight people, rented by the bed, at about 4 ¥ per day. A new restaurant has just opened on the hotel's first floor and is quite reasonable.

The Snowland Hotel and the Number Two Municipal Guesthouse also provide reasonable accommodation for individual travellers.

Although the food in Lhasa is not good, it is not so bad that you should feel the need to bring your own. A passable Chinese restaurant (known to foreigners as the Orange Table Restaurant) is located in front and to the left of the entrance to the Potala. There is even an English menu stashed in a drawer where the cashier sits. The procedure is to point out what you want, pay, get a slip of paper with the order on it, and present it to the cook via a hole in the wall at the rear of the establishment. If you are concerned about cleanliness you are advised to carry your own chopsticks when dining here. Just around the corner from the Number One Guest House, is another small eatery, which often offers excellent noodles. Closer to the Tibetan Guest House, you can find a whole host of tea and dumpling shops.

Those wishing to cook their own food will find the market full of vegetables, rice, noodles, and, should you want to try it, yak meat, butter and cheese. Cooking facilities are not available at any of the guest houses, although it is possible to purchase a small kerosene stove and fuel locally. It is probably not worth bringing your own stove unless you expect to camp out during some other part of your journey. Unleaded fuel is completely unknown in these parts so you should either bring your own, or expect to spend some time traversing the bureaucracy to purchase the leaded kind at the station just outside of town on the airport road.

The **Potala**, perched on a hill overlooking the city, still dominates the entire landscape. While it is not clear how much power the lamas have here, at least they, rather than their Chinese overlords, seem to be running the day-to-day operation of the building. As a result the hours are not predictable, especially during Tibetan holidays when buildings may be closed for a week or more. It is best to try in the morning around 9 am, keeping an eye out for locals making their way up the long set of zig-zag steps that climb the front of the building. Only a small part of the Potala is open to visitors, and rooms seem to open and close at the whim of the lamas. Depending on their 'pull', escorted tours may see more or less than you do on your own. While it is possible to tag along with most tours, be discreet to avoid irritating the Chinese tour guides. Also, watch out for large groups of Tibetans who may be waiting for a lama to open some important room not usually opened for foreign visitors. Do not miss the Dalai Lama's private chambers, a cluster of rooms on the roof, of which only a few are shown unless you ask to see the rest. Also a must are the main meeting chamber and accompanying stupas containing the remains of past Dalai Lamas. Some of these are made of gold or silver and most are covered with semi-precious stones. You could also try to find the legendary torture chamber, described and even photographed by various visitors to Lhasa before 1950.

Be aware that, as of October 1984, the electric lights in much of the building are not being used due to nervousness after an electrical fire some months earlier. It can be very dark inside, so a strong flashlight is essential (do not depend on the locally manufactured variety). Photography is officially prohibited inside the Potala without payment of an extortionate picture fee of around Rmb. 20 per picture.

Other major sights of Lhasa are still the **Jokhang** in the centre of town and **Sera** and **Drepung** monasteries outside. It is less easy to see the daily open-air burial rites at Sera. Recently foreign visitors have been chased away, and not always politely.

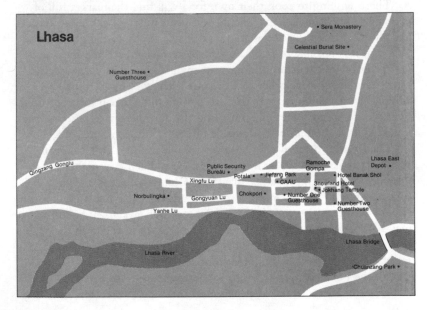

One of the more unpleasant side effects of Lhasa's newfound openness is that getting out can now be rather difficult. Air tickets can be impossible to obtain unless you make a reservation (small fee required) some days ahead. Even then the planes are often overbooked, and it is not uncommon to travel the two hours to the airport only to find out there are no seats.

Those hoping to maximize their chances of getting a seat should opt for the free CAAC bus that leaves Lhasa for the airport at 5:30 pm the day before your flight. Unfortunately this forces you to spend a night at the somewhat dirty airport hotel. The only alternative is to pool a few traveller's resources and hire a car.

For any of you travelling from Lhasa to Nepal by road, there is theoretically a monthly bus from Lhasa to the border. However, it is very irregular and it is hard to discover when during the month is is supposed to leave. Worse, it does not stop at either Gyangze or Xigaze, both of which are worth seeing. There are frequent buses as far as these cities, but picking up transport to the border can be difficult. Try trucks. Make sure the truck is going at least as far as you are, since drivers are inclined to ignore the roadside hitchhikers. Expect to be asked to pay for your ride.

During 1982 and 1983 there were at least two well-guarded gates along the road between Lhasa and the border. This is considered a militarily sensitive border and it is not worth making a run for it without proper permission.

Once you reach the Nepalese side it is easy to catch a ride to the first major town. From there you can get a bus to Kathmandu. Note that customs inspectors have been known to thoroughly search the belongings of foreigners leaving Tibet for 'cultural relics'. Anything that looks old or interesting is subject to seizure.

Central China

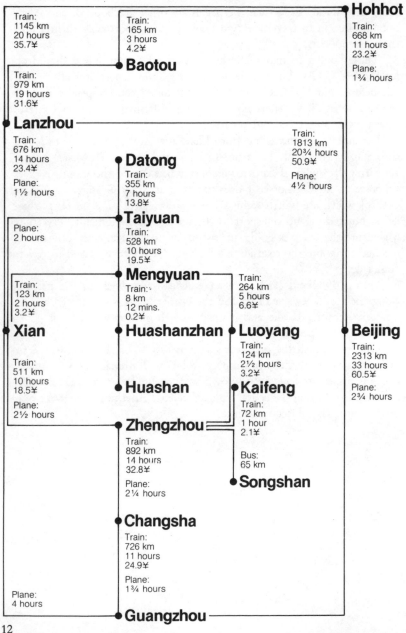

Hohhot

Train:
668 km
11 hours
23.2¥

Plane:
1¾ hours

Train:
1145 km
20 hours
35.7¥

Train:
165 km
3 hours
4.2¥

Baotou

Train:
979 km
19 hours
31.6¥

Lanzhou

Train:
676 km
14 hours
23.4¥

Plane:
1½ hours

Datong

Train:
355 km
7 hours
13.8¥

Train:
1813 km
20¾ hours
50.9¥

Plane:
4½ hours

Taiyuan

Plane:
2 hours

Train:
528 km
10 hours
19.5¥

Mengyuan

Train:
123 km
2 hours
3.2¥

Train:·
8 km
12 mins.
0.2¥

Train:
264 km
5 hours
6.6¥

Xian

Huashanzhan

Luoyang

Beijing

Train:
511 km
10 hours
18.5¥

Plane:
2½ hours

Huashan

Train:
124 km
2½ hours
3.2¥

Kaifeng

Train:
2313 km
33 hours
60.5¥

Plane:
2¾ hours

Zhengzhou

Train:
72 km
1 hour
2.1¥

Train:
892 km
14 hours
32.8¥

Plane:
2¼ hours

Bus:
65 km

Songshan

Changsha

Train:
726 km
11 hours
24.9¥

Plane:
1¾ hours

Plane:
4 hours

Guangzhou

Eastern China

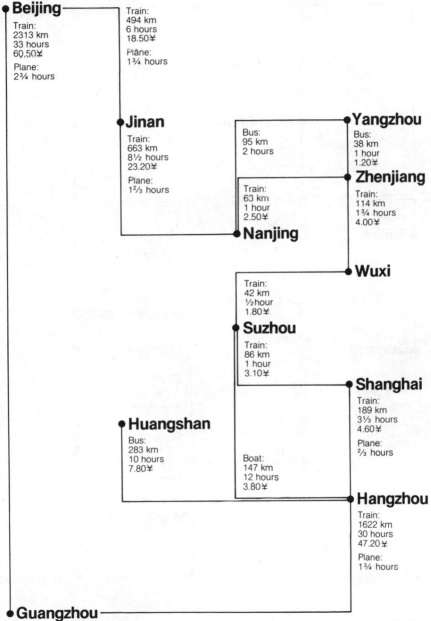

Beijing

Train:
2313 km
33 hours
60.50¥

Plane:
2¾ hours

Train:
494 km
6 hours
18.50¥

Plane:
1¾ hours

Jinan

Train:
663 km
8½ hours
23.20¥

Plane:
1⅔ hours

Bus:
95 km
2 hours

Yangzhou

Bus:
38 km
1 hour
1.20¥

Zhenjiang

Train:
114 km
1¾ hours
4.00¥

Train:
63 km
1 hour
2.50¥

Nanjing

Wuxi

Train:
42 km
½ hour
1.80¥

Suzhou

Train:
86 km
1 hour
3.10¥

Shanghai

Train:
189 km
3⅓ hours
4.60¥

Plane:
⅔ hours

Huangshan

Bus:
283 km
10 hours
7.80¥

Boat:
147 km
12 hours
3.80¥

Hangzhou

Train:
1622 km
30 hours
47.20¥

Plane:
1¾ hours

Guangzhou

South Western China

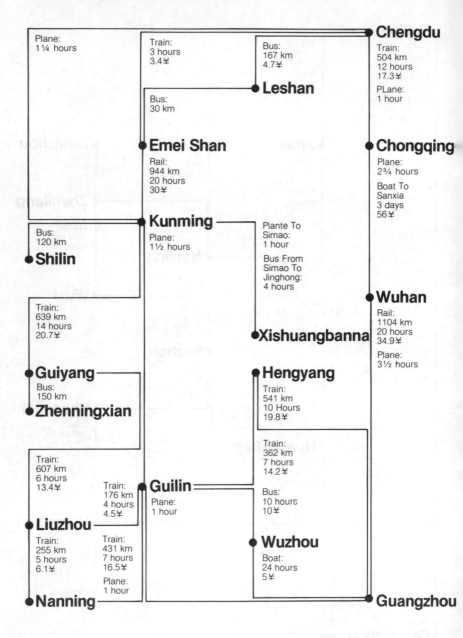

Plane:
1¼ hours

Train:
3 hours
3.4¥

Bus:
167 km
4.7¥

● Chengdu

Train:
504 km
12 hours
17.3¥

PLane:
1 hour

● Leshan

Bus:
30 km

● Emei Shan

Rail:
944 km
20 hours
30¥

● Chongqing

Plane:
2¾ hours

Boat To
Sanxia
3 days
56¥

● Kunming

Plane:
1½ hours

Plante To
Simao:
1 hour

Bus From
Simao To
Jinghong:
4 hours

Bus:
120 km

● Shilin

● Wuhan

Rail:
1104 km
20 hours
34.9¥

Plane:
3½ hours

Train:
639 km
14 hours
20.7¥

● Xishuangbanna

● Guiyang

Bus:
150 km

● Zhenningxian

● Hengyang

Train:
541 km
10 Hours
19.8¥

Train:
362 km
7 hours
14.2¥

Train:
607 km
6 hours
13.4¥

Train:
176 km
4 hours
4.5¥

● Guilin

Plane:
1 hour

Bus:
10 hours
10¥

● Liuzhou

Train:
255 km
5 hours
6.1¥

Train:
431 km
7 hours
16.5¥

Plane:
1 hour

● Wuzhou

Boat:
24 hours
5¥

● Nanning

● Guangzhou

North Eastern China

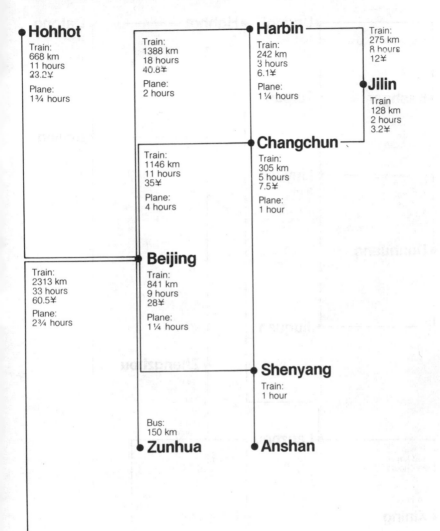

Hohhot

Train:
668 km
11 hours
23.2¥

Plane:
1¾ hours

Train:
1388 km
18 hours
40.8¥

Plane:
2 hours

Harbin

Train:
242 km
3 hours
6.1¥

Plane:
1¼ hours

Train:
275 km
8 hours
12¥

Jilin

Train:
128 km
2 hours
3.2¥

Train:
1146 km
11 hours
35¥

Plane:
4 hours

Changchun

Train:
305 km
5 hours
7.5¥

Plane:
1 hour

Beijing

Train:
2313 km
33 hours
60.5¥

Plane:
2¾ hours

Train:
841 km
9 hours
28¥

Plane:
1¼ hours

Shenyang

Train:
1 hour

Bus:
150 km

Zunhua

Anshan

Guangzhou

North Western China

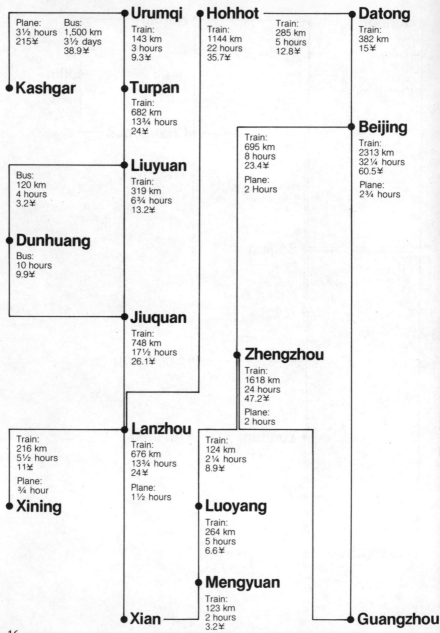

Kashgar

Urumqi

Plane:
3½ hours
215¥

Bus:
1,500 km
3½ days
38.9¥

Turpan

Train:
143 km
3 hours
9.3¥

Train:
682 km
13¾ hours
24¥

Hohhot

Train:
1144 km
22 hours
35.7¥

Train:
285 km
5 hours
12.8¥

Datong

Train:
382 km
15¥

Liuyuan

Train:
319 km
6¾ hours
13.2¥

Beijing

Train:
695 km
8 hours
23.4¥

Plane:
2 Hours

Train:
2313 km
32¼ hours
60.5¥

Plane:
2¾ hours

Bus:
120 km
4 hours
3.2¥

Dunhuang

Bus:
10 hours
9.9¥

Jiuquan

Train:
748 km
17½ hours
26.1¥

Zhengzhou

Train:
1618 km
24 hours
47.2¥

Plane:
2 hours

Lanzhou

Train:
216 km
5½ hours
11¥

Plane:
¾ hour

Xining

Train:
676 km
13¾ hours
24¥

Plane:
1½ hours

Train:
124 km
2¼ hours
8.9¥

Luoyang

Train:
264 km
5 hours
6.6¥

Mengyuan

Train:
123 km
2 hours
3.2¥

Xian

Guangzhou